AMERICA:
Once the United States?

Revised Edition

Ralph "PETE" Peters Jr.

AMERICA: Once the United States?
Revised Edition
Copyright © 2019 by Ralph "PETE" PETERS JR.

Library of Congress Control Number: 2019936974
ISBN-13:   Paperback: 978-1-64674-052-9
       PDF: 978-1-64674-053-6
       ePub: 978-1-64674-054-3
       Kindle: 978-1-64674-055-0

Printed in the United States of America

LitFire
PUBLISHING

LitFire LLC
1-800-511-9787
www.litfirepublishing.com
order@litfirepublishing.com

CONTENTS

DEDICATED TO GALE LEWIS BURNS

In Loving Remembrance

FOREWORD: Dedicated to Lewis Gale Burns, this is a collection of "things" which means **THINGS** = True Hopefully? but Incredibly, Noteworthy Good Stories! This book has been on my bucket list for some time now. This collection includes many e-mails from Lewis Burns and others; some are humorous, inspirational, religious and politically sensitive **THINGS** since 2004. As I begin this book, which is dedicated to Lewis Burns, believe me that Lou was truly without question one of the **"Nice Guys of the World"**, a true American patriot and was a true friend to all he met. And for me he was really more like another brother to me rather than being my brother-in-law.

And I know this for sure!

Lou Served His State and Nation: Lou proudly served both his nation and the State of North Carolina. Following 22 years of service, he retired from the US Air Force in 1982. Later he serviced with the NC Department of Corrections as a Corrections Officer retiring in 2009 as he found out he had leukemia. Something else is more important than his military service. That is his dedication to his wife Nancy, his friends and families. Everyone he met seemed to become a friend when they first meet Lou.

The Favorite Uncle: I think Lou holds the world's record for being the "favorite uncle" of every one of his seven nieces and nephews. He was a "maker of good memories" along the way during his many adventures. Personally, I think Lou invented and NIKE stole from him their brand slogan; "JUST DO IT! Before Nike swooped down with this slogan, Lou was "JUST DOING IT"; with a loving life, family, friends, his country and taking off on many adventurous trips. For example, one thing he would do is take off with Nancy from Durham, NC drive to Carolina Beach and pick up a few dozens of Brit's donuts. If Joyce and I were at our place on Oak Island, he would drop off a dozen for us and then go back to Durham afraid his two Siamese cats would miss him too much.

Final Journey: When Lou made his final journey in life to Heaven on 1/11/11 at 11am, we all knew Lou would later have a smile on his face in heaven (which he always had) and love in his heart for Nancy, his family, his friends and his country. He always loved significant numbers since I bragged about being born on 01/23/45 and our first granddaughter Olivia was born 04/04/04. So his passing on 1/11/11 @ 11am was amazing.

Lewis--- we still miss you and "We Love You Man!!"

America: Once the United States? Is dedicated to a modern day American Patriot.... Gale Lewis Burns. We called him Lou!! He is not at all like the many "American Media Patriots" now popular on TV and radio. Lou really served his nation. You might ask, "Who was this Lou?" He was not like Lou Dobbs on TV and fired by CNN and hired by FOX. Lou was not a Gale Sayers for sure. But this Lou was very much like George Burns, remember him? Lou was one funny guy!

Lewis Was a Modern Day Adventurer: But bottom-line, he is much like Marco Polo way back in 1269 and most recently Lewis and Clark in 1804. Lou was an adventurer, one that you will have fun with you during all your trips and adventures with him. Back in 1269, it would have been "Marco Polo & Lou" meeting Kublai Khan. On November 4, 1804, it would have been "Lewis & Clark (L & C and Lewis)" meeting Sacagawea for the first time. Gale Lewis Burns is really an adventurous American. But...Why is Gale Lewis Burns so adventurous? Well in the picture you see our two sons; Jay (L) and Brian (R) with their bowie knives that Lewis gave them for his last Christmas alive in 2010. He and Nancy made a special trip almost to Dolly Parton's Dollywood in The Great Smokiest Mountains to buy four knives, two of which he gave to his other two nephews; Chad and Trevor Helms.

Lewis, Clark and Lou: Maybe it was his name Lewis and his knowledge of Lewis & Clark's place in history. Lou would have worked well together with L & C as they arrived in North Dakota and stayed Fort Mandan near Bismarck, ND. Lou really hated being cold and would have educated L & C about dealing with the cold. Lou being retired US Air Force, would have somehow had L & C in modern-like USAF cold weather gear, except for the camping stuff. Lou was not a camper and he too would have needed the warm of Fort Mandan as well.

Things about Lou: Let me now tell you some more interesting *things* about Lou. Many of the *things* included in this collection came from him via e-mails to me through the electronic magic of the internet. Yes, Lou helped Al Gore invent and refine the internet. My e-mail collection started about the time when Al Gore was trying to figure out his own e-mail system and Lou got big Al straightened out. But now, more about Gale Lewis Burns.

Lou Served Very Proudly: Lou proudly served both his nation and the State of North Carolina. Following 22 years of service he retired from the US Air Force in 1982. Later he serviced with the NC Department of Corrections as a Corrections Officer retiring in 2009 as he found out he had leukemia. Something else is more important than his military service. That is his dedication to his wife Nancy, his friends and families. Everyone he met seemed to become a friend when they first meet Lou.

Favorite Uncle: I think Lou holds the world's record for being the "favorite uncle" of every one of his seven nieces and nephews. He was a "maker of good memories" along the way during his many adventures. Personally, I think Lou invented and NIKE stole from him their brand slogan; "JUST DO IT! Before Nike swooped down with this slogan, Lou was "JUST DOING IT"; loving life, family, friends, his country and taking off on adventurous trips.

The Durham, NC to Raleigh, NC Walk: One hot summer day in Durham, Lou and Brian Peters (our youngest of two fine sons) sat talking about hiking, now called *trekking*. Brian said to Lou, "Have you ever thought about walking 27 miles from Durham to my house in North Raleigh?" Lou looked back at Brian and quickly said, "No, but let's "Just Do It." And that is what they did with very little discussion, planning and...water. They found water on the way. But with Lewis they "Just Did It".

Brian's Sense of Adventure and Desire to Climb: That one experience triggered Brian's sense of adventure and helped mold him into a true mountain climber. On his first climb he ascended Mount Rainer to complete his first ever climbing attempt on his 40th birthday June 26, 2012. His second climb of Mount Rainer was completed in September 2013 and raised $7000 for our family non-profit: *Adventures for Special Needs (AFSN)* www.adventurers4specialneeds.com. The end of summer conditions has much ice and snow on the peak at 14,410' on this magnificent mountain. His next major goal in is Mount McKinley in Alaska after some good practice in the Colorado, Rockies. Lewis sparked the fire for trekking that lead to mountain biking and then to mountain climbing for Brian, all starting when he was just a little boy hiking with Lewis.

The Grand Canyon Climb: Another time Lewis was at the north rim of the Grand Canyon, watching all the mule trains carrying people down to the bottom. Trevor Helms, another nephew with him said, "Lou do you think we can walk down this Canyon trail and back up without a mule?" Lou looked back at Trevor and quickly said, "Yes, let's "Just Do It?" And that is what they did. Also like with Brian's walk from Durham to Raleigh, there was very little discussion, planning and again little water. They found water on the way and had one Baby Ruth candy bar between them for the climb down and back up the narrow path of the Grand Canyon. As before with Brian they "Just Did It".

I can see Lewis so vividly now with Lewis & Clark on that historical expedition. When they finally got to see the Pacific Ocean, Lewis would have wanted to go "North to Alaska" instead of back tracking over what they had seen before.

First Parachute Jump from A Plane: Ten years back, Lewis said, "Pete, let's make our first jump out of a plane here at Oak Island, NC. Since I never done it while in the US Army Corps of Engineers!" I said "Okay let's "Just Do It" Lou!" This short story ends here with me being too heavy/fat at 250 pounds plus for him to jump with me. Now in November 2014 at 320 pounds I may never get this bucket list item accomplished. But maybe I could get one of my buddies at Fort Bragg to set me up with a cargo parachute drop and get this one off that "bucket list".

Bucket List Item: This book has been a bucket list of mine for some time. This is a fun collection includes many e-mails from Lewis; some humorous, inspirational, religious and politically correct *things* since 2004. And I even added some personal comments leading to the title; *AMERICA-Once the United States?* You may hear Lewis laughing when he reads some of the crazy *things* in this book. You will see some noted politician frown as they read some of the political sessions. Pro-Death advocates calling themselves Pro-Choice will object. Those who have religious beliefs will find some reinforcement on GOD's Word, some will laugh at the" Bubba" jokes and many Veterans may shed a tear on some of the inspiring military stories. FOX may frown at some of my opinion but they are still the best source of news available.

Bottom-line: As I close this section, believe me that Lou was truly without question one of the **"Nice Guys of the World"**, a true American Patriot and he was a true friend to all he met. And for me he was really more like another brother to me rather than being my brother-in-law. And I know this for sure! When Lou made his final journey in life to Heaven on 1/11/11 at 11am, we all knew Lou would have a smile on his face (which he always had) and love in his heart for Nancy, his family, his friends and his country. He always loved significant numbers since I bragged about being born on 01/23/45 and our first granddaughter was born 04/04/04. So his passing on at 1/11/11 @ 11am was amazing.

ACKNOWLEDGEMENTS:

Lewis Burns, Ron Cabell, Dan Fritz, Clay Kimrey, Wayne Yeargan, Spencer Satterfield, John Foley, Robert Gaskins, Robert Schuller, et al and Anne Copeland-Editorial Consultant

INTRODUCTION-
WHERE DOES
AMERICA GO NOW?

RWP2: This book is a collection of articles, letters, antidotes, and jokes, religious and motivational material for you to consider, enjoy and apply in many cases. It is like a book of poems or quotes somewhat like the amusing *Uncle John's Biggest Ever Bathroom Reader* by the Bathroom Reader's Institute; a favorite of Lewis Burns.

My book also reflects my basic views; Pro Country, Pro God, Pro Gun, Pro Life and Pro Values. It is something you can pick up, randomly open it and enjoy something as you from A to ZZ!

This treasure trove of e-mails, articles, letters, antidotes and facts for you to consider because many are life lessons from the past for use today. The words from my mouth will denoted by **RWP2** and all are from true American patriots as far as I can determine. You will read about many different ****THINGS**** from A to ZZ.

People are concerned about the future of *AMERICA: Once the United States*? As a baby boomer, I sure am concerned. Please do not be concerned that this book has somewhat a negative title. There are many, many very positive topics and lessons learned from history. America is the best place to live and work." **But the key is to work"**.

The FOX News and: Mud Wrestling: In this collection you will see how AMERICANS really feel! It is in their own words, their true words without any editorial censorship or political correctness (PC) as to the real meaning of their words. Now I love FOX news except when they break into mud wrestling between the Socialist Democratic Party and the Party of Lincoln-Republicans. The Socialist Democratic Party has its own Mud Wresting Team and it more like a tag match because they so many knuckle heads to pick from. Personally I would bet the Fox News any day of the week.

This entire book is without Rush Limboo-Bimboo, Bill O'Really or HandNutty and Clones (Clones got fired) telling you the real story from Fox News. It really looks like they staged political mud wrestling at times...

CNN/MSNBC Fake News: It is all fake news at specifically CNN/MSNBC. **NOTICE** that I have only mentioned **Trump's** name once. Let us pretend that H. Clinton had won the final 2016 election if you will. Let that soak as for a while as I plan write *AMERICA II: Once Made Good Again!* As of this edition ---dated October 6 I predict Trump will win a landslide. rather.

Do They Help or Hurt: A personal note which very well may not be true is....that these people especially LimBoo-BimBoo have often hurt rather than bring America back to a United States of America. They want to keep "stirring the political pot" and thus keeping their ratings high. Now do not get me wrong FOX News is my absolute favorite. But the same "stirring of the political pot" goes for the socialistic opposition networks CNN, MSNBC and all of the liberal media that exist in November 2014. **Just that it might be November 3, 2020 sooner**

Does Political Mud Wrestling Help? However what seems like "than is a lot like " mud wrestling" between the Fox "stars" at times has helped uncover the smelly under belly of progressive liberals and the socialist trends of our current President Barrack Hussain Obama that the liberal media ignores. Maybe some of the FOX "rock stars" should consider running for office as

American Media Patriots. But why do that when book deals are so good. More power to them as I sit here self-publishing my first non-engineering book. But also, in my opinion, they are good media people, but they are vapor-ware American patriots and very little else. Which one served anyone, except radio, TV and the Neilson ratings?

The FOX Five-A Formal Political Mud Wrestling Team: I added this section on November 5, 2014, while watching the FOX Five today. Lewis has not here to experience and see this formally organized mud wrestling tag team show on FOX from 5:00 -6:00pm. Here they have 5 mud wrestlers and I won't mention their names because they are not that important. But their roles are really interesting. Let's start with how they are staged before the bout.

On the immediate left is a leggy, buxom brunette that dances in her seat when going to a TV break. She was a former blonde..... I would wager she is the dumbest but the one you would not want to fight one on one. And she would be the one of the Five, the guys would want in see in a wet T-Shirt wrestling event.

Next is a fat Democratic, who is the one they try to pick on whenever they can. He was a former football player somewhere and had some brain damage it appears. In the middle, is the referee who also fights at times, especially with the Fat Democrat was often plays the "bully role" against the two lady wrestlers. He is former professional baseball player, I think, and he also appears to be the smartest. Next is a fragile blonde (as compared to the brunette) who was a press secretary under President Bush. She is very, very smart!

Last but not least to the right is the 30-something, funny man on the team. Evidently he is doing well since he takes over for O'Really at times. I think he is the dumbest but he is loud and can be a pure a- - hole at times so evidently has a good following.

But this one was smart enough to "write a book". When one of these five main mud wrestlers needs a break they pull from the FOX bench of "non-stars" for a bout or two. Is really amusing to watch! So that is the official FOX news mud wrestling team. Like all the others they want to continue stirring the pot to keep or improve their ratings. **(By the way, three of five have been missing in action as of October, 2019**).

The Democratic Socialist Party: Many countries like Italy have an official a "Democratic Socialist" party. In some countries, also in Italy, one minority party such as the "Communist" party was somewhat of a positive factor. Most all political items are politically correct except a few Obama facts not uttered in the liberal press. Fact is that Obama today (November 5, 2015 in one of his longest news conference) said almost nothing new. He called for working together. He said he would listen to the new leaders from the Senate and Congress and then basically after six week for example, would solve the immigration issue by Executive Order. He said in essence that I will listen to Republican ideas and act on those I like. But politics aside, the words shared in this book are uncensored, mostly positive and are facts.

Mentors of Presidents: Here is something I have been concerned about. Read for yourself about Obama's key mentor **Franklin Marshall Davis** in **Dr. Paul Kengor's** book entitled *The Communist*. Obama only speaks of "Frank" in his own book; *Dreams from My Father*. Most of us in life have all have mentors in sports, religion and politics etc. Read *The Communist* because most American would never have nor admit that they had positive impact from an avowed communist like Frank Davis Marshal.

In 2008, *The Guardian's* Rob Woodard wrote that *Dreams from My Father* **"is easily the most honest, daring, and ambitious volume put out by a major US politician in the last 50 years."** Michiko Kakutani, the Pulitzer Prize-winning critic for *The New*

York Times, described it as **"the most evocative, lyrical and candid autobiography written by a future president'.**

Mentors Matter: Mentors in my life have mattered to me; my Mom and Dad, my elementary school principal and first baseball coach Dr. Leonard Schmitt, my pastor in Tyner, TN who showed me how to throw a curve ball, James Traylor my first and best basketball coach for our 20-0 team at Tyner Junior High school, the first pastor at North Raleigh Methodist Church, Sid Huggins plus all my college and high school coaches. Most of my entire life, my wife Joyce has mentored me now for over 54 years. But **"Look at the mentors of our past presidents", Dr. Paul Kengor concludes.** His book's back cover info states; **"The people who influence our president matter!"** **Frank Marshall Davis was "The Communist" who was Obama's key mentor in life after his father's death.**

"Nothing but Net" and Facts Here: Nothing but net--- is a basketball term for a good, swisk shot. Every word included has been said or sent to me. For many items the real author is unknown to me. Most everything was sent to me via e-mail, or gained from personal research. I have researched some of the ****THINGS**** I selected for this collection. But most all of these pages came from longtime friends, true Americans. If you have believed all of LimBoo BimBoo, O'Really & HandNutty, you can believe my friends opinion as well.

Sad for America: You may surmise from my previous comments that I am absolutely not a member of the current Democratic Socialist Party here in the USA. I am a Moderate to Right Wing Conservative bordering upon being on becoming a Right Wing Extremist. No not really! I have said that line before the Clinton years up to right now. But just one example... when I hear and see Pro-Death/Pro-Choice people protecting salamanders, milk cows & gorillas yet advocate mutilating and then killing real people in the womb I am very sad and I get enraged at the same time. I grew up on Guernsey dairy farms in NC, TN and SC and I like cows, nature and salamanders!!

Do you realize that we have aborted/killed over 54,000,000 (30% of this total were black) Americans since Roe vs. Wade passed in 1973. This is more killed than in all of our wars combined. Personally there should be a memorial to these unborn right outside the Supreme Court Building in Washington, DC that passed this law. More sad facts on Pro-Choice/Pro-Death under the P's.

Why This Book Is Just a Collection of **Things**: Simple! We need to formally recognize and document what the internet e-mails have provided to us. E-mails become electronic vapor and are like smoke gone forever when not put into "the written word" or made into an e-book version for Kindle and others. The many E-mails and other is in this collection does say many good things about *America, Once the United States?* I hope you have fun reading this A to ZZ collection patterned somewhat after the Robert Townsend (former AVIS CEO) first book entitled an "Up the Organization with a sequel entitled "Further up the Organization'...

THINGS = True Hopefully!! but Incredibly, Noteworthy Good Stories! There are some words from my mouth and they will all be denoted by **RWP2**. Most of the material in this collection is from true American patriots as far as I can determine. You will read about many different ****THINGS**** arranged from A to ZZ.

Many people are concerned about the future of *America- Once the United States?* As a baby boomer myself, I am very concerned. Please do not be concerned that this book's title is somewhat negative. It is can be a very positive one, based on many of the ****THINGS**** you will read from A to ZZ. Now go to the outline and take your pick from A to ZZ .

A

ADVENTURERS FOR SPECIAL NEEDS (AFSN):

RWP2: I discussed during the intro, how Lewis Burns made a tremendous positive impact on Brian our youngest son and also our other oldest son Jay during their early years. Brian is one of two fine sons Joyce have. But Brian is a real mountain climber and true adventurer. Brian had an idea!

*Dad he said one day, "Let's start a fund raiser for special needs children." We kicked it around quickly and decided to set up a non-profit corporation that we initially called "Climbers for Special Needs". So we began the process. Before we filed our bylaws Brian said. "Let's call it **Adventurers for Special Needs** instead because we can cover a broader scope of ordinary people doing extraordinary things. Then we can feature them on our web site at www.Adventurers4SpecialNeeds.com and even sponsor some of them on special events they accomplish". Our first fund raising*

event in 2013 was a climb of Mount Rainier (at top) of 14, 410 feet and provided a nice donation to The Frankie Lemon Development School in Raleigh, NC. So that is the genesis of AFSN and that is where <u>all</u> net profits from this book will go! You can always donate at: http://www.adventurers4specialneeds.com/donation.html.

Your donations are tax deductible and 100% of donations go for good causes because AFSN has **zero overhead,** no Executive Director's salary and an all-volunteer staff.

100% 0F ALL PROFITS FROM *AMERICA-Once the United States?* WILL GO TO Adventurers for Special Needs (AFSN

Very briefly our Mission-Vision-Value is below;

- *Mission-Serve special needs people with both financial and personal support.*

- *Vision- Never give up on the God given value of people with special needs*

- *Value-Maximize service and funding to special needs people and minimize AFSN cost of doing business*

Now for Some Fun **THINGS**!

ABBOTT SELLS COSTELLO A COMPUTER

You have to be old enough to remember Abbott and Costello and too old to REALLY understand computers, to fully appreciate this. For those of us who sometimes get flustered by our computers, please read on. If Bud Abbott and Lou Costello were alive today, their infamous sketch, 'Who's on First?' might have turned out something like the following dialogue.

Costello Calls To Buy A Computer From Abbott

ABBOTT: Super Duper computer store. Can I help you?
COSTELLO: Thanks I'm setting up an office in my den and I'm thinking about buying a computer.
ABBOTT: Mac?
COSTELLO: No, the name's Lou.
ABBOTT: Your computer?
COSTELLO: I don't own a computer. I want to buy one.
ABBOTT: Mac?
COSTELLO: I told you, my name's Lou.
ABBOTT: What about Windows?
COSTELLO: Why? Will it get stuffy in here?
ABBOTT: Do you want a computer with Windows?
COSTELLO: I don't know. What will I see when I look at the windows?
ABBOTT: Wallpaper.
COSTELLO: Never mind the windows. I need a computer and software.
ABBOTT: Software for Windows?
COSTELLO: No. On the computer! I need something I can use to write proposals, track expenses and run my business. What do you have?
ABBOTT: Office.
COSTELLO: Yeah, for my office. Can you recommend anything?
ABBOTT: I just did.
COSTELLO: You just did what?
ABBOTT: Recommend something.
COSTELLO: You recommended something?
ABBOTT: Yes
COSTELLO: For my office?
ABBOTT: Yes.
COSTELLO: OK, what did you recommend for my office?
ABBOTT: Office.
COSTELLO: Yes, for my office!
ABBOTT: I recommend Office with Windows.

COSTELLO: *I already have an office with windows! OK, let's just say I'm sitting at my computer and I want to type a proposal. What do I need?*
ABBOTT: Word.
COSTELLO: *What word?*
ABBOTT: Word in Office.
COSTELLO: The only word in office is office.
ABBOTT: The Word in Office for Windows.
COSTELLO: *Which word in office for windows?*
ABBOTT: The Word you get when you click the blue 'W'.
COSTELLO: *I'm going to click your blue 'W' if you don't start with some straight answers. What about financial bookkeeping? Do you have anything I can track my money with?*
ABBOTT: *Money.*
COSTELLO: *That's right. What do you have?*
ABBOTT: Money.
COSTELLO: *I need money to track my money?*
ABBOTT: It comes bundled with your computer.
COSTELLO: *What's bundled with my computer?*
ABBOTT: Money.
COSTELLO: *Money comes with my computer?*
ABBOTT: Yes. At no extra charge.
COSTELLO: *I get a bundle of money with my computer? How much?*
ABBOTT: One copy.
COSTELLO: *Isn't it illegal to copy money?*
ABBOTT: Microsoft gave us a license to copy Money.
COSTELLO: *They can give you a license to copy money?*
ABBOTT: Why not? THEY OWN IT!
(A----- FEW----- DAYS------ LATER)
ABBOTT: Super Duper computer store. Can I help you?
COSTELLO: *How do I turn my computer off?*
ABBOTT: Click on 'START.'

ATTITUDE

An old man lived alone in Minnesota. He wanted to spade his potato garden, but it was very hard work. His only son, who would have helped him, was in prison. The old man wrote a letter to his son and mentioned his situation:

Dear Son,

I am feeling pretty bad because it looks like I won't be able to plant my potato garden this year. I hate to mess up the garden plot, because your mother always loved planting time. I'm just getting too old to be digging up a garden plot. If you were here; all my troubles would be over. I know you would dig the plot, for me if you weren't in the prison

Love,

Dad

Shortly, the old man received this telegram: "For Heaven's sake, Dad, don't dig up the garden!! That's where I buried the GUNS!!"

So at 4 am the next morning, a dozen FBI agents and local police officers showed up and dug up the entire garden without finding any guns. Confused, the old man wrote another note to his son telling him what happened and asked him what to do next.

His son's reply was: "Go ahead and plant your potatoes, Dad it's the best I could do for you from here in prison."

NO MATTER WHERE YOU ARE IN THE WORLD, IF YOU HAVE DECIDED TO DO SOMETHING DEEP FROM YOUR HEART, YOU CAN DO IT. IT IS THE THOUGHT THAT MATTERS NOT WHERE YOU ARE. **THAT'S ATTITUDE!!**

<u>AGING: GEORGE CARLIN'S VIEWS (IN MEMORY OF)</u>

Do you realize that the only time in our lives when we like to get old is when we're kids? If you're less than 10 years old, you're so excited about aging that you think in fractions.

'How old are you?' 'I'm four **and a half!**' You're never thirty-six and a half. You're four and a half, going on five! That's the key.

You get into your teens, now they can't hold you back. You jump to the next number, or even a few ahead. 'How old are you?' 'I'm **gonna be** 16!' You could be 13, but hey, you're gonna be 16! And then the greatest day of your life.

You **become** 21. Even the words sound like a ceremony. **YOU BECOME 21. YESSSS!!!**

But then you **turn** 30. Oooohh, what happened there? Makes you sound like bad milk! He TURNED; we had to throw him out. There's no fun now, you're Just a sour-dumpling. What's wrong? What's changed?

You **BECOME** 21, you **TURN** 30, then you're **PUSHING** 40. Whoa! Put on the brakes, it's all slipping away. Before you know it, you **REACH** 50 and your dreams are gone.

But wait!!! You **MAKE** it to 60. You didn't think you would! So you **BECOME** 21, **TURN** 30, **PUSH** 40, **REACH** 50 and **MAKE it** to 60.

You've built up so much speed that you **HIT 70!** After that it's a day-by-day thing; you HIT Wednesday!

You **get into** your 80's and every day is a complete cycle; you HIT lunch; you TURN 4:30; you REACH bedtime. And it doesn't end there. Into the 90s, you start going backwards; 'I **Was JUST** 92!' Then a strange thing happens. If you make it over 100, you become a little kid again. 'I'm 100 and a half!' **May you all make it to a healthy 100 and a half!!**

Aging Continued: How to Stay Young by George Carlen

Throw out nonessential numbers. This includes age, weight and height. Let the doctors worry about them. That is why you pay 'them.'

Keep only cheerful friends. The grouches pull you down.

Keep learning. Learn more about the computer, crafts, gardening, whatever. **Never let the brain idle.** 'An idle mind is the devil's workshop.' And the **devil's** name is **Alzheimer's.**

Enjoy the simple things.

Laugh often, long and loud. Laugh until you gasp for breath.

The tears happen. Endure, grieve, and move on. The only person, who is with us our entire life, is ourselves. Be ALIVE while you are alive.

Surround yourself with what you love, whether it's family, pets, keepsakes, music, plants, and hobbies, whatever. **Your home is your refuge.**

Cherish your health: If it is good, preserve it. If it is unstable, improve it. If it is beyond what you can improve, get help.

Don't take guilt trips. Take a trip to the mall, even to the next county; to a foreign country but NOT to where the guilt is.

Tell the people you love that you love them, at every opportunity.

ALWAYS REMEMBER: Life is not measured by the number of breaths we take, **but** by the moments that take our breath away. And if you don't send this by e-mail to at least 8 people - **who cares?** Please do share this with someone. We all need to live life to its fullest each day.

IN MEMORY OF GEORGE CARLIN

ALABAMA JUDGE ROY MOORE'S STORY: SOME GREAT GOOD NEWS AT THE END

Some of you may be wondering what Judge Roy Moore has been doing since he was removed from the bench in 2003 for refusing to remove the Ten Commandments from his courtroom wall. Please read the poem he wrote. The following is a poem written by Judge Roy Moore from Alabama.

Judge Moore was sued by the ACLU for displaying the Ten Commandments in his courtroom foyer. He has been stripped of his judgeship and now they are trying to strip his right to practice law in Alabama! The judge's poem sums it up quite well.

America the beautiful, or so you used to be.
Land of the Pilgrims' pride; I'm glad they'll never see.
Babies piled in dumpsters, abortion on demand,
Oh, sweet land of liberty; your house is on the sand.
Our children wander aimlessly poisoned by cocaine
Choosing to indulge their lusts, when God has said abstain

From sea to shining sea, our Nation turns away
From the teaching of God's love and a need to always pray
We've kept God in our temples, how callous we have grown.
When earth is but His footstool, and Heaven is His throne.
We've voted in a government that's rotting at the core,
Appointing Godless Judges; who throw reason out the door,
Too soft to place a killer in a well-deserved tomb,
But, brave enough to kill a baby before he leaves the womb.
You think that God's not angry, that our land's a moral slum?
How much longer will He wait before His judgment comes?
How are we to face our God, from Whom we cannot hide?
What then is left for us to do, but stem this evil tide?
If we who are His children, will humbly turn and pray;
Seek His holy face and mend our evil way:
Then God will hear from Heaven; and forgive us of our sins,
He'll heal our sickly land and those who live within.
But, America the Beautiful, If you don't - then you will see,
A sad but Holy God withdraw His hand from Thee.
~~Judge Roy Moore~~

This says it all. May we all forward this message and offer our prayers for Judge Moore to be blessed and for America to wake up and realize what we need to do to keep OUR America the Beautiful. Pass this on and let's lift Judge Moore up in Prayer. He has stood firm and needs our support. IN GOD WE TRUST!

GOD does answer prayer and Judge Moore was re-elected after almost 10 years off the bench. But Wait!!

MONTGOMERY, Ala. — Roy Moore, forever known as Alabama's Ten Commandments judge, has been re-elected chief justice in a triumphant political resurrection after being ousted from that office nearly a decade ago.

Republican Moore defeated Jefferson County Circuit Judge Bob Vance, a Democrat, to win back his former office. "It's clear the people have voted to return me to the office of chief justice,"

Moore said. "I have no doubt this is a vindication. I look forward to being the next chief justice," Moore told a crowd of sign-waving supporters.

Moore thanked supporters at his party for sticking with him through what had been an up-and-down night that had Vance out to an early lead. Moore eventually won the race with 52 percent of the vote with 99 percent of precincts reporting. "Go home with the knowledge that we are going to stand for the acknowledgment of God," Moore said to shouts of "Amen" from supporters. Moore was elected chief justice in 2000, but a state judicial panel removed him three years later after he refused to obey a federal judge's order to remove a 5,200-pound granite Ten Commandments monument from the lobby of the Alabama Judicial Building.

ALL PUNS ARE INTENDED

1. The roundest knight at King Arthur's round table was Sir Cumference. He acquired his size from too much pi   i.e. F P
2. I thought I saw an eye doctor on an Alaskan island, but it turned out to be an optical Aleutian
3. She was only a whisky maker, but he loved her still.
4. A rubber band pistol was confiscated from algebra class because it was a weapon of math disruption.
5. The butcher backed into the meat grinder and got a little behind in his work.
6. No matter how much you push the envelope, it'll still be stationery.
7. A dog gave birth to puppies near the road and was cited for littering.
8. A grenade thrown into a kitchen in France would result in Linoleum Blownapart.
9. Two silk worms had a race. They ended up in a tie.

10. Time flies like an arrow. Fruit flies like a banana
11. A hole has been found in the nudist camp wall. The police are looking into it.
12. Atheism is a non-prophet organization.
13. Two hats were hanging on a hat rack in the hallway.
14. One hat said to the other,
15. 'You stay here; I'll go on a head.'
16. I wondered why the baseball kept getting bigger. Then it hit me.
17. A sign on the lawn at a drug rehab center said: 'Keep off the Grass.'
18. A small boy swallowed some coins and was taken to a hospital. When his grandmother telephoned to ask how he was, a nurse said, 'No change yet.'
19. A chicken crossing the road is poultry in motion.
20. The short fortune-teller who escaped from prison was a small medium at large.
21. The man who survived mustard gas and pepper spray is now a seasoned veteran.
22. A backward poet writes inverse.
23. In democracy it's your vote that counts. In feudalism it's your count that votes.
24. When cannibals ate a missionary, they got a taste of religion.
25. Don't join dangerous cults: Practice safe sects!

AMMO AND BUBBA

Several years ago, I traveled to Pennsylvania and Ohio, and took my "Travel Gun", which was a Mossberg 500, which was a 12 gauge pump shotgun, with an 18 inch barrel and a pistol grip, (basically a sawed off shotgun loaded with 00 Buckshot). I bought the gun across the counter in a department store in North Carolina, but learned after I got there, that in Ohio, it was considered to be a "Weapon of Mass Destruction". As luck would have it, I got back home without being sentenced to 100 years in a federal prison. Some states don't cotton to us patriotic and freedom loving Americans arming ourselves as we see fit.

You may have heard on the news about a Southern California man who was put under 72-hour psychiatric observation when it was found he owned 100 guns and allegedly had 100,000 rounds of ammunition stored in his home. The house also featured a secret escape tunnel.

By Southern California standards, someone owning 100,000 rounds is considered "mentally unstable."

In Michigan, he'd be called "The last white guy still living in Detroit."

In Arizona, he'd be called "an avid gun collector."

In Arkansas, he'd be called "a novice gun collector."

In Utah, he'd be called "moderately well prepared," but they'd probably reserve judgment until they made sure that he had a corresponding quantity of stored food."

In Kansas, he'd be "A guy down the road you would want to have for a friend."

In Montana, he'd be called "The neighborhood 'Go-To' guy."

In Idaho, he'd be called "a likely gubernatorial candidate."

In Georgia, he'd be called "an eligible bachelor."

In North Carolina, Virginia, Mississippi, Tennessee, Kentucky and South Carolina he would be called "a deer hunting buddy."

And, in Texas he'd just be "Bubba, who's a little short on ammo."

ANDY ROONEY SAID THIS ON "60 MINUTES": (IN MEMORY)

So the late Andy Rooney said; "I don't think being a minority makes you a victim of anything except numbers. The only things I can think of that are truly discriminatory are things like the United Negro College Fund, Jet Magazine, Black Entertainment Television, and Miss Black America.

Try to have things like the United Caucasian College Fund, Cloud Magazine, White Entertainment Television, or Miss White America; and see what happens...Jesse Jackson will be knocking down your door.

Guns do not make you a killer. I think killing makes you a killer. You can kill someone with a baseball bat or a car, but no one is trying to ban you from driving to the ball game.

I believe they are called the Boy Scouts for a reason and that is why there are no girls allowed. Girls belong in the Girl Scouts! ARE YOU LISTENING MARTHA BURKE?

I think that if you feel homosexuality is wrong, it is not a phobia, it is an opinion. I have the right "NOT" to be tolerant of others because they are different, weird, or tick me off.

When 70% of the people who get arrested are black, in cities where 70% of the population is black, that is not racial profiling; it is the Law of Probability.

I believe that if you are selling me a milkshake, a pack of cigarettes, a newspaper or a hotel room, you must do it in

English! As a matter of fact, if you want to be an American citizen, you should have to speak English!

My father and grandfather didn't die in vain so you can leave the countries you were born in to come over and disrespect ours. I think the police should have every right to shoot your sorry a-- if you threaten them after they tell you to stop. If you can't understand the word "freeze" or "stop" in English, see the above lines.

I don't think just because you were not born in this country, you are qualified for any special loan programs, government sponsored bank loans or tax breaks, etc., so you can open a hotel, coffee shop, trinket store, or any other business.

We did not go to the aid of certain foreign countries and risk our lives in wars to defend their freedoms, so that decades later they could come over here and tell us our constitution is a living document and open to their interpretations.

I don't hate the rich. I don't pity the poor.

I know pro wrestling is fake, but so are movies and network television. That doesn't stop you from watching them.

I think Bill Gates has every right to keep every penny he made and continue to make more. If it ticks you off, go and invent the next operating system that's better, and put your name on the building.

It doesn't take a whole village to raise a child right, but it does take a parent to stand up to the kid; and smack their little behinds when necessary, and say "NO!"

I think tattoos and piercing are fine if you want them, but please don't pretend they are a political statement. And, please, stay home until that new lip ring heals. I don't want to look at your ugly infected mouth as you serve me French fries!

I am sick of **"Political Correctness."** I know a lot of black people, and not a single one of them was born in Africa; so how can they be "African-Americans"? Besides, Africa is a continent. I don't go around saying I am a European-American because my great, great, great, great, great, great grandfather was from Europe. I am proud to be from America and <u>nowhere else</u>!

I PLEDGE ALLEGIANCE TO THE FLAG, OF THE UNITED STATES OF AMERICA, AND TO THE REPUBLIC, FOR WHICH IT STANDS, <u>ONE NATION UNDER GOD</u>, INDIVISIBLE, WITH LIBERTY AND JUSTICE FOR ALL!

I was asked to send this on if I agree or delete if I don't. It is said that 86% of Americans believe in God. Therefore, I have a very hard time understanding why there is such a problem in having "In God We Trust" on our money and having "God" in the Pledge of Allegiance.

Why don't we just tell the 14% to Shut Up and BE QUIET!!! If you agree, pass this on, if not delete. I AGREE!"

In Memory of Andy Rooney

ASPIRIN: WHY KEEP ASPIRIN BY YOUR BEDSIDE?

This is something that we can do to help ourselves and it is nice to know. FYI: Bayer is making crystal aspirin to dissolve under the tongue. They work much faster than the tablets. First something *About Heart Attacks* There are other symptoms of a heart attack besides *the pain on the left arm.* One must also be aware of *an intense pain on the chin,* as well as *nausea* and lots of *sweating*, however these symptoms may also occur less frequently .*Note:* There may be no pain in the chest during a heart attack. The majority of people (about 60%) who had a heart attack during their sleep and did not wake up. However, if it occurs, the chest pain may wake you up from your deep sleep. If that happens, ***immediately dissolve two aspirins in your mouth*** and swallow them with a bit of water. Now here is what you must do afterwards.

Afterwards:

1. ***Phone a neighbor** or a family member who lives very close by*
2. *Say "heart attack!"*
3. *Say that you have **taken 2 aspirins.***
4. ***Take a seat on a chair or sofa** near the front door, and*
5. ***Wait for their arrival** and...*

DO NOT LIE Down A Cardiologist has stated that, if each person, after receiving this e-mail, sends it to 10 people, probably one life can be saved! *I have already shared the information- - What about you? <u>Do</u> forward this message; it may save lives!*

<u>AT BIRTH</u>-Send this one to a Friend

At birth we boarded the train and met our parents, and we believe they will always travel on our side. However, at some station our parents will step down from the train, leaving us on this journey alone.

As time goes by, other people will board the train; and they will be significant i.e. our siblings, friends, children, and even the love of your life. Many will step down and leave a permanent vacuum. Others will go so unnoticed that we don't realize they vacated their seats.

This train ride will be full of joy, sorrow, fantasy, expectations, hellos, goodbyes, and farewells. Success consists of having a good relationship with all passengers requiring that we give the best of ourselves.

The mystery to everyone is: We do not know at which station we ourselves will step down. So, we must live in the best way, love, forgive, and offer the best of who we are. It is important to do this because when the time comes for us to step down and leave our seat empty we should leave behind beautiful memories for those who will continue to travel on the train of life.

I wish you a joyful journey on the train of life. Reap success and give lots of love. More importantly, thank God for the journey. Lastly, I thank you for being one of the passengers on my train.

B

BADGES: THE POWER OF THE BADGE

-A DEA officer stops at a ranch in West Texas, and talks with an old rancher. He tells the rancher, "I need to inspect your ranch for illegally grown drugs." The rancher says, "Okay, but do not go in that field over there," as he points out the location.

-The DEA officer verbally explodes saying, "Mister, I have the authority of the Federal Government with me."

-Reaching into his rear pants pocket, he removes his badge and proudly displays it to the rancher. "See this badge? This badge means I am allowed to go wherever I wish and on anyone's land. No questions asked or answers given. Have I made myself clear? Do you understand?

-The rancher nods politely, apologizes, and goes about his chores.

-A short time later, the old rancher hears loud screams and sees the DEA officer running for his life chased by the rancher's big Santa Gertrudis bull.

-With every step the bull is gaining ground on the officer, and it seems likely that he'll get gored before he reaches safety. The officer is clearly terrified. The rancher throws down his tools, runs to the fence and yells at the top of his lungs..... *"Your BADGE... Show him your BADGE ! "*

BELIEVE: A GUIDE FOR THE LIVING

A Birth Certificate shows that we were born A Death Certificate shows that we died

Pictures show that we lived! Have a seat . . . Relax . . . And read this slowly.

I Believe....That just because two people argue; it doesn't mean they don't love each other. And just because they don't argue, it doesn't mean they do love each other.

I Believe... That we don't have to change friends if we understand that friends change.

I Believe... That no matter how good a friend is, they're going to hurt you every once in a while and you must forgive them for that.

I Believe... That true friendship continues to grow, even over the longest distance. Same goes for true love.

I Believe... That you can do something in an instant. That will give you heartache for life.

I Believe... That it's taking me a long time to become the person I want to be.

I Believe... That you should always leave loved ones with Loving words. It may be the last time you see them.

I Believe... That you can keep going long after you think you can't.

I Believe... That we are responsible for what we do, no matter how we feel.

I Believe... That either you control your attitude or it controls you.

I Believe... That heroes are the people who do what has to be done when it needs to be done, regardless of the consequences.

I Believe... That money is a lousy way of keeping score.

I Believe... That my best friend and I, can do anything, or nothing and have the best time.

I Believe.. .That sometimes the people you expect to kick you when you're down, will be the ones to help you get back up.

I Believe... That sometimes when I'm angry I have the right to be angry, but that doesn't give me the right to be cruel.

I Believe.. .That maturity has more to do with what types of experiences you've had and what you've learned from them and less to do with how many birthdays you've celebrated.

I Believe... That it isn't always enough, to be forgiven by others. Sometimes, you have to learn to forgive yourself.

I Believe... That no matter how bad your heart is broken the world doesn't stop for your grief.

I Believe... That our background and circumstances may have influenced who we are, But, we are responsible for who we become.

I Believe... That you shouldn't be so eager to find out a secret. It could change your life Forever.

I Believe... Two people can look at the exact same thing and see something totally different.

I Believe... That your life can be changed in a matter of hours by people who don't even know you.

I Believe... That even when you think you have no more to give, if a friend cries out to you...you will find the strength to help.

I Believe... That credentials on the wall do not make you a decent human being.

I Believe... That the people you care about most in life are taken from you too soon.

I Believe... That you should send this to all of the people that you believe in. I just did.

The happiest of people don't necessarily have the best of everything; they just make the most of everything.

Thank you God for all the wonderful people who help us throughout the journey of life...

BENJAMIN FRANKLIN CALL FOR *GOD*

Benjamin Franklin's call for God's leadership at the 1787 Constitutional Convention: "I have lived, Sir, a long time, and the longer I live, the more convincing proofs I see of this truth – that God governs in the affairs of men.

And if a sparrow cannot fall to the ground without his notice, is it probable that an empire can rise without his aid? We have been assured, Sir, in the sacred writings, that 'except the Lord build the House they labor in vain that build it.'

I therefore beg leave to move, that henceforth prayers imploring the assistance of Heaven, and its blessings on our deliberations, be held in this assembly every morning before we proceed to business."

BEYOND BEARINGS

RWP2: Tim Gaffney's statement "Because of my passion for our trade and what we do" says much about him as a professional and for what we simply call PRIDE-in-Maintenance. We need more people like Tim in every plant. I know many like Tim's around the World. They are what I call CRAFT LEADERS as compared to TOP LEADERS and MAINTENANCE LEADERS.

In over 45 years in this business, we still have much to learn, when we truly listen to our CRAFT LEADERS. I saw it first in US ARMY Engineers (one year in Vietnam and support to Desert Storm as MP + time during my two tours of duty as a plant manager and now as consultant/trainer/author. Last "REMEMBER WHO YOU WORK FOR": as a MAINTENANCE LEADER and even as a TOP LEADER related to your physical assets. We all should be working for the millwrights/technicians that do real THE WORK!

Supporting them with the best "tools" possible to work smarter - not harder, to work safer and to be work productively in this GREAT PROFESSION. This is very important because MAINTENANCE IS FOR EVER like gravity, taxes and extinction!!

BIBLICAL HUMOR

It doesn't hurt to have a little Biblical humor to start the day.

NOTE: Now sit back, relax, push FS for Fun Stuff and pretend you are the Sunday school teacher for your 9 year old grandson or your own child just starting to learn the Bible.

Q. What kind of man was Boaz before he married Ruth?
A. Ruthless.

Q. What do they call pastors in Germany?
A. German Shepherds.

Q. Who was the greatest financier/stock broker in the Bible?
A. Noah He was floating his stock while everyone else was in liquidation.

Q. Who was the greatest female financier in the Bible?
A. Pharaoh's daughter. She went down to the bank of the Nile and drew out a little prophet.

Q. What kind of motor vehicles are in the Bible?
A. Jehovah drove Adam and Eve out of the Garden in a Fury. David's Triumph was heard throughout the land. Also, probably a Honda was there too, because the apostles were all in one Accord.

Q. Who was the greatest comedian in the Bible?
A. Samson. He brought the house down.

Q. What excuse did Adam give to his children as to why he no longer lived in Eden?
A. Your mother ate us out of house and home. *Guys, now that is funny!*

Q. Which servant of God was the most flagrant lawbreaker in the Bible?
A. Moses. He broke all 10 commandments at once.

Q. Which area of Palestine was especially wealthy?
A. The area around Jordan was because..... The banks were always overflowing.

Q. Who is the greatest babysitter mentioned in the Bible?
A. David, he rocked Goliath to a very deep sleep. *Military guys..... Now that is really Funny!*

Q. Which Bible character had no parents?
A. Joshua, son of Nun. You Gotta Know Your Bible for This One!

Q. Why didn't they play cards on the Ark?
A. Because Noah was standing on the deck. (.)

PS... *Guys* Did you know it's a sin for a woman to make coffee?

Yup, it's in the Bible. It says... 'He-brews'

KEEP SMILING!!!! GOD LOVES YOU BUNCHES AND BUNCHES!!!!

Friends are God's way of taking care of us. Faith, Hope & Love -- but the greatest of these is LOVE.   *1Corinthians13:13*

BILL CLINTON'S ABORTED MILITARY CAREER

Bill Clinton registers for the draft on September 08, 1964, accepting all contractual conditions of registering for the draft. Selective Service Number is 326 46 228.

Bill Clinton classified 2-S on November 17, 1964.

Bill Clinton reclassified 1-A on March 20, 1968.

Bill Clinton ordered to report for induction on July 28, 1969.

Bill Clinton refuses to report and is not inducted into the military.

Bill Clinton reclassified 1-D after enlisting in the United States Army Reserves on August 07, 1969, under authority of COL. E. Holmes.

Clinton signs enlistment papers and takes oath of enlistment.

Bill Clinton fails to report to his duty station at the University of Arkansas ROTC, September 1969.

Bill Clinton reclassified 1-A on October 30, 1969, as enlistment with Army Reserves is revoked by Colonel E. Holmes and Clinton now AWOL and subject to arrest under Public Law 90-40 (2) (a) - registrant who has failed to report...remain liable for induction.

Bill Clinton's birth date lottery number is 311, drawn December 1, 1969, but anyone who has already been ordered to report for induction is INELIGIBLE!

Bill Clinton runs for Congress (1974), while a fugitive from justice under Public Law 90-40.

Bill Clinton runs for Arkansas Attorney General (1976), while a fugitive from justice.

Bill Clinton receives pardon on January 21, 1977, from President Carter.

Bill Clinton becomes the FIRST PARDONED FEDERAL FELON ever to serve as President of the United States.

All these facts come from Freedom of Information requests, public laws, and various books that have been published, and have not been refuted by Clinton.

After the 1993 World Trade Center bombing, President Clinton promised that those responsible would be hunted down and punished.

After the 1995 bombing in Saudi Arabia, which killed five U.S. military personnel, Clinton promised that those responsible would be hunted down and punished.

After the 1996 Khobar Towers bombing in Saudi Arabia, which killed 19 and injured 200 U.S. military personnel, Clinton promised that those responsible would be hunted down and punished.

After the 1998 bombing of U.S. embassies in Africa, which killed 224 and injured 5,000, Clinton promised that those responsible would be hunted down and punished.

After the 2000 bombing of the USS Cole, which killed 17 and injured 39 U.S. sailors, Clinton promised that those responsible be hunted down and punished.

Maybe if Clinton had kept those promises, an estimated 3,000 people in New York and Washington, DC, who are now dead, would be alive today.

THINK ABOUT IT! It is a strange turn of events. Hillary gets $8Million for her forthcoming memoir. Bill gets about $12 Million for his memoir yet to be written. This from two people who spent 8 years being unable to recall anything about past events while under oath.

Sincerely,

Cdr. Hamilton McWhorter USN (ret)

P.S. Please forward this to as many people as you can! We don't want this woman to even THINK of running for President!

BLONDE GUYS:

It's not too often that you hear a joke about blonde guys, *but here is one for you.*

Two blonde guys were working for the city works department. One would dig a hole and the other would follow behind him and fill the hole in. They worked up one side of the street, then down the other, then they moved on to the next street, working furiously all day without rest, one guy digging a hole, the other guy filling it in again.

An onlooker was amazed at their hard work, but couldn't understand what they were doing. So he asked the hole digger, 'I'm impressed by the effort you two are putting into your work, but I don't get it -- why do you dig a hole, only to have your partner follow behind and fill it up again?'

The hole digger wiped his brow and sighed, 'Well, I suppose it probably looks odd because we're normally a three-man team. But today the guy who plants the trees called in sick.

BUBBA #1:

RWP2: *Okay now ...everyone knows a Bubba and loves at least one Bubba in this World.*

Bubba died in a real bad fire while was smoking in bed and his body was burned pretty badly. So badly burned that the morgue needed someone to identify the body, so they sent for his two best friends; Cooter and Gomer. These three men Bubba, Cooter and Gomer had always done everything together.

Cooter arrived first, and when the mortician pulled back the sheet Cooter said, 'Yup, his face is burned up pretty bad. You better roll him over.' The mortician rolled him over and Cooter said, 'Nope, that ain't Bubba.'

The mortician thought this was rather strange. So he brought Gomer in to confirm the identity of the body. Gomer looked at the body and said, 'Yup, he's pretty well burnt up. Roll him over.' The mortician rolled him over and Gomer said, 'No, it ain't Bubba.'

The mortician asked, 'How can you tell?' Gomer said, **'Well, Bubba had two a- -holes.'**

'What? He had two a- - holes?' asked the mortician. 'Yup, we had never seen 'em, but everybody used to say;

'There's Bubba with them two a- -holes.'

BUBBA # 2 AND COPPER WIRE

After having dug to a depth of 10 feet last year, New York scientists found traces of a copper-wire system dating back 100 years, and they came to the conclusion that their ancestors already had a telephone network more than 100 years ago.

Not to be outdone by New Yorkers, in the weeks that followed, California scientists dug to a depth of 20 feet, and shortly after, headlines in the LA Times newspaper read; "California archaeologists have found traces of a 200 year old copper-wire system and have concluded that their ancestors already had an advanced high-tech communications network a hundred years earlier than the New Yorkers."

One week later, "The Redneck Rebel Gazette" in Arlamsas, Arkansas reported the following;

After digging as deep as 30 feet in a cornfield, **Bubba Ray Johnson**, a self-taught archaeologist, reported that he found absolutely nothing. Bubba has therefore concluded that 300 years ago, concluded that Arkansas had already gone wireless. *I REALLY LIKE BUBBA'S!!!!! Another SMILE FOR YOUR DAY!*

BUBBA # 3 AND A TRUE STORY:

RWP2: OUR FAMILY LIVED IN THE SUBURBS OF HELL IN SUMTER, SC (WE COULD SEE THE LIGHTS FROM THE FLAMES) IN THE 1980's, WHEN OUR TWO SONS WERE JUST GETTING STARTED IN SPORTS. THE MAYOR OF SUMTER WAS NAMED BUBBA PLUS MANY MORE PEOPLE THERE. IF YOU WENT ANYWHERE (BAR MALL OR CHURCH) AND SHOUTED, "HEY BUBBA!' You would have 79% of the males turn, look at you and wave! Most times at least two females would do the same.

BUBBA # 4 FINE DINING

As the story goes Bubba won a dinner in the finest restaurant in Chattanooga, TN from a trade show drawing

As Bubba was dining away in this fancy restaurant and there was a gorgeous redhead sitting at the next table. He was been really checking her out since he sat down, but Bubba lacked the nerve to talk with her.

Suddenly she sneezes, and her glass eye comes flying out of its socket towards the Bubba.

Bubba being quick as greased lightning, reflexively reaches out, grabs it right out of the air before it hits the floor, and hands it back.

"Oh my, I am so sorry", the red headed voluptuous woman says as she pops her eye back in place.

"Let me buy your dinner to make it up to you," she says. They enjoy a wonderful dinner together, and afterwards they go to the theater, his first with live people, followed by drinks. They talk, they laugh, she shares her deepest dreams and he shares his. She listens.

After paying for everything, she asks Bubba if he would like to come to her place for a nightcap and stay for breakfast. They had a wonderful, wonderful time. Bubba was in "hog heaven" for a while.

The next morning, she cooks a gourmet meal with all the trimmings. Now Bubba is really amazed!! Everything had been SO incredible!

"You know," Bubba said, "you are the perfect woman. Are you this nice to every guy you meet?"

"No" she replies, "You just happened to catch my eye Bubba"!

BUBBA'S GOOD STUFF TO KNOW

HOW TO INSTALL A SOUTHERN HOME SECURITY SYSTEM

1. Go to the Goodwill and buy a pair of size 14-16 men's work boots
2. Place them on your front porch, along with a copy of Guns and Ammo Magazine.
3. Put four giant dog dishes next to the boots and magazines
4. Leave a note that reads....**Bubba**, Me and Marcel, Donnie Ray and Jimmy Earl went for more ammo. Back in an hour. Don't mess with the pit bulls. They got the mailman this morning and messed him up bad. I don't think Killer took part, but it was hard to tell from all the blood. Anyway, I locked all four of 'em in the house. Better wait outside. ***Be right back, Cooter***

BROOKLYN BRIDGE: AN IMPOSSIBLE DREAM THAT BECAME A REALITY

March 02, 2010

Robert H. Schuller

"Jesus told them, '...if you have faith and don't doubt, you can do things like this and much more....'"–Matthew 21:21, NLT

John Roebling was the engineer who came up with the idea of building a bridge across the river to tie Manhattan Island with Brooklyn. It was a fabulous idea, but all the bridge-building experts and structural engineers said it was impossible. Some agreed that the river might be spanned, but that a 1,595-foot span would never stand up against the winds and the tides. But John Roebling and his son Washington figured out how the problems could be solved and how the obstacles would be overcome.

And then, as construction began, John Roebling was killed on the job and in the same accident, his son Washington suffered the bends underneath the water. The son survived, but was left with permanent brain damage so that he never walked or talked again.

Everybody said to forget the project. But Washington would not. He developed a code of communication by touching one finger to the arm of his wife. And he communicated the dream through her to the engineers on the project. For thirteen years, Washington Roebling supervised construction that way. And finally in 1883, traffic streamed across the completed Brooklyn Bridge.

When Washington Roebling was told the news, he wept for joy. The impossible dream had become a reality!

Prayer:

Today, read aloud "The Possibility Thinker's Creed" as your own prayer of faith: "When faced with a mountain I WILL NOT QUIT! I will keep on striving until I climb over, find a pass through, tunnel underneath—or simply stay and turn the mountain into a gold mine, with God's help!"

What is the biggest problem you are facing today? Briefly describe your "impossible problem." Now look again at the problem you just described and complete this statement: It might be possible if ....?!

C

CAJUN PREGNANCY

Way down in Louisiana, Boudreaux's old lady had been pregnant for some time and now the time had come. So he brought her to the doctor and the doctor began to deliver the baby.

She had a little boy and the doctor looked over at Boudreaux and said, "Hey, Boudreaux, you just had you-sef a son! Ain't dat grand!"

Boudreaux got excited by dis, but just then the doctor spoke up and said, "Hold on! We ain't finished yet!" The doctor then delivered a little girl. He said, "Hey, Boudreaux, you got you-sef a daughter too! She a pretty lil ting." Boudreaux got kind of puzzled by this and then the doctor said, "Hold on, we still ain't got done yet!" The doctor then delivered another boy and said, "Boudreaux, you just had you-sef another boy!"

When Boudreaux and his wife went home with their 3 children, he sat down with his wife and said, "Mama, you remember dat night what we run out of Vaseline and we had to use dat dere Tree-in-One Oil?"

His wife said, "Yeah, I do!" Boudreaux said, "Man, it's a good ting we didn't use no WD-Forty!"

CALIFORNIA IN 1850:

Do you know what happened this week back in 1850, 159 YEARS AGO THIS WEEK?

- California became a state.

- The State had no electricity.

- The State had no money.

- Almost everyone spoke Spanish.

- There were gunfights in the streets.

So basically, it was just like CALIFORNIA is TODAY; except the women had real breasts and the men didn't hold hands.

CHANGE?

Not long ago I read a joke ... It said all the politicians running for president are promising change to the American people. We send them billions and billions of tax dollars and they send us the change. That's Not Funny?

Not really; there is too much truth in it to be funny. That got me to thinking ... They all promise change. How about if they run on a promise of restoration rather than change?

A restoration that would take us back in time to a place where things ran better, smoother and life was more enjoyable. Change? That, in truth, is what they have been giving us all along.

We used to have a strong dollar; Politicians changed that.

Marriage used to be sacred; Politicians are changing that.

We used to be respected around the world, Politicians changed that.

We used to have a strong manufacturing economy, Politicians changed that.

We used to have lower tax structures, Politicians changed that.

We used to enjoy more freedoms, Politicians changed that.

We used to be a large exporter of American made goods, Politicians changed that.

We used to teach patriotism in schools, Politicians changed that.

We used to educate children in schools, Politicians changed that.

We used to enforce LEGAL citizenship, Politicians changed that.

We used to have affordable food & gas prices, Politicians changed that, too!

We could go on and on with this list. What hasn't been changed, politicians are promising to change that as well, if you will elect them.

When, oh when, is America going to sit back with open eyes and look at what we once were and where we have come and say, enough is enough?

The trouble is *and sad truth is*, America s youthful voters today don't know of the great America that existed forty and fifty years ago. They see the world as if it has always existed, as it is now.

When will we wake up? Tomorrow may be too late. When will America realize that *some* Politicians are what is wrong with America?

What is needed is for the constitution to be amended to limit all Senators and Representatives to TWO terms in office like the president. Oh, by the way, no big pension either, social security just like the rest of us.

Being a politician shouldn't be a person's life work but rather a call to service then back to being an honest hard working citizen. PASS THIS ONE AROUND FOR A CHANGE.

COYOTE POPULATION CONTROL

The Alberta Government and the Alberta Forest Service were presenting an alternative to Alberta ranchers for controlling the coyote population. It seems that after years of the ranchers using the tried and true methods of shooting and/or trapping the predators, the tree-huggers had a 'more humane' solution.

What they proposed was for the animals to be captured alive; the males would then be castrated and let loose again. Therefore the population would be controlled. This was ACTUALLY proposed to the Alberta Ranching Association and Farming Association by the Alberta Government and the Alberta Forest Service.

All of the ranchers thought about this amazing idea for a couple of minutes. Finally, one of the old boys in the back of the conference room stood up, tipped his hat back and said, **'Son, I don't think you understand our problem. *THOSE COYOTES AIN'T FU- KING OUR SHEEP -THEY'RE EATIN'-EM!!***

You should have been there to hear the roar of laughter! **A small coyote problem!**

CHICAGO:

Body count: In the last six months 292 killed (murdered) in Chicago. 221 killed in Iraq AND Chicago has one of the strictest gun laws in the entire US. (To left is Deon Gilbert, Jr. age 15, killed on November 7, 2014)

President: Barack Hussein Obama
Senator: Dick Durbin
House Representative: Jesse Jackson Jr.
Governor: Pat Quinn
House leader: Mike Madigan
Atty. Gen.: Lisa Madigan (daughter of Mike)
Mayor: Rahm Emanuel
The leadership in Illinois - all Democrats.
Thank you for the combat zone in Chicago.
Of course, they're all blaming each other.
Can't blame Republicans; there aren't any!
Chicago school system rated one of the worst in the country.
Can't blame Republicans; there aren't any!
State pension fund $78 Billion in debt, worst in country.
Can't blame Republicans; there aren't any!
Cook County (Chicago) sales tax 10.25% highest in country.
Can't blame Republicans; there aren't any!
This is the political culture that Obama comes from Illinois.
And he is going to 'fix' Washington politics for us???
George Ryan is no longer Governor; he is in the big house. Of course he was replaced by Rob Blajegovitch who is...that's right, also in the big house.

And Representative Jesse Jackson Jr. resigned a couple of weeks ago. That is because he is fighting being sent to...that's right, the big house.

The Land of Lincoln, where our governors make our license plates.

But you know what? As long as they keep providing entitlements to the population of Chicago, nothing is going to change, except the state will go broke before the country does.

While We're at It Consider These Facts?

TEN POOR CITIES

The top ten cities with estimated percentages of people below the Poverty Level

1. Detroit, MI 32.5%
2. Buffalo, NY 29.9%
3. Cincinnati, OH 27.8%
4. Cleveland, OH 27.0%
5. Miami, FL 26.9%
6. St. Louis, MO 26.8%
7. El Paso, TX 26.4%
8. Milwaukee, WI 26.2%
9. Philadelphia, Pa 25.1%
10. Newark , NJ 24.2%

What do all these top ten cities with a population of over 250,000 with the highest poverty rate have in common?

1. Detroit, MI (1st) hasn't elected a Republican mayor since 1961.
2. Buffalo, NY (2nd) hasn't elected a Republican mayor since 1954.
3. Cincinnati, OH (3rd) hasn't elected a Republican mayor since 1984.
4. Cleveland, OH (4th) hasn't elected a Republican mayor since 1989.
5. Miami, FL (5th) has never had a Republican mayor.
6. St. Louis, MO (6th) hasn't elected a Republican mayor since 1949.

7. El Paso, TX (7th) has never had a Republican mayor.
8. Milwaukee, WI (8th) hasn't elected a Republican mayor since 1908.
9. Philadelphia, PA (9th) hasn't elected a Republican mayor since 1952.
10. Newark, NJ (10th) hasn't elected a Republican mayor since 1907.

Abraham Lincoln said the following: "You cannot help the poor by destroying the rich. You cannot strengthen the weak by weakening the strong. You cannot bring about prosperity by discouraging thrift. You cannot lift the wage earner up by pulling the wage payer down. You cannot further the brotherhood of man by inciting class hatred. You cannot build character and courage by taking away people's initiative and independence. You cannot help people permanently by doing for them, what they could and should do for themselves."

Einstein once said, 'The definition of insanity is doing the same thing over and over again and expecting different results.' It is the poor who habitually elect Democrats yet they are still POOR! *RWP2: Well maybe many got the message and voted on November 4, 2014. Only time will tell after January 3, 2015 when the new Congress comes to Washington, DC.*

And Mr. Obama, you are no Abe Lincoln!--and certainly no Einstein.

CHRISTMAS PAGEANT

My husband and I had been happily married (most of the time) for five years but hadn't been blessed with a baby.

I decided to do some serious praying and promised God that if he would give us a child, I would be a perfect mother, love it with all my heart and raise it with His word as my guide.

God answered my prayers and blessed us with a son. The next year God blessed us with another son.

The following year, He blessed us with yet another son.

The year after that we were blessed with a daughter.

My husband thought we'd been blessed right into poverty. We now had four children, and the oldest was only four years old.

I learned never to ask God for anything unless I meant it. As a minister once told me, "If you pray for rain, make sure you carry an umbrella."

I began reading a few verses of the Bible to the children each day as they lay in their cribs.

I was off to a good start. God had entrusted me with four children and I didn't want to disappoint Him.

I tried to be patient the day the children smashed two dozen eggs on the kitchen floor searching for baby chicks.

I tried to be understanding... when they started a hotel for homeless frogs in the spare bedroom, although it took me nearly two hours to catch all twenty-three frogs.

When my daughter poured ketchup all over herself and rolled up in a blanket to see how it felt to be a hot dog, I tried to see the humor rather than the mess.

In spite of changing over twenty-five thousand diapers, never eating a hot meal and never sleeping for more than thirty minutes at a time, I still thank God daily for my children.

While I couldn't keep my promise to be a perfect mother - I didn't even come close...I did keep my promise to raise them in the Word of God.

I knew I was missing the mark just a little when I told my daughter we were going to church to worship God, and she wanted to bring a bar of soap along to "wash up" Jesus, too.

Something was lost in the translation when I explained that God gave us everlasting life, and my son thought it was generous of God to give us his "last wife."

My proudest moment came during the children's Christmas pageant.

My daughter was playing Mary, two of my sons were shepherds and my youngest son was a wise man.

This was their moment to shine.

My five-year-old shepherd had practiced his line, "We found the babe wrapped in swaddling clothes."

But he was nervous and said, "The baby was wrapped in wrinkled clothes."

My four-year-old "Mary" said, "That's not 'wrinkled clothes,' silly.

That's dirty, rotten clothes."

A wrestling match broke out between Mary and the shepherd and was stopped by an angel, who bent her halo and lost her left wing.

I slouched a little lower in my seat when Mary dropped the doll representing Baby Jesus, and it bounced down the aisle crying, "Mama-mama."

Mary grabbed the doll, wrapped it back up and held it tightly as the wise men arrived.

My other son stepped forward wearing a bathrobe and a paper crown, knelt at the manger and announced, "We are the three wise men, and we are bringing gifts of gold, common sense and fur."

The congregation dissolved into laughter, and the pageant got a standing ovation.

"I've never enjoyed a Christmas program as much as this one," laughed the pastor, wiping tears from his eyes

"For the rest of my life, I'll never hear the Christmas story without thinking of gold, common sense and fur."

"My children are my pride and my joy and my greatest blessing," I said as I dug through my purse for an aspirin.

Jesus had no servants, yet they called Him Master.

Had no degree, yet they called Him Teacher.

Had no medicines, yet they called Him Healer.

Had no army, yet kings feared Him.

He won no military battles, yet He conquered the world.

He committed no crime, yet they crucified Him.

He was buried in a tomb, yet He lives today.

Feel honored to serve such a Leader who loves us.

If you believe in God and in Jesus Christ His Son, send this to all on your buddy list.

GOD BLESS YOU ALL!

CHRISTMAS ADVENTURE WITH GRANDMA:

I remember my first Christmas adventure with Grandma. I was just a kid. I remember tearing across town on my bike to visit her on the day my big sister dropped the bomb: "There is no Santa Claus," she jeered. "Even dummies know that!"

My Grandma was not the gushy kind, never had been. I fled to her that day because I knew she would be straight with me. I knew Grandma always told the truth, and I knew that the truth always went down a whole lot easier when swallowed with one of her world-famous cinnamon buns. I knew they were world-famous, because Grandma said so. It had to be true.

Grandma was home, and the buns were still warm. Between bites, I told her everything. She was ready for me. "No Santa Claus!" she snorted. "Ridiculous! Don't believe it. That rumor has been going around for years, and it makes me mad, plain mad. Now, put on your coat, and let's go."

"Go? Go where, Grandma?" I asked. I hadn't even finished my second world-famous, cinnamon bun. "Where" turned out to be Kerby's General Store, the one store in town that had a little bit of just about everything. As we walked through its doors,

Grandma handed me ten dollars. That was a bundle in those days. "Take this money," she said, "and buy something for someone who needs it.

I'll wait for you in the car." Then she turned and walked out of Kerby's.

I was only eight years old. I'd often gone shopping with my mother, but never had I shopped for anything all by myself. The store seemed big and crowded, full of people scrambling to finish their Christmas shopping. For a few moments I just stood there, confused, clutching that ten-dollar bill, wondering what to buy, and who on earth to buy it for.

I thought of everybody I knew: my family, my friends, my neighbors, the kids at school, and the people who went to my church. I was just about thought out, when I suddenly thought of Bobby Decker. He was a kid with bad breath and messy hair, and he sat right behind me in Mrs. Pollock's grade-two class.

Bobby Decker didn't have a coat. I knew that because he never went out for recess during the winter. His mother always wrote a note, telling the teacher that he had a cough, but all we kids knew that Bobby Decker didn't have a cough, and he didn't have a coat. I fingered the ten-dollar bill with growing excitement. I would buy Bobby Decker a coat!

I settled on a red corduroy one that had a hood to it. It looked real warm, and he would like that. "Is this a Christmas present for someone?" the lady b*ehind the counter asked kindly, as I laid my ten dollars down. "Yes," I* replied shyly. "It's .... For Bobby." The nice lady smiled at me. I didn't get any change, but she put the coat in a bag and wished me a Merry Christmas.

That evening, Grandma helped me wrap the coat in Christmas paper and ribbons (a little tag fell out of the coat, and Grandma tucked it in her *Bible)* and wrote on the package, "To Bobby, From Santa Claus" -- Grandma said that Santa always insisted on secrecy. Then she drove me over to Bobby Decker's house, explaining as we went that I was now and forever officially one of Santa's helpers.

Grandma parked down the street from Bobby's house, and she and I crept noiselessly and hid in the bushes by his front walk. Then Grandma gave me a nudge. "All right, Santa Claus," she whispered, "get going."

I took a deep breath, dashed for his front door, threw the present down on his step, pounded his doorbell and flew back to the safety of the bushes and Grandma. Together we waited breathlessly in the darkness for the front door to open. Finally it did, and there stood Bobby.

Fifty years haven't dimmed the thrill of those moments spent shivering, beside my Grandma, in Bobby Decker's bushes. That night, I realized that those awful rumors about Santa Claus were just what Grandma said they were: ridiculous. Santa was alive and well, and we were on his team.

I still have the Bible, with the tag tucked inside: $19.95.

He who has no Christmas in his heart will never find Christmas under a tree.

CLUNKERS: AM I ON THE WRONG PAGE?

REMEMBER WHEN THE USA SPENT $3,000,000,000 BUYING CLUNKERS?

A vehicle at 15 mpg and 12,000 miles per year uses 800 gallons a year of gasoline.

A vehicle at 25 mpg and 12,000 miles per year uses 480 gallons a year.

So, the average clunker transaction will reduce US gasoline consumption by **320** gallons per year.

They claim 700,000 vehicles – so that's 224 million gallons / year.

That equates to a bit over 5 million barrels of oil.

- 5 million barrels of oil is about ¼ of one day's US consumption.

- 5 million barrels of oil costs about $350 million dollars at $75/bbl. +

- *__So, we all contributed to spending $3 billion buy"clunkers" to save $350 million.__*

Now...How Good a Deal Was That?

RWP2: Just a little more about Cash for Clunkers. Researchers at Texas A&M, in a recently released report, measured the impact of Cash for Clunkers on sales and found the program actually decreased industry revenue by $3 billion over a nine-to-11-month period. Meanwhile, the "stimulus" also cost taxpayers $3 billion. The Car Allowance Rebate System, commonly called Cash for Clunkers, was part of a 2009 economic stimulus program that was sold as a lifeline from the federal government to a sinking U.S. auto industry.

The program let people turn in their old cars for up to $4,500 in cash to be used toward the purchase of a more fuel-efficient alternative. Nearly 700,000 vehicles were traded in through the program. But the Texas A&M University study, for the National Bureau of Economic Research, shows the program may have actually created a drag on the economy. While the program's fuel-efficiency restrictions led to the purchase of more fuel-efficient cars, Americans ended up buying cheaper cars than they otherwise would have, the study found.

"Strikingly, we find that Cash for Clunkers actually reduced overall spending on new vehicles," the researchers reported, noting households "tended to purchase less expensive and smaller vehicles such as the Toyota Corolla, which was the most popular new vehicle purchased under the program." They found buyers who participated "spent an average of $4,600 less on a new vehicle than they otherwise would have."

During the two months of the program, the frequency of purchasing a new vehicle was around 50 percent higher for those who qualified for the program compared with those who did not. But after the program ended, the researchers found, car-buying habits returned to normal. Congress originally appropriated $1 billion to the program but was forced to add another $2 billion when the program ran out of money a month after it started and two months sooner than the government expected.

CONGRESSIONAL REFORM PROPOSAL

This needs to grow legs and move across America thru everyone's email friends.

The proposal is to promote a "Congressional Reform Act of 2009." It would contain eight provisions, all of which would probably be strongly endorsed by those who drafted the Constitution and the Bill of Rights.

I know many of you will say, "this is impossible." Remember, Congress has the lowest approval of any entity in Government, now is the time when Americans will join together to reform Congress - the entity that represents us.

We need a Senator to introduce this bill in the US Senate and a Representative to introduce a similar bill in the US House. Please add any ideas on how to get this done.

If all else fails, something like this needs to be added to the ballot for the next election. After what's been going on for the past few years, I'm certain the American public will vote for these changes.

CONGRESSIONAL REFORM ACT OF 2009

1. Term Limits: 12 years only, one of the possible options below.

> **A. Two Six-year Senate terms**
> **B. Six Two-year House terms**
> **C. One Six-year Senate term and three Two-Year House terms**

Serving in Congress is an honor, not a career. The Founding Fathers envisioned citizen legislators, serve your term(s), then go home and back to work.

2. No Tenure / No Pension: A congressman collects a salary while in office and receives no pay when they are out of office.

Serving in Congress is an honor, not a career. The Founding Fathers envisioned citizen legislators, serve your term(s), then go home and back to work.

3. Congress (past, present & future) participates in Social Security: All funds in the Congressional retirement fund moves to the Social Security system immediately. All future funds flow into the Social Security system, Congress participates with the American people.

Serving in Congress is an honor, not a career. The Founding Fathers envisioned citizen legislators, server your term(s), then go home and back to work.

4. Congress can purchase their own retirement plan just as all Americans...

Serving in Congress is an honor, not a career. The Founding Fathers envisioned citizen legislators, serve your term(s), then go home and back to work.

5. Congress will no longer vote themselves a pay raise. Congressional pay will rise by the lower of CPI or 3%.

Serving in Congress is an honor, not a career. The Founding Fathers envisioned citizen legislators, serve your term(s), then go home and back to work.

6. Congress loses their current health care system and participates in the same health care system as the American people.

Serving in Congress is an honor, not a career. The Founding Fathers envisioned citizen legislators, serve your term(s), then go home and back to work.

7. Congress must equally abide in all laws they impose on the American people.

Serving in Congress is an honor, not a career. The Founding Fathers envisioned citizen legislators, serve your term(s), then go home and back to work.

8. All contracts with past and present congressmen are void effective 1/1/10.

PLEASE REMEMBER: The American people did not give all these perks to congressmen; congressmen gave all these sweetheart deals to themselves. We need to take back the Congress.

They all seem to have forgotten: Serving in Congress is an honor, not a career. The Founding Fathers envisioned citizen legislators, serve your term(s), then go home and back to work.

DIFFERENT CHRISTMAS POEM:

The embers glowed softly, and in their dim light, I gazed round the room and I cherished the sight.

My wife was asleep, her head on my chest, my daughter beside me, angelic in rest.

Outside the snow fell, a blanket of white, transforming the yard to a winter delight.

The sparkling lights in the tree I believe, Completed the magic that was Christmas Eve.

My eyelids were heavy, my breathing was deep, Secure and surrounded by love I would sleep.

In perfect contentment, or so it would seem, So I slumbered, perhaps I started to dream.

The sound wasn't loud, and it wasn't too near, But I opened my eyes when it tickled my ear.

Perhaps just a cough, I didn't quite know, Then the sure sound of footsteps outside in the snow.

My soul gave a tremble, I struggled to hear, And I crept to the door just to see who was near.

Standing out in the cold and the dark of the night, a lone figure stood, his face weary and tight.

A soldier, I puzzled, some twenty years old, Perhaps a Marine, huddled here in the cold.

Alone in the dark, he looked up and smiled, Standing watch over me, and my wife and my child.

"What are you doing?" I asked without fear, "Come in this moment, it's freezing out here!"

Put down your pack, brush the snow from your sleeve, You should be at home on a cold Christmas Eve!"

For barely a moment I saw his eyes shift, Away from the cold and the snow blown in drifts.

To the window that danced with a warm fire's light. Then he sighed and he said "It's really all right,

I'm out here by choice. I'm here every night." "It's my duty to stand at the front of the line. That separates you from the darkest of times.

No one had to ask or beg or implore me, I'm proud to stand here like my father's before me.

My Gramps died at ' Pearl on a day in December," Then he sighed, "That's a Christmas 'Gram always remembers."

"My dad stood his watch in the jungles of ' Nam ', And now it is my turn and so, here I am.

I've not seen my own son in more than a while, But my wife sends me pictures, he's sure got her smile."

Then he bent and he carefully pulled from his bag, the red, white, and blue... an American flag. "I can live through the cold and the being alone, Away from my family, my house and my home.

I can stand at my post through the rain and the sleet; I can sleep in a foxhole with little to eat.

I can carry the weight of killing another, Or lay down my life with my sister and brother.

"Who stand at the front against any and all? To ensure for all time that this flag will not fall."

"So go back inside," he said, "harbor no fright, Your family is waiting and I'll be all right."

"But isn't there something I can do, at the least, "Give you money," I asked, "or prepare you a feast?

It seems all too little for all that you've done, or being away from your wife and your son."

Then his eye welled a tear that held no regret, "Just tell us you love us, and never forget."

To fight for our rights back at home while we're gone. To stand your own watch, no matter how long.

For when we come home, either standing or dead. To know you remember we fought and we bled.

Is payment enough, and with that we will trust. That we mattered to you as you mattered to us."

PLEASE: Would you do me the kind favor of sending this to as many people as you can? Christmas will be coming soon and some credit is due to our U.S. service men and women for our being able to celebrate these festivities. Let's try in this small way to pay a tiny bit of what we owe. Make people stop and think of our heroes, living and dead, who sacrificed themselves for us. By: LCDR Jeff Giles, SC, USN, 30th Naval Construction Regiment, OIC, Logistics Cell One, Al Taqqadum, Iraq

CIRCUMCISION: GET IT DONE EARLY"!

Two little boys are going to the hospital the next day for operations.

Theirs will be first on the schedule.

The older boy leans over and asks, "What are you having done?"

The younger boy says, "I'm getting my tonsils out, and I'm afraid."

The first boy says, "You've got nothing to worry about. I had that done when I was four. They put you to sleep, and when you wake up, they give you lots of Jell-O and ice cream. It's a breeze.

The younger boy then asks, "What are you going in for?

The older boy says, "Circumcision."

"Whoa!" the smaller boy replies. "Good luck, buddy. I had that done when I was born. Couldn't walk for a year."

D

DOCTORS: DEADLY DOCTORS BY BETSY MCCAUGHEY

THE health bills coming out of Congress would put the decisions about your care in the hands of presidential appointees. They'd decide what plans cover, how much leeway your doctor will have and what seniors get under Medicare.

Yet at least two of President Obama's top health advisers should never be trusted with that power. Start with Dr. Ezekiel Emanuel, the brother of White House Chief of Staff Rahm Emanuel. He has already been appointed to two key positions: health-policy adviser at the Office of Management and Budget and a member of Federal Council on Comparative Effectiveness Research. Emanuel bluntly admits that the cuts will not be pain-free.

"Vague promises of savings from cutting waste, enhancing prevention and wellness, installing electronic medical records and improving quality are merely 'lipstick' cost control, more for show and public relations than for true change," he wrote last year (Health Affairs Feb. 27, 2008).

Savings, he writes, will require changing how doctors think about their patients: Doctors take the Hippocratic Oath too seriously, "as an imperative to do everything for the patient regardless of the cost or effects on others" (Journal of the American Medical Association, June 18, 2008).

Yes, that's what patients want their doctors to do. But Emanuel wants doctors to look beyond the needs of their patients and consider social justice, such as whether the money could be better spent on somebody else. Many doctors are horrified by this notion; they'll tell you that a doctor's job is to achieve social justice one patient at a time.

Emanuel, however, believes that "communitarianism" should guide decisions on who gets care. He says medical care should be reserved for the non-disabled, not given to those "who are irreversibly prevented from being or becoming participating citizens . . . An obvious example is not guaranteeing health services to patients with dementia" (Hastings Center Report, Nov.-Dec. '96). Translation: Don't give much care to a grandmother with Parkinson's or a child with cerebral palsy.

He explicitly defends discrimination against older patients: "Unlike allocation by sex or race, allocation by age is not invidious discrimination; every person lives through different life stages rather than being a single age. Even if 25-year-olds receive priority over 65-year-olds, everyone who is 65 years now was previously 25 years" (Lancet, Jan. 31). The bills being rushed through Congress will be paid for largely by a $500 billion-plus cut in Medicare over 10 years.

Knowing how unpopular the cuts will be, the president's budget director, Peter Orszag, urged Congress this week to delegate its own authority over Medicare to a new, presidentially-appointed bureaucracy that wouldn't be accountable to the public. Since Medicare was founded in 1965, seniors' lives have been transformed by new medical treatments such as angioplasty, bypass surgery and hip and knee replacements. These innovations allow the elderly to lead active lives.

But Emanuel criticizes Americans for being too "enamored with technology" and is determined to reduce access to it. Dr. David Blumenthal, another key Obama adviser, agrees. He recommends slowing medical innovation to control health spending. Blumenthal has long advocated government health-spending controls, though he concedes they're "associated with longer waits" and "reduced availability of new and expensive treatments and devices" (New England Journal of Medicine, March 8, 2001). But he calls it "debatable" whether the timely care Americans get is worth the cost. (Ask a cancer patient, and you'll get a different answer.

Delay lowers your chances of survival.) Obama appointed Blumenthal as national coordinator of health-information technology, a job that involves making sure doctors obey electronically delivered guidelines about what care the government deems appropriate and cost effective. In the April 9 New England Journal of Medicine,

Blumenthal predicted that many doctors would resist "embedded clinical decision support" -- a euphemism for computers telling doctors what to do. Americans need to know what the president's health advisers have in mind for them. Emanuel sees even basic amenities as luxuries and says Americans expect too much: "Hospital rooms in the United States offer more privacy . . . physicians' offices are typically more conveniently located and have parking nearby and more attractive waiting rooms" (JAMA, June 18, 2008).

No one has leveled with the public about these dangerous views. Nor have most people heard about the arm-twisting, Chicago-style tactics being used to force support. In a Nov. 16, 2008, Health Care Watch column, Emanuel explained how business should be done: "Every favor to a constituency should be linked to support for the health-care reform agenda. If the automakers want a bailout, then they and their suppliers have to agree to support and lobby for the administration's health-reform effort.

"Do we want a "reform" that empowers people like this to decide for us? Betsy McCaughey is founder of the Committee to Reduce Infection Deaths and a former New York lieutenant governor. To sign up for Daily Newsletter Alerts, please visit: www.nypost.com/php/newsletter/classify_newsletter_clicks.php

DEAR ABBY ADMITTED SHE WAS AT A LOSS TO ANSWER THE FOLLOWING:

Dear Abby,

A couple of women moved in across the hall from me. One is a middle-aged gym teacher and the other is a social worker in her mid-twenties. These two women go everywhere together and I've never seen a man go into or leave their apartment. Do you think they could be Lebanese?

Dear Abby,

What can I do about all the Sex, Nudity, Foul Language and Violence on my VCR?

Dear Abby,

I have a man I can't trust. He cheats so much, I'm not even sure the baby I'm carrying is his.

Dear Abby,

I am a twenty-three year old liberated woman who has been on the pill for two years. It's getting expensive and I think my boyfriend should share half the cost, but I don't know him well enough to discuss money with him.

Dear Abby,

I've suspected that my husband has been fooling around, and when confronted with the evidence, he denied everything and said it would never happen again.

Dear Abby,

Our son writes that he is taking Judo. Why would a boy who was raised in a good Christian home turn against his own?

Dear Abby,

I joined the Navy to see the world. I've seen it. Now how do I get out?

Dear Abby,

My forty-year old son has been paying a psychiatrist $50.00 an hour every week for two and a half years. He must be crazy.

Dear Abby,

I was married to Bill for three months and I didn't know he drank until one night he came home sober.

Dear Abby,

My mother is mean and short tempered. I think she is going through mental pause.

Dear Abby,

You told some woman whose husband had lost all interest in sex to send him to a doctor. Well, my husband lost all interest in sex and he is a doctor. Now what do I do?

Remember These People Can Vote!!

DODGE DEALER LETTER

May 19, 2009 to Editor

My name is XXXXXXXXX. I am the sole owner of XXXXXX Dodge-Isuzu; a family owned and operated business in XXXX, Florida. My family bought and paid for this automobile franchise 35 years ago in 1974. I am the second generation to manage this business.

We currently employ 50+ people and before the economic slowdown we employed over 70 local people. We are active in the community and the local chamber of commerce. We deal with several dozen local vendors on a day to day basis and many more during a month. All depend on our business for part of their livelihood. We are financially strong with great respect in the market place and community. We have strong local presence and stability. I work every day the store is open, nine to ten hours a day. I know most of our customers and all our employees. XXXXXX Dodge is my life.

On Thursday, May 14, 2009 I was notified that my Dodge franchise, that we purchased, will be taken away from my family on June 9, 2009 without compensation and given to another dealer at no cost to them. My new vehicle inventory consists of 125 vehicles with a financed balance of 3 million dollars. This inventory becomes impossible to sell with no factory incentives beyond June 9, 2009. Without the Dodge franchise we can no longer sell a new Dodge as "new," nor will we be able to do any warranty service work.

Additionally, my Dodge parts inventory, (approximately $300,000.) is virtually worthless without the ability to perform warranty service. There is no offer from Chrysler to buy back the vehicles or parts inventory.

Our facility was recently totally renovated at Chrysler's insistence, incurring a multi-million dollar debt in the form of a mortgage at Sun Trust Bank.

HOW IN THE UNITED STATES OF AMERICA CAN THIS HAPPEN?

THIS IS A PRIVATE BUSINESS NOT A GOVERNMENT ENTITY

This is beyond imagination! My business is being stolen from me through NO FAULT OF OUR OWN. We did NOTHING wrong. This atrocity will most likely force my family into bankruptcy. This will also cause our 50+ employees to be unemployed. How will they provide for their families? This is a total economic disaster.

HOW CAN THIS HAPPEN IN A FREE MARKET ECONOMY IN THE UNITED STATES OF AMERICA?

I beseech your help, and look forward to your reply. Thank you.

Sincerely,
XXXXXXX
President & Owner
XXXXX Dodge-Isuzu

DOGS AND CATS

Excerpts from a Dog's Diary

8:00 am - Dog food! My favorite thing!
9:30 am - A car ride! My favorite thing!
9:40 am - A walk in the park! My favorite thing!

10:30am - Got rubbed and petted! My favorite thing!
12:00pm - Lunch! My favorite thing!
1:00 pm - Played in the yard! My favorite thing!
3:00 pm - Wagged my tail! My favorite thing!
5:00 pm - Milk bones! My favorite thing!
7:00 pm - Got to play ball! My favorite thing!
8:00 pm - Wow! Watched TV with the people! My favorite thing!
11:00 pm - Sleeping on the bed! My favorite thing!

Excerpts from a Cat's Diary

It is Day 983 of my captivity. My captors continue to taunt me with bizarre little dangling objects. They dine lavishly on fresh meat, while the other inmates and I are fed hash or some sort of dry nuggets. Although I make my contempt for the rations perfectly clear, I nevertheless must eat something in order to keep up my strength. The only thing that keeps me going is my dream of escape. In an attempt to disgust them, I once again vomit on the carpet.

Today I decapitated a mouse and dropped its headless body at their feet. I had hoped this would strike fear into their hearts, since it clearly demonstrates what I am capable of. However, they merely made condescending comments about what a "good little hunter" I am. Bastards! There was some sort of assembly of their accomplices tonight. I was placed in solitary confinement for the duration of the event. However, I could hear the noises and smell the food. I overheard that my confinement was due to the power of "allergies." I must learn what this means, and how to use it to my advantage.

Today I was almost successful in an attempt to assassinate one of my tormentors by weaving around his feet as he was walking. I must try this again tomorrow -- but at the top of the stairs.

I am convinced that the other prisoners here are flunkies and snitches. The dog receives special privileges. He is regularly released - and seems to be more than willing to return. He is obviously retarded. The bird has got to be an informant. I observe him communicate with the guards regularly. I am certain that he reports my every move. My captors have arranged protective custody for him in an elevated cell, so he is safe. For now...

DOLLARS: SO, HERE'S HOW IT ALL WORKS:

It's a slow day in a little East Texas town the sun is beating down, and the streets are deserted. Times are tough, everybody is in debt, and everybody lives on credit.

On this particular day a rich tourist from back east is driving through town. He stops at the motel and lays a $100 bill on the desk saying he wants to inspect the rooms upstairs in order to pick one to spend the night.

As soon as the man walks upstairs, the owner grabs the bill and runs next door to pay his debt to the butcher.

The butcher takes the $100 and runs down the street to retire his debt to the pig farmer.

The pig farmer takes the $100 and heads off to pay his bill at the supplier of feed and fuel.

The guy at the Farmer's Co-op takes the $100 and runs to pay his debt to the local prostitute, who has also been facing hard times and has had to offer her "services" on credit.

The hooker rushes to the hotel and pays off her room bill with the hotel owner.

The hotel proprietor then places the $100 back on the counter so the rich traveler will not suspect anything.

At that moment the traveler comes down the stairs, picks up the $100 bill, states that the rooms are not satisfactory, pockets the money, and leaves town.

No one produced anything. No one earned anything.

However, the whole town is now out of debt and now looks to the future with a lot more optimism.

And that, ladies and gentlemen, is how the United States Government is conducting business today.

DOOLITTLE RAID ON TOKYO:

This is a really excellent firsthand account by the pilot of **Aircraft #13** on the Doolittle Raid off the USS Hornet in **1942**. You will enjoy this bit of extraordinary history.

My name is Edgar McElroy. My friends call me "Mac." I was born and raised in **Ennis, Texas**, the youngest of five children, son of Harry and Jennie McElroy.

Folks say that I was the quiet one. We lived at 609 North Dallas Street and attended the Presbyterian Church. My dad had an auto mechanic's shop downtown close to the main fire station. My family was a hard working bunch, and I was expected to work at dad's garage after school and on Saturdays, so I grew up in an atmosphere of machinery, oil and grease. Occasionally I would hear a lone plane fly over, and would run out in the street and strain my eyes against the sun to watch it.

Someday, that would be me up there! I really like cars, and I was always busy on some project, and it wasn't long before I decided to build my very own Model-T out of spare parts. I got an engine from over here, a frame from over there, and wheels from someplace else, using only the good parts from old cars that were otherwise shot. It wasn't very pretty, but it was all mine. I enjoyed driving on the dirt roads around town and the feeling of freedom and speed. That car of mine could really go fast. 40 miles per hour!

In high school, I played football and tennis, and was good enough at football to receive an athletic scholarship from Trinity University in San Antonio. I have to admit that sometimes I daydreamed in class, and often times I thought about flying my very own airplane and being up there in the clouds.

That is when I even decided to take a correspondence course in aircraft engines. Whenever I got the chance, I would take my girl on a date up to Love Field in Dallas. We would watch the airplanes and listen to those mighty piston engines roar. I just loved it and if she didn't, well that was just too bad.

After my schooling, I operated a filling station with my brother, then drove a bus, and later had a job as a machinist in Longview, but I never lost my love of airplanes and my dream of flying.

With what was going on in Europe and in Asia, I figured that our country would be drawn into war someday, so I decided to join the Army Air Corps in November of 1940. This way I could finally follow my dream. I reported for primary training in California.

The training was rigorous and frustrating at times. We trained at airfields all over California. It was tough going, and many of the guys washed out. When I finally saw that I was going to make it, I wrote to my girl back in Longview, Texas... Her name is Agnes Gill. I asked her to come out to California for my graduation... and oh yeah, also to marry me. I graduated on July 11, 1941. I was now a real, honest-to-goodness Army Air Corps pilot. Two days later, I married "Aggie" in Reno, Nevada. We were starting a new life together and were very happy.

I received my orders to report to Pendleton, Oregon and join the 17th Bomb Group. Neither of us had traveled much before, and the drive north through the Cascade Range of the Sierra Nevada's was interesting and beautiful. It was an exciting time for us. My unit was the first to receive the **new B-25** medium bomber. When I saw it for the first time, I was in awe. It looked so huge. It was so sleek and powerful. The guys started calling it the "rocket plane," and I could hardly wait to get my hands on it. I told Aggie that it was really something! Reminded me of a big old scorpion, just ready to sting! Man, I could barely wait!

We were transferred to another airfield in Washington State, where we spent a lot a time flying practice missions and attacking imaginary targets. Then, there were other assignments in Mississippi and Georgia, for more maneuvers and more practice.

We were on our way back to California on December 7th when we got word of a Japanese attack on Pearl Harbor. We listened with mixed emotions to the announcements on the radio, and the next day to the declaration of war. What the President said, it just rang over and over in my head, "With confidence in our armed forces, with the unbounding termination of our people, we will gain the inevitable triumph. So help us God." By gosh, I felt as though he was talking straight to me! I didn't know what would happen to us, but we all knew that we would be going somewhere now.

The first weeks of the war, we were back in Oregon flying patrols at sea looking for possible Japanese submarines. We had to be up at 0330 hours to warm up the engines of our planes. There was 18 inches of snow on the ground, and it was so cold that our engine oil congealed overnight. We placed big tarps over the engines that reached down to the ground. Inside this tent we used plumbers' blow torches to thaw out the engines. I figured that my dad would be proud of me, if he could see me inside this tent with all this machinery, oil and grease. After about an hour of this, the engines were warm enough to start.

We flew patrols over the coasts of Oregon and Washington from dawn until dusk. Once I thought I spotted a sub, and started my bomb run, even had my bomb doors open, but I pulled out of it when I realized that it was just a big whale. Lucky for me, I would have never heard the end of that! Actually it was lucky for us that the Japanese didn't attack the west coast, because we just didn't have a strong enough force to beat them off. Our country was in a real fix now, and overall things looked pretty bleak to most folks. In early February, we were ordered to report to Columbus (Columbia?), South Carolina. Man, this Air Corps sure moves a fellow around a lot! Little did I know what was coming next!

After we got settled in Columbus, my squadron commander called us all together. He told us that an awfully hazardous mission was being planned, and then he asked for volunteers. There were some of the guys that did not step forward, but I was one of the ones that did. My co-pilot was shocked. He said, "You can't volunteer, Mac! You're married, and you and Aggie are expecting a baby soon. Don't do it!" I told him that "I got into the Air Force to do what I can, and Aggie understands how I feel. The war won't be easy for any of us." We that volunteered were transferred to Eglin Field near Valparaiso, Florida in late February. When we all got together, there were about 140 of us volunteers, and we were told that we were now part of the "Special B-25 Project.

We set about our training, but none of us knew what it was all about. We were ordered not to talk about it, not even to our wives. In early March, we were all called in for a briefing, and gathered together in a big building there on the base. Somebody said that the fellow who's head of this thing is coming to talk to us, and in walks **Lieutenant Colonel Jimmy Doolittle.** He was already an aviation legend, and there he stood right in front of us. I was truly amazed just to meet him.

Colonel Doolittle explained that this mission would be extremely dangerous, and that only volunteers could take part. He said that he could not tell us where we were going, but he could say that some of us would not be coming back. Here was a silent pause; you could have heard a pin drop. Then Doolittle said that anyone of us could withdraw now, and that no one would criticize us for this decision. No one backed out! From the outset, all volunteers worked from the early morning hours until well after sunset. All excess weight was stripped from the planes and extra gas tanks were added. The lower gun turret was removed, the heavy liaison radio was removed, and then the tail guns were taken out and more gas tanks were put aboard. We extended the range of that plane from 1000 miles out to 2500 miles.

Then I was assigned my crew. There was **Richard Knobloch** the co-pilot, **Clayton Campbell**, the navigator, **Robert Bourgeois**, the bombardier, **Adam Williams**, the flight engineer and gunner, and me, **Mac McElroy**, the pilot. Over the coming days, I came to respect them a lot. They were a swell bunch of guys, just regular All-American boys.

We got a few ideas from the training as to what type of mission that we had signed on for. A Navy pilot had joined our group to coach us at short takeoffs and also in shipboard etiquette. We began our short takeoff practice. Taking off with first a light load, then a normal load, and finally overloaded up to 31,000 lbs. The shortest possible take-off was obtained with flaps full down, stabilizer set three-fourths, tail heavy, full power against the brakes and releasing the brakes simultaneously as the engine revved up to max power. We pulled back gradually on the stick and the airplane left the ground with the tail skid about one foot from the runway. It was a very unnatural and scary way to get airborne! I could hardly believe it myself, the first time as I took off with a full gas load and dummy bombs within just 700 feet of runway in a near stall condition. We were, for all practical purposes, a slow flying gasoline bomb!

In addition to take-off practice, we refined our skills in day and night navigation, gunnery, bombing, and low level flying. We made cross country flights at tree-top level, night flights and navigational flights over the Gulf of Mexico without the use of a radio. After we started that short-field takeoff routine, we had some pretty fancy competition between the crews. I think that one crew got it down to about 300 feet on a hot day. We were told that only the best crews would actually go on the mission, and the rest would be held in reserve. One crew did stall on takeoff, slipped back to the ground, busting up their landing gear. They were eliminated from the mission.

Doolittle emphasized again and again the extreme danger of this operation, and made it clear that anyone of us who so desired could drop out with no questions asked. No one did.

On one of our cross country flights, we landed at **Barksdale Field** in Shreveport, and I was able to catch a bus over to Longview to see Aggie. We had a few hours together, and then we had to say our goodbyes. I told her I hoped to be back in time for the baby's birth, but I couldn't tell her where I was going. As I walked away, I turned and walked backwards for a ways, taking one last look at my beautiful pregnant Aggie.

Part 2

Within a few days of returning to our base in Florida, we were abruptly told to pack our things. After just three weeks of practice, we were on our way. This was it. It was time to go. It was the middle of March 1942, and I was 30 years old. Our orders were to fly to **McClellan Air Base** in Sacramento, California, on our own, at the lowest possible level. So here we went on our way west, scraping the tree tops at 160 miles per hour, and skimming along just 50 feet above plowed fields. We crossed North Texas and then the panhandle, scaring the dickens out of livestock, buzzing farm houses and a many a barn along the way. Over the Rocky Mountains and across the Mojave Desert dodging thunderstorms, we enjoyed the flight immensely and although tempted, I didn't do too much dare-devil stuff. We didn't know it at the time, but it was good practice for what lay ahead of us. It proved to be our last fling. Once we arrived in Sacramento, the mechanics went over our plane with a fine-tooth comb. Of the twenty-two planes that made it, only those whose pilots reported no mechanical problems were allowed to go on. The others were shunted aside.

After having our plane serviced, we flew on to Alameda Naval Air Station in Oakland. As I came in for final approach, we saw it! I excitedly called the rest of the crew to take a look. There below us was a huge aircraft carrier. It was the USS Hornet, and it looked so gigantic! Man, I had never even seen a carrier until this moment. There were already two B-25s parked on the flight deck.

Now we knew! My heart was racing, and I thought about how puny my plane would look on board this mighty ship. As soon as we landed and taxied off the runway, a jeep pulled in front of me with a big "Follow Me" sign on the back. We followed it straight up to the wharf, alongside the towering Hornet. All five of us were looking up and just in awe, scarcely believing the size of this thing.

As we left the plane, there was already a Navy work crew swarming around attaching cables to the lifting rings on top of the wings and the fuselage. As we walked towards our quarters, I looked back and saw them lifting my plane up into the air and swing it over the ship's deck. It looked so small and lonely. Later that afternoon, all crews met with **Colonel Doolittle** and he gave last minute assignments. He told me to go to the **Presidio** and pick up two hundred extra "C" rations. I saluted, turned, and left, not having any idea where the Presidio was, and not exactly sure what a "C" ration was. I commandeered a Navy staff car and told the driver to take me to the Presidio, and he did. On the way over, I realized that I had no written signed orders and that this might get a little sticky. So in I walked into the Army supply depot and made my request, trying to look poised and confident. The supply officer asked, "What is your authorization for this request, sir?" I told him that I could not give him one. "And what is the destination?" he asked. I answered, "The aircraft carrier, Hornet, docked at Alameda." He said, "Can you tell me who ordered the rations, sir?" And I replied with a smile, "No, I cannot." The supply officers huddled together, talking and glanced back over towards me. Then he walked back over and assured me that the rations would be delivered that afternoon. Guess they figured that something big was up. They were right.

The next morning we all boarded the ship. Trying to remember my naval etiquette, I saluted the Officer of the Deck and said, "Lt. McElroy, requesting permission to come aboard." The officer returned the salute and said, "Permission granted." Then I turned aft and saluted the flag. I made it, without messing up. It was April 2, and in full sunlight, we left San Francisco Bay. The whole task force of ships, two cruisers, four destroyers, and a fleet oiler, moved slowly with us under the Golden Gate Bridge.

Thousands of people looked on. Many stopped their cars on the bridge, and waved to us as we passed underneath. I thought to myself, I hope there aren't any spies up there waving.

Once at sea, **Doolittle** called us together. "Only a few of you know our destination, and you others have guessed about various targets. Gentlemen, your target is Japan!" A sudden cheer exploded among the men. "Specifically, Yokohama, Tokyo, Nagoya, Kobe, Nagasaki, and Osaka. The Navy task force will get us as close as possible and we'll launch our planes. We will hit our targets and proceed to airfields in China." After the cheering stopped, he asked again, if any of us desired to back out, no questions asked. Not one did, not one. Then the ship's Captain went over the intercom to the whole ship's company. The loudspeaker blared, "The destination is Tokyo!"

A tremendous cheer broke out from everyone on board. I could hear metal banging together and wild screams from down below decks. It was quite a rush! I felt relieved actually. We finally knew where we were going.

I set up quarters with two Navy pilots, putting my cot between their two bunks. They couldn't get out of bed without stepping on me. It was just fairly cozy in there, yes it was. Those guys were part of the Torpedo Squadron Eight and were just swell fellows. The rest of the guys bedded down in similar fashion to me, some had to sleep on bedrolls in the Admiral's chartroom. As big as this ship was, there wasn't any extra room anywhere. Every square foot had a purpose. A few days later, we discovered where they had an ice cream machine!

There were sixteen B-25s tied down on the flight deck, and I was flying **number 13**. All the carrier's fighter planes were stored away helplessly in the hangar deck. They couldn't move until we were gone. Our Army mechanics were all on board, as well as our munitions loaders and several back up crews, in case any of us got sick or backed out. We settled into a daily routine of checking our planes. The aircraft were grouped so closely together on deck that it wouldn't take much for them to get damaged. Knowing that my life depended on this plane, I kept a close eye on her.

Day after day, we met with the intelligence officer and studied our mission plan. Our targets were assigned, and maps and objective folders were furnished for study. We went over approach routes and our escape route towards China. I never studied this hard back at Trinity. Every day at dawn and at dusk, the ship was called to general quarters and we practiced finding the quickest way to our planes. If at any point along the way, we were discovered by the enemy fleet, we were to launch our bombers immediately so the Hornet could bring up its fighter planes. We would then be on our own, and try to make it to the nearest land, either Hawaii or Midway Island.

Dr. Thomas White, a volunteer member of **plane number 15**, went over our medical records and gave us inoculations for a whole bunch of diseases that hopefully I wouldn't catch. He gave us training sessions in emergency first aid, and lectured us at length about water purification and such. Tom, a medical doctor, had learned how to be a gunner just so he could go on this mission. We put some new tail guns in place of the ones that had been taken out to save weight. Not exactly functional, **they were two broom handles, painted black.** The thinking was they might help scare any Jap fighter planes. Maybe, maybe not.

On Sunday, April 14, we met up with Admiral Bull Halsey's task force just out of Hawaii and joined into one big force. The carrier Enterprise was now with us, another two heavy cruisers, four more destroyers and another oiler. We were designated as **Task Force 16**. It was quite an impressive sight to see, and represented the **bulk of what was left of the U.S. Navy** after the devastation of Pearl Harbor. There were over **10,000 Navy**

personnel sailing into harm's way, just to deliver us **sixteen Army planes** to the Japs, orders of the President.

As we steamed further west, tension was rising as we drew nearer and nearer to Japan. Someone thought of arming us with some old .45 pistols that they had on board. I went through that box of 1911 pistols; they were in such bad condition that I took several of them apart, using the good parts from several useless guns until I built a serviceable weapon. Several of the other pilots did the same. Admiring my "new" pistol, I held it up, and thought about my old Model-T.

Colonel Doolittle called us together on the flight deck. We all gathered round, as well as many Navy personnel. He pulled out some medals and told us how these friendship medals from the Japanese government had been given to some of our Navy officers several years back. And now the Secretary of the Navy had requested for us to return them. **Doolittle wired them to a bomb** while we all posed for pictures.

Something to cheer up the folks back home!

I began to pack my things for the flight, scheduled for the 19th. I packed some extra clothes and a little brown bag that Aggie had given me, inside were some toilet items and a few candy bars. No letters or identity cards were allowed, only our dog-tags. I went down to the wardroom to have some ice cream and settle up my mess bill. It only amounted to $5 a day and with my per diem of $6 per day, I came out a little ahead. By now, my Navy pilot roommates were about ready to get rid of me, but I enjoyed my time with them. They were alright. Later on, I learned that **both of them were killed** at the Battle of Midway. They were good men. Yes, very good men.

Colonel Doolittle let each crew pick our own target. We chose the **Yokosuka Naval Base** about twenty miles from Tokyo. We loaded 1450 rounds of ammo and four 500-pound bombs. A little payback, direct from Ellis County, Texas! We checked and re-checked our plane several times. Everything was now ready. I felt relaxed, yet tensed up at the same time. Day after tomorrow, we will launch when we are **400 miles out**. I lay in my cot that night, and rehearsed the mission over and over in my head. It was hard to sleep as I listened to sounds of the ship.

Part 3

Early the next morning, I was enjoying a leisurely breakfast, expecting another full day on board, and I noticed that the ship was pitching and rolling quite a bit this morning, more than normal. I was reading through the April 18th day plan of the **Hornet**, and there was a message in it which said, "**From the Hornet to the Army - Good luck, good hunting, and God bless you.**" I still had a large lump in my throat from reading this, when all of a sudden, the intercom blared, "**General Quarters, General Quarters,** All hands man your battle stations! **Army pilots, man your planes!!!**" There was instant reaction from everyone in the room and food trays went crashing to the floor. I ran down to my room jumping through the hatches along the way, grabbed my bag, and ran as fast as I could go to the flight deck. I met with my crew at the plane, my heart was pounding. Someone said, "What's going on?" The word was that the Enterprise had spotted an enemy trawler. It had been sunk, but it had transmitted radio messages. **We had been found out!**

The weather was crummy, the seas were running heavy, and the ship was pitching up and down like I had never seen before. Great waves were crashing against the bow and washing over the front of the deck this wasn't going to be easy! Last minute instructions were given. We were reminded to avoid non-military targets, especially the Emperor's Palace. Do not fly to Russia, but fly as far west as possible, land on the water and launch our rubber raft. This was going to be a one-way trip! We were still much too far out and we all knew that our chances of making land were somewhere between slim and none. Then at the last minute, each plane loaded an extra ten 5-gallon gas cans to give us a fighting chance of reaching China.

We all climbed aboard, started our engines and warmed them up, just feet away from the plane in front of us and the plane behind us. Knobby, Campbell, Bourgeois and me in the front, Williams, the gunner was in the back, separated from us by a big rubber gas tank. I called back to Williams on the intercom and told him to look sharp and don't take a nap! He answered dryly, "Don't worry about me, Lieutenant. If they jump us, **I'll just use my little black broomsticks to keep the Japs off our tail.**"

The ship headed into the wind and picked up speed. There was now a near gale force wind and water spray coming straight over the deck. I looked down at my instruments as my engines revved up. My mind was racing. I went over my mental checklist, and said a prayer? God please, help us! Past the twelve planes in front of us, I strained to see the flight deck officer as he leaned into the wind and signaled with his arms for **Colonel Doolittle** to come to full power. I looked over at Knobby and we looked each other in the eye. He just nodded to me and we both understood.

With the deck heaving up and down, the deck officer had to time this just right. Then I saw him wave **Doolittle** to go, and we watched breathlessly to see what happened. When his plane pulled up above the deck, Knobby just let out with, "Yes! Yes!" The second plane, piloted by Lt. **Hoover**, appeared to stall with its nose up and began falling toward the waves. We groaned and called out, "Up! Up! Pull it up!" Finally, he pulled out of it, staggering back up into the air, much to our relief!

One by one, the planes in front of us took off. The deck pitched wildly, 60 feet or more, it looked like. One plane seemed to drop down into the drink and disappeared for a moment, then pulled back up into sight. There was sense of relief with each one that made it. We gunned our engines and started to roll forward. **Off to the right, I saw the men on deck cheering and waving their covers!** We continued inching forward, careful to keep my left main wheel and my nose wheel on the white guidelines that had been painted on the deck for us. Get off a little bit too far left and we go off the edge of the deck. A little too far to the right and our wing-tip will smack the island of the ship. With the best seat on the ship, we watched Lt. Bower take off in plane number 12, and I taxied up to the starting line, put on my the brakes and looked down to my left. My main wheel was right on the line. Applied more power to the engines, and I turned my complete attention to the deck officer on my left, who was circling his paddles. Now my adrenaline was really pumping! We went to full power, and the noise and vibration inside the plane went way up. He circled the paddles furiously while watching forward for the pitch of the deck. Then he dropped them, and I said, "Here We Go!" I released the brakes and we started rolling forward, and as I looked down the flight-deck, you could see straight down into the angry churning water.

As we slowly gained speed, the deck gradually began to pitch back up. I pulled up and our plane slowly strained up and away from the ship. There was a big cheer and whoops from the crew, but I just felt relieved and muttered to myself, "Boy, that was short!"

We made a wide circle above our fleet to check our compass headings and get our bearings. I looked down as we passed low over one of our cruisers and could see the men on deck waving to us. I dropped down to low level, so low we could see the whitecap waves breaking. It was just after 0900, there were broken clouds at 5,000 feet and visibility of about thirty miles due to haze or something. Up ahead and barely in sight, I could see **Captain Greening**, our flight leader, and **Bower** on his right wing. Flying at 170 mph, I was able; to catch up to them in about 30 minutes. We were to stay in this formation until reaching landfall, and then break on our separate ways.

Now we settled in for the **five hour flight**. Tokyo, here we come! Williams was in the back emptying the extra gas cans into the gas tank as fast as we had burned off enough fuel. He then punched holes in the tins and pushed then out the hatch against the wind. Some of the fellows ate sandwiches and other goodies that the Navy had put aboard for us. I wasn't hungry. I held onto the controls with a firm grip as we raced along westward just fifty feet above the cold rolling ocean, as low as I dared to fly. Being so close to the choppy waves gave you a true sense of speed. Occasionally our windshield was even sprayed with a little saltwater. It was an exhilarating feeling, and I felt as though the will and spirit of our whole country was pushing us along. I didn't feel too scared, just anxious. There was a lot riding on this thing, and on me.

As we began to near land, we saw an occasional ship here and there. None of them close enough to be threatening, but just the same, we were feeling more edgy. Then at 1330 we sighted land, the Eastern shore of **Honshu**. With Williams now on his guns in the top turret and Campbell on the nose gun, we came ashore still flying low as possible, and were **surprised to see people on**

the ground waving to us as we flew in over the farmland. It was beautiful countryside.

Campbell, our navigator, said, "Mac, I think we're going to be about sixty miles too far north. I'm not positive, but pretty sure." I decided that he was absolutely right and turned left ninety degrees, went back just offshore and followed the coast line south. When I thought we had gone far enough, I climbed up to two thousand feet to find out where we were. We started getting fire from anti-aircraft guns. Then we spotted Tokyo Bay, turned west and put our nose down diving toward the water. Once over the bay, I could see our target, **Yokosuka Naval Base.** Off to the right there was already smoke visible over Tokyo. Coming in low over the water, I increased speed to 200 mph and told everyone, "Get Ready!"

Part 4

When we were close enough, I pulled up to 1300 feet and opened the bomb doors. There were **furious black bursts of anti-aircraft fire all around us,** but I flew straight on through them, spotting our target, the torpedo works and the dry-docks. I saw a big ship in the dry-dock just as we flew over it...

Those flak bursts were really getting close and bouncing us around, when I heard Bourgeois shouting, "Bombs away!"

I couldn't see it, but Williams had a bird's eye view from the back and he shouted jubilantly, "We got an aircraft carrier! The whole dock is burning!"

I started turning to the south and strained my neck to look back and at that moment saw a large crane blow up and start falling over! Take that! There was loud yelling and clapping each other on the back. We were all just ecstatic, and still alive! But there wasn't much time to celebrate. We had to get out of here and fast! When we were some thirty miles out to sea, we took one last look back at our target, and could still see huge billows of black smoke. Up until now, we had been flying for Uncle Sam, but now we were flying for ourselves.

We flew south over open ocean, parallel to the Japanese coast all afternoon. We saw a large submarine apparently at rest, and then in another fifteen miles, we spotted three large enemy cruisers headed for Japan. There were no more bombs, so we just let them be and kept on going. By late afternoon, Campbell calculated that it was time to turn and make for China. Across the East China Sea, the weather out ahead of us looked bad and overcast. Up until now, we had not had time to think much about our gasoline supply, but the math did not look good. We just didn't have enough fuel to make it!

Each man took turns cranking the little hand radio to see if we could pick up the promised radio beacon. **There was no signal.** This is not good. The weather turned bad and it was getting dark, so we climbed up. I was now flying on instruments, through a dark misty rain. Just when it really looked hopeless of reaching land, we suddenly picked up a strong tailwind. It was an answer to a prayer. Maybe, just maybe, we can make it!

In total darkness at 2100 hours, we figured that we must be crossing the coastline, so I began a slow, slow climb to be sure of not hitting any high ground or anything. I conserved as much fuel as I could, getting real low on gas now. The guys were still cranking on the radio, but after five hours of hand cranking with aching hands and backs, there was utter silence. **No radio beacon!** Then the **red light** started blinking, indicating twenty minutes of fuel left. We started getting ready to bail out. I turned the controls over to Knobby and crawled to the back of the plane, past the now collapsed rubber gas tank. I dumped everything out of my bag and repacked just what I really needed, **my .45 pistol, ammunition, flashlight, compass,**

medical kit, fishing tackle, chocolate bars, peanut butter and crackers. I told Williams to come forward with me so we could all be together for this. There was no other choice. I had to get us as far west as possible, and then we had to jump.

At 2230, we were up to sixty-five hundred feet. We were over land but still above the Japanese Army in China. We couldn't see the stars, so Campbell couldn't get a good fix on our position. We were flying on fumes now and I didn't want to run out of gas before we were ready to go. Each man filled his canteen, put on his Mae West life jacket and parachute, and filled his bag with rations, those "C" rations from the Presidio. I put her on auto-pilot and we all gathered in the navigator's compartment around the hatch in the floor. We checked each other's parachute harness. Everyone was scared, without a doubt. None of us had ever done this before! I said, "Williams first, Bourgeois second, Campbell third, Knobloch fourth, and I'll follow you guys! Go fast, two seconds apart! Then count three seconds off and pull your rip-cord!"

We kicked open the hatch and gathered around the hole looking down into the blackness. It did not look very inviting! Then I looked up at Williams and gave the order, "JUMP!!!" Within seconds, they were all gone. I turned and reached back for the auto-pilot, but could not reach it, so I pulled the throttles back, then turned and jumped. Counting quickly, thousand one, thousand two, thousand three, I pulled my rip-cord and jerked back up with a terrific shock. At first, I thought that I was hung on the plane, but after a few agonizing seconds that seemed like hours, realized that I was free and drifting down. Being in the total dark, I was disoriented at first but figured my feet must be pointed toward the ground. I looked down through the black mist to see what was coming up. I was in a thick mist or fog, and the silence was so eerie **after nearly thirteen hours inside that noisy plane.** I could only hear the whoosh, whoosh sound of the wind blowing through my shroud lines, and then I heard a loud crash and explosion. My planc!

Looking for my flashlight, I groped through my bag with my right hand, finally pulled it out and shined it down toward the ground, which I still could not see. Finally I picked up a glimmer of water and thought I was landing in a lake. We're too far inland for this to be ocean. I hope! I relaxed my legs a little, thinking I was about to splash into water and would have to swim out, and then bang. I jolted suddenly and crashed over onto my side. Lying there in just a few inches of water, I raised my head and put my hands down into thick mud. **It was rice paddy!**

There was a burning pain, as if someone had stuck a knife in my stomach. I must have torn a muscle or broke something. I laid there dazed for a few minutes, and after a while struggled up to my feet. I dug a hole and buried my parachute in the mud. Then started trying to walk, holding my stomach, but every direction I moved the water got deeper. Then, I saw some lights off in the distance. I fished around for my flashlight and signaled one time. Sensing something wrong, I got out my compass and to my horror saw that those lights were off to my west. That must be a Jap patrol! How dumb could I be! Knobby had to be back to my east, so I sat still and quiet and did not move.

It was a cold dark lonely night. At 0100 hours I saw a single light off to the east. I flashed my light in that direction, one time. It had to be Knobby! I waited a while, and then called out softly, **"Knobby?"** And a voice replied, **"Mac,** is that you?" Thank goodness, what a relief! Separated by a wide stream, we sat on opposite banks of the water communicating in low voices. After daybreak, Knobby found a small rowboat and came across to get me. We started walking east toward the rest of the crew and away from that Japanese patrol.

Knobby had cut his hip when he went through the hatch, but it wasn't too awful bad. We walked together toward a small village and several Chinese came out to meet us, they seemed friendly enough. I said, **"Luchu hoo megwa fugi! Luchu hoo megwa fugi!"** meaning, <u>"I am an American! I am an American!"</u>

Later that morning we found the others. Williams had wrenched his knee when he landed in a tree, but he was limping along just fine. There were hugs all around. I have never been so happy to see four guys in all my life!

Well, the five of us eventually made it out of China with the help of the local Chinese people and the Catholic missions along the way. They were all very good to us, and later they were made to pay terribly for it, so we found out afterward. For a couple of weeks, we traveled across country. Strafed a couple of times by enemy planes, we kept on moving, by foot, by pony, by car, by train, and by airplane. But we finally made it to India.

I did not make it home for the baby's birth. I stayed on their flying a DC-3 "Gooney Bird" in the China-Burma-India Theatre for the next several months. I flew supplies over the Himalaya Mountains, or as we called it, over "The Hump" into China. When B-25s finally arrived in India, I flew combat missions over Burma, and then later in the war, flew a B-29 out of the Marianna Islands to bomb Japan again and again.

After the war, I remained in the Air Force until 1962, when I retired from the service as a Lt. Colonel, and then came back to Texas, my beautiful Texas. First moving to Abilene and then we settled in Lubbock, where Aggie taught school at Mackenzie Junior High. I worked at the S & R Auto Supply, once again in an atmosphere of machinery, oil and grease.

I lived a good life and raised two wonderful sons that I am very proud of. I feel blessed in many ways. We have a great country, better than most folks know. It is worth fighting for. Some people call me a hero, but I have never thought of myself that way, no.

But I did serve in the company of heroes. What we did will never leave me. It will always be there in my fondest memories. I will always think of the fine and brave men that I was privileged to serve with.

Remember us, for we were soldiers once and young. With the loss of all 16 aircraft, **Doolittle** believed that the raid had been a failure, and that **he would be court-martialed** upon returning to the states. Quite to the contrary, the raid proved to be a tremendous boost to American morale, which had plunged following the Pearl Harbor attack. It also caused serious doubts in the minds of Japanese war planners. They in turn recalled many seasoned fighter plane units back to defend the home islands, which resulted in Japan's weakened air capabilities at the upcoming Battle of Midway and other South Pacific campaigns.

Edgar "Mac" Mc Elroy, LTC., U.S.A.F. (Ret.) passed away at his residence in Lubbock, Texas early on the morning of Friday, April 4, 2003.

In Memory of LTC Mac Elroy

ED FREEMAN- MEDAL OF HONOR WINNER

You're a 19 year old kid.
You're critically wounded and dying in the jungle in the Ia Drang Valley.
November 11, 1965.

LZ X-ray, Vietnam .

Your infantry unit is outnumbered 8-1 and the enemy fire is so intense, from 100 or 200 yards away,

that your own Infantry Commander has ordered the MediVac helicopters to stop coming in. You're lying there, listening to the enemy machine guns and you know you're not getting out. Your family is 1/2 way around the world, 12,000 miles away, and you'll never see them again. As the world starts to fade in and out, you know this is the day. Then - over the machine gun noise - you faintly hear that sound of a helicopter.

You look up to see an unarmed Huey. But ... it doesn't seem real because no Medi-Vac markings are on it.

Ed Freeman is coming for you.

He's not Medi-Vac so it's not his job, but he's flying his Huey down into the machine gun fire anyway.

Even after the Medi-Vacs were ordered not to come. He's coming anyway.

And he drops it in and sits there in the machine gun fire, as they load 2 or 3 of you on board.

Then he flies you up and out through the gunfire to the doctors and nurses.

And, Ed Freeman kept coming back!! 13 more times!!

He took about 30 of you and your buddies out who would never have gotten out.

Medal of Honor Recipient, Ed Freeman, died last Wednesday at the age of 80, in Boise, Idaho.

May God Rest His Soul. I bet you didn't hear about this hero's passing, but we've sure seen a whole bunch about Michael Jackson. Shame on the American media !!! **Now** *...Please. Do Not Forget the Ed Freemans!*

In Memory of *Ed Freeman*

ENGINEERS

COMPREHENDING ENGINEERS - TAKE ONE

Two engineering students were walking across campus when one said, "Where did you get such a great bike?"

The second engineer replied, "Well, I was walking along yesterday minding my own business when a beautiful woman rode up on this bike.

She threw the bike to the ground, took off all her clothes and said, "Take what you want."

The second engineer nodded approvingly, "Good choice; the clothes probably wouldn't have fit."

COMPREHENDING ENGINEERS - TAKE TWO

· To the optimist, the glass is half full.

· To the pessimist, the glass is half-empty.

· But to the engineer - no matter how you look at it - the glass is *still* twice as big as it needs to be.

COMPREHENDING ENGINEERS - TAKE THREE

A pastor, a doctor and an engineer were waiting one morning for a particularly slow group of golfers.

The engineer fumed, "What's with these guys? We must have been waiting for 15 minutes!"

The doctor chimed in, "I don't know, but I've never seen such ineptitude!"

The pastor said, "Hey, here comes the greens keeper. Let's have a word with him."

"Hey George. Say, what's with that group ahead of us? They're rather slow, aren't they?"

The greens keeper replied, "Oh, yes, that's a group of blind firefighters. They lost their sight saving our clubhouse from a fire last year, so we always let them play for free anytime."

The group was silent for a moment.

The pastor said, "That's so sad. I think I will say a special prayer for them tonight."

The doctor said, "Good idea. And I'm going to contact my ophthalmologist buddy and see if there's anything he can do for them."

The engineer simply asked "Well that is all well and good; but why can't these guys play at night?"

COMPREHENDING ENGINEERS - TAKE FOUR

There was an engineer who had an exceptional gift for fixing all things mechanical.

After serving his company loyally for over 30 years, he happily retired.

Several years later the company contacted him regarding a seemingly impossible problem they were having with one of their multi-million-dollar machines.

They had tried everything and everyone else to get the machine to work but to no avail.

In desperation, they called on the retired, engineer who had solved so many of their problems in the past.

The engineer reluctantly took the challenge. He spent a day studying the huge machine.

At the end of the day, he marked a small "x" in chalk on particular component of the machine and stated, "This is where your problem is".

The part was replaced and the machine worked perfectly again.

The company received a bill for $50,000 from the engineer for his service.

They demanded an itemized accounting of his charges.

The engineer responded briefly:

One chalk mark $1 - knowing where to put it $49,999.

COMPREHENDING ENGINEERS - TAKE FIVE

What is the difference between Mechanical Engineers and Civil Engineers?

Mechanical Engineers build weapons. Civil Engineers build targets.

COMPREHENDING ENGINEERS - TAKE SIX

· The graduate with a Science degree asks, "Why does it work?"

· The graduate with an Engineering degree asks, "How does it work?"

· The graduate with an Accounting degree asks, "How much will it cost?"

· The graduate with a Liberal Arts degree asks, "Do you want fries with that?"

COMPREHENDING ENGINEERS - TAKE SEVEN

"Normal people ... believe that if it ain't broke, don't fix it. Engineers believe that if it ain't broke, it doesn't have enough features yet."

COMPREHENDING ENGINEERS - TAKE EIGHT

An engineer was crossing a road one-day when a frog called out to him and said, "If you kiss me, I'll turn into a beautiful princess".

He bent over, picked up the frog and put it in his pocket.

The frog spoke up again and said, "If you kiss me and turn me back into a beautiful princess, I will stay with you for one week."

The engineer took the frog out of his pocket, smiled at it and returned it to the pocket.

The frog then cried out, "If you kiss me and turn me back into a princess, I'll stay with you and do ANYTHING you want."

Again the engineer took the frog out, smiled at it and put it back into his pocket.

Finally, the frog asked, "What is the matter? I've told you I'm a beautiful princess that I'll stay with you for a week and do anything you want. Why won't you kiss me?"

The engineer said, "Look I'm an engineer. I don't have time for a girlfriend, but a talking frog, now that's cool."

ESSENTIAL TRUTHS-POLITICAL ONES

If God wanted us to vote, he would have given us candidates. ~ Jay Leno

The problem with political jokes is they get elected. ~ Henry Cate, VII

We hang the petty thieves and appoint the great ones to public office. ~ Aesop

If we got one-tenth of what was promised to us in these State of the Union speeches, there wouldn't be any inducement to go to heaven. ~ Will Rogers

Politicians are the same all over. They promise to build a bridge even where there is no river. ~ Nikita Khrushchev

When I was a boy I was told that anybody could become President; I'm beginning to believe it. ~ Clarence Darrow

Why pay money to have your family tree traced; go into politics and your opponents will do it for you. ~ Author unknown

Politicians are people who, when they see light at the end of the tunnel, go out and buy some more tunnel. ~ John Quinton

Politics is the gentle art of getting votes from the poor and campaign funds from the rich, by promising to protect each from the other. ~ Oscar Ameringer

I offer my opponents a bargain: if they will stop telling lies about us, I will stop telling the truth about them. ~ Adlai Stevenson, campaign speech, 1952

A politician is a fellow who will lay down your life for his country. ~ Tex Guinan

I have come to the conclusion that politics is too serious a matter to be left to the politicians. ~ Charles de Gaulle

Instead of giving a politician the keys to the city, it might be better to change the locks. ~ Doug Larson

There ought to be one day -- just one -- when there is open season on senators. ~ Will Rogers

EXPLANATION OF GOD

THIS IS FABULOUS!!!

It was written by an 8-year-old named Danny Dutton, who lives in Chula Vista, CA. He wrote it for his third grade homework assignment, to 'explain God.' I wonder if any of us could have done as well.

[.... and he had such an assignment, in California, and someone published it, I guess miracles do happen ! ...]

EXPLANATION OF GOD:

'One of God's main jobs is making people. He makes them to replace the ones that die, so there will be enough people to take care of things on earth. He doesn't make grownups, just babies. I think because they are smaller and easier to make. That way he doesn't have to take up his valuable time teaching them to talk and walk. He can just leave that to mothers and fathers.'

'God's second most important job is listening to prayers. An awful lot of this goes on, since some people, like preachers and things, pray at times beside bedtime. God doesn't have time to listen to the radio or TV because of this. Because he hears everything, there must be a terrible lot of noise in his ears, unless he has thought of a way to turn it off.'

'God sees everything and hears everything and is everywhere which keeps Him pretty busy. So you shouldn't go wasting his time by going over your mom and dad's head asking for something they said you couldn't have.'

'Atheists are people who don't believe in God. I don't think there are any in Chula Vista. At least there aren't any who come to our church.'

'Jesus is God's Son. He used to do all the hard work, like walking on water and performing miracles and trying to teach the people who didn't want to learn about God. They finally got tired of him preaching to them and they crucified him But he was good and kind, like his father, and he told his father that they didn't know what they were doing and to forgive them and God said O.K.'

'His dad (God) appreciated everything that he had done and all his hard work on earth so he told him he didn't have to go out on the road anymore. He could stay in heaven. So he did. And now he helps his dad out by listening to prayers and seeing things which are important for God to take care of and which ones he can take care of himself without having to bother God. Like a secretary, only more important.'

'You can pray anytime you want and they are sure to help you because they got it worked out so one of them is on duty all the time.'

'You should always go to church on Sunday because it makes God happy, and if there's anybody you want to make happy, it's God!

Don't skip church to do something you think will be more fun like going to the beach. This is wrong. And besides the sun doesn't come out at the beach until noon anyway.'

'If you don't believe in God, besides being an atheist, you will be very lonely, because your parents can't go everywhere with you, like to camp, but God can. It is good to know He's around you when you're scared, in the dark or when you can't swim and you get thrown into real deep water by big kids.'

'But...you shouldn't just always think of what God can do for you. I figure God put me here and he can take me back anytime he pleases.

And...that's why I believe in God.'

F

FAMOUS BIBLE QUOTES

Proverbs 3:5-6: "Trust in the LORD with all your heart, And lean not on your own understanding; In all your ways acknowledge Him, And He shall direct your paths." (NKJV)

Psalm 46:10: "Be still, and know that I am God: I will be exalted among the heathen, I will be exalted in the earth." (KJV)

Psalm 119:89: For ever, O LORD, thy word is settled in heaven.

Psalm 34:8: O taste and see that the LORD is good: blessed is the man that trusteth in him.

1 Corinthians 13:13: So now faith, hope, and love abide, these three; but the greatest of these is love. (ESV)

John 3:16: "For God so loved the world that he gave his one and only Son, that whoever believes in him shall not perish but have eternal life." (NIV)

Jeremiah 32:27: "Behold, I am the LORD, the God of all flesh; is anything too difficult for Me?" (NASB)

Isaiah 50:10: "Who is among you that fears the LORD, That obeys the voice of His servant, That walks in darkness and has no light? Let him trust in the name of the LORD and rely on his God." (NASB)

Philippians 1:21: For to me to live is Christ, and to die is gain. (KJV)

Matthew 7:7: Ask, and it shall be given you; seek, and ye shall find; knock, and it shall be opened unto you: For every one that asketh receiveth; and he that seeketh findeth; and to him that knocketh it shall be opened.

1 Corinthians 15:57-58: "But thanks be to God! He gives us the victory through our Lord Jesus Christ. Therefore, my dear brothers, stand firm. Let nothing move you. Always give yourselves fully to the work of the Lord, because you know that your labor in the Lord is not in vain." (NIV)

Galatians 2:20: I am crucified with Christ: nevertheless I live; yet not I, but Christ liveth in me: and the life which I now live in the flesh I live by the faith of the Son of God, who loved me, and gave himself for me.

Psalm 23:4: Yea, though I walk through the valley of the shadow of death, I will fear no evil: for thou art with me; thy rod and thy staff they comfort me.

Isaiah 40:31: But they that wait upon the LORD shall renew their strength; they shall mount up with wings as eagles; they shall run, and not be weary; and they shall walk, and not faint.

Psalm 119:9-11: "How can a young man keep his way pure? By living according to your word. I seek you with all my heart; do not let me stray from your commands. I have hidden your word in my heart that I might not sin against you." (NIV)

Matthew 25:40: "The King will reply, 'I tell you the truth, whatever you did for one of the least of these brothers of mine, you did for me." (NIV)

Joshua 1:9: "Have I not commanded you? Be strong and courageous. Do not be terrified; do not be discouraged, for the LORD your God will be with you wherever you go." (NIV)

Proverbs 1:7: The fear of the LORD is the beginning of knowledge: but fools despise wisdom and instruction.

John 8:32: And ye shall know the truth, and the truth shall make you free.

Psalm 19:14: Let the words of my mouth, and the meditation of my heart, be acceptable in thy sight, O LORD, my strength, and my redeemer.

1 Peter 5:6: Humble yourselves therefore under the mighty hand of God, that he may exalt you in due time.

1 Thessalonians 5:18: In everything give thanks: for this is the will of God in Christ Jesus concerning you.

Isaiah 12:2: Behold, God is my salvation; I will trust, and not be afraid: for the LORD JEHOVAH is my strength and my song; he also is become my salvation.

Proverbs 28:1: The wicked flee when no man pursueth: but the righteous are bold as a lion.

Romans 8:1: There is therefore now no condemnation to them which are in Christ Jesus, who walk not after the flesh, but after the Spirit.

Romans 10:9: That if thou shalt confess with thy mouth the Lord Jesus, and shalt believe in thine heart that God hath raised him from the dead, thou shalt be saved.

John 14:19: "Yet a little while and the world will see me no more, but you will see me. Because I live, you also will live." (ESV)

Psalm 34:18: The LORD is nigh unto them that are of a broken heart; and saveth such as be of a contrite spirit.

John 16:33: "I have told you these things, so that in me you may have peace. In this world you will have trouble. But take heart! I have overcome the world." (NIV)

Isaiah 53:5: But he was wounded for our transgressions, he was bruised for our iniquities: the chastisement of our peace was upon him; and with his stripes we are healed.

1 Corintians 15:58: Therefore, my beloved brethren, be ye stedfast, unmoveable, always abounding in the work of the Lord, forasmuch as ye know that your labour is not in vain in the Lord.

Matthew 6:9-13: Our Father which art in heaven, Hallowed be thy name. Thy kingdom come. Thy will be done in earth, as it is in heaven. Give us this day our daily bread. And forgive us our debts, as we forgive our debtors. And lead us not into temptation, but deliver us from evil: For thine is the kingdom, and the power, and the glory, forever. Amen. *(The Lord's Prayer)*

Isaiah 43:1-3: Fear not: for I have redeemed thee, I have called thee by thy name; thou art mine. When thou passest through the waters, I will be with thee; and through the rivers, they shall not overflow thee: when thou walkest through the fire, thou shalt not be burned; neither shall the flame kindle upon thee. For I am the LORD thy God.

Isaiah 30:21: And thine ears shall hear a word behind thee, saying, This is the way, walk ye in it, when ye turn to the right hand, and when ye turn to the left.

Romans 5:3 – 5: And not only so, but we glory in tribulations also: knowing that tribulation worketh patience; And patience, experience; and experience, hope; And hope maketh not ashamed; because the love of God is shed abroad in our hearts by the Holy Ghost which is given unto us.

Philippians 4:13: I can do all things through Christ who strengthens me.

Psalm 127:1: Except the LORD build the house, they labour in vain that build it: except the LORD keep the city, the watchman waketh but in vain.

Matthew 6:19-21: Lay not up for yourselves treasures upon earth, where moth and rust doth corrupt, and where thieves break through and steal: But lay up for yourselves treasures in heaven, where neither moth nor rust doth corrupt, and where thieves do not break through nor steal: For where your treasure is, there will your heart be also.

Mark 8:38: Whosoever therefore shall be ashamed of me and of my words in this adulterous and sinful generation; of him also shall the Son of man be ashamed, when he cometh in the glory of his Father with the holy angels.

Romans 12:1-2: I beseech you therefore, brethren, by the mercies of God, that ye present your bodies a living sacrifice, holy, acceptable unto God, which is your reasonable service. And be not conformed to this world: but be ye transformed by the renewing of your mind, that ye may prove what is that good, and acceptable, and perfect, will of God.

Psalms 88:2: Let my prayer come before thee: incline thine ear unto my cry

Ephesians 2:8: For by grace are ye saved through faith; and that not of yourselves: it is the gift of God.

Proverbs 3: 5-6: Trust in the Lord with all thine heart, and lean not unto thine own understanding. In all thy ways acknowledge Him, and He shall direct thy paths.

Matthew 24:34-35: Verily I say unto you, This generation shall not pass, till all these things be fulfilled. Heaven and earth shall pass away, but my words shall not pass

Luke 10:19: I give unto you power to tread on serpents and scorpions, and over all the power of the enemy: and nothing shall by any means hurt you.

Psalm 119:11: Thy word have I hid in mine heart, that I might not sin against thee.

1 John 3:18: My little children, let us not love in word, neither in tongue; but in deed and in truth.

Proverbs 30:5 Every word of God is pure: he is a shield unto them that put their trust in him.

John 14:1: Let not your heart be troubled: ye believe in God, believe also in me.

Psalm 125:1: They that trust in the LORD shall be as mount Zion, which cannot be removed, but abideth for ever.

Nahum 1:7: The Lord is good, a strong hold in the day of trouble; and He knoweth them that trust in Him.

Romans 8:28: And we know that all things work together for good to them that love God, to them who are the called according to his purpose.

John 14:27: Peace I leave with you, my peace I give unto you: not as the world giveth, give I unto you. Let not your heart be troubled, neither let it be afraid.

Genesis 1:1: In the beginning God created the heaven and the earth.

Psalm 145:21: My mouth shall speak the praise of the LORD: and let all flesh bless his holy name forever and ever.

1 John 4:8: He that loveth not knoweth not God; for God is love.

Jeremiah 33:3: Call unto me, and I will answer thee, and shew thee great and mighty things, which thou knowest not.

Ecclesiastes 3:1: To everything there is a season, and a time to every purpose under the heaven.

Psalm 23:1: The LORD is my shepherd; I shall not want.

1 Corinthians 4:5: Therefore judge nothing before the time, until the Lord come, who both will bring to light the hidden things of darkness, and will make manifest the counsels of the hearts: and then shall every man have praise of God.

Jeremiah 29:11: For I know the thoughts that I think toward you, saith the LORD, thoughts of peace, and not of evil, to give you an expected end.

2 Samuel 23:5: Yet he hath made with me an everlasting covenant.

John 11:35: Jesus wept.

Job 27:6: My righteousness I hold fast, and will not let it go: my heart shall not reproach me so long as I live.

Psalm 117:1 & 2: O praise the LORD, all ye nations: praise him, all ye people. For his merciful kindness is great toward us: and the truth of the LORD endureth for ever. Praise ye the LORD.

Matthew 7:2: For with what judgment ye judge, ye shall be judged: and with what measure ye mete, it shall be measured to you again.

Acts 2:38: Repent, and be baptized every one of you in the name of Jesus Christ for the remission of sins, and ye shall receive the gift of the Holy Ghost.

Isaiah 55:11: So shall my word be that goeth forth out of my mouth: it shall not return unto me void, but it shall accomplish that which I please, and it shall prosper in the thing whereto I sent it.

Philippians 3:13 "Brothers, I do not consider myself yet to have taken hold of it. But one thing I do: Forgetting what is behind and straining toward what is ahead, I press on toward the goal to win the prize for which God has called me heavenward in Christ Jesus." (NIV)

Psalm 23:1-6 The LORD is my shepherd; I shall not want. He maketh me to lie down in green pastures: he leadeth me beside the still waters. He restoreth my soul: he leadeth me in the paths of righteousness for his name's sake. Yea, though I walk through the valley of the shadow of death, I will fear no evil: for thou art with me; thy rod and thy staff they comfort me. Thou preparest a table before me in the presence of mine enemies: thou anointest my head with oil; my cup runneth over. Surely goodness and mercy shall follow me all the days of my life: and I will dwell in the house of the LORD forever.

1 John 4:20: If a man say, "I love God," and hateth his brother, he is a liar. For he that loveth not his brother whom he hath seen, how can he love God whom he hath not seen?

Romans 6:23: For the wages of sin is death, but the gift of God is eternal life through Jesus Christ our Lord.

Jeremiah 33:3: "Call unto me, and I will answer thee, and shew thee great and mighty things, which thou knowest not." (KJV)

Finally, brethren, whatsoever things are true, whatsoever things are honest, whatsoever things are just, whatsoever things are pure, whatsoever things are lovely, whatsoever things are of good report; if there be any virtue, and if there be any praise, think on these things." (KJV)

Isaiah 43:18-19: Forget the former things; do not dwell on the past. See, I am doing a new thing! Now it springs up; do you not perceive it? I am making a way in the desert and streams in the wasteland. (NIV)

Romans 12:1: "Therefore I urge you, brethren, by the mercies of God, to present your bodies a living and holy sacrifice, acceptable to God, which is your spiritual service of worship." (NASB)

FLEMING- STORY OF SIR ALEXANDER FLEMING, THE DISCOVERER OF PENICILLIN:

His name was Fleming, and he was a poor Scottish farmer. One day, while trying to make a living for his family, he heard a cry for help coming from a nearby bog. He dropped his tools and ran to the bog.

There, mired to his waist in black muck, was a terrified boy, screaming and struggling to free himself. Farmer Fleming saved the lad from what could have been a slow and terrifying death.

The next day, a fancy carriage pulled up to the Scotsman's sparse surroundings An elegantly dressed nobleman stepped out and introduced himself as the father of the boy Farmer Fleming had saved.

'I want to repay you,' said the nobleman. 'You saved my son's life.'

'No, I can't accept payment for what I did,' the Scottish farmer replied waving off the offer.. At that moment, the farmer's own son came to the door of the family hovel.

'Is that your son?' the nobleman asked.

'Yes,' the farmer replied proudly.

'I'll make you a deal. Let me provide him with the level of education my own son will enjoy. If the lad is anything like his father, he'll no doubt grow to be a man we both will be proud of.' And that he did.

Farmer Fleming's son attended the very best schools and in time, graduated from St. Mary's Hospital Medical School in London, and went on to become known throughout the world as the noted Sir Alexander Fleming, the discoverer of Penicillin.

Years afterward, the same nobleman's son who was saved from the bog was stricken with pneumonia.

WHAT SAVED HIS LIFE THIS TIME? PENICILLIN.

THE NAME OF THE NOBLEMAN? LORD RANDOLPH
CHURCHILL.
HIS SON'S NAME?
SIR WINSTON CHURCHILL.
**SOMEONE ONCE SAID: WHAT GOES AROUND
COMES AROUND.**
WORK LIKE YOU DON'T NEED THE MONEY.
LOVE LIKE YOU'VE NEVER BEEN HURT.
DANCE LIKE NOBODY'S WATCHING...
SING LIKE NOBODY'S LISTENING...
LIVE LIKE IT'S HEAVEN ON EARTH.
IT'S NATIONAL FRIENDSHIP WEEK. SEND THIS TO
EVERYONE YOU CONSIDER A FRIEND.
PASS THIS ON, AND BRIGHTEN SOMEONE'S DAY.

AN IRISH FRIENDSHIP WISH:
MAY THERE ALWAYS BE WORK FOR YOUR HANDS TO DO;
MAY YOUR PURSE ALWAYS HOLD A COIN OR TWO;
MAY THE SUN ALWAYS SHINE ON YOUR WINDOWPANE;
MAY A RAINBOW BE CERTAIN TO FOLLOW EACH RAIN;
MAY THE HAND OF A FRIEND ALWAYS BE NEAR YOU;
MAY GOD FILL YOUR HEART WITH GLADNESS TO
CHEER YOU.

FORTUNATE SON: LYRICS BY CREDENCE CLEARWATER REVIVAL (CCR)

RWP2: Below are the words to One of my favorite songs by my favorite group CCR .The first verse "Ooo, they point the cannon at you, Lord" is what many who want more war are all about i.e. pointing the cannon at someone else. Also this verse "Some folks inherit star spangled eyes, Ooh, they send you down to war, Lord,

And when you ask 'em, "How much should we give?"and Ooh, they only answer "More! More! More!", y'all." This stanza also relates to me that many Veterans today and in past centuries have truly given More - Their Life in Support of America: The United States. So this Veterans Day, November 11, 2014 celebrate all that have truly given More for America.

Some folks are born, made to wave the flag
Ooo, their red, white and blue
And when the band plays "Hail to the Chief"
Ooo, they point the cannon at you, Lord
It ain't me, it ain't me, I ain't no senator's son, son
It ain't me, it ain't me, I ain't no fortunate one, no
Some folks are born, silver spoon in hand
Lord, don't they help themselves, y'all
But when the taxman comes to the door
Lord, the house looks like a rummage sale, yeah

It ain't me, it ain't me, I ain't no millionaire's son, no, no
It ain't me, it ain't me, I ain't no fortunate one, no
Yeah, yeah
Some folks inherit star spangled eyes
Ooh, they send you down to war, Lord
And when you ask 'em, "How much should we give?"
Ooh, they only answer "More! More! More!", y'all
It ain't me, it ain't me, I ain't no military son, son
It ain't me, it ain't me, I ain't no fortunate one, one
It ain't me, it ain't me, I ain't no fortunate one, no, no, no
It ain't me, it ain't me, I ain't no fortunate son, no, no, no
Songwriters: JOHN C. FOGERTY
Fortunate Son lyrics © JONDORA MUSIC

FOX News Spin: This is worth repeating!

RWP2:This alphabetically correct listing of topics from A to G so far will allow you to read what AMERICANS really feel! It is in their own words, their true words without an editorial censorship as to the real meaning of these words. There is fun stuff, religious stuff for all religions, serious attitude adjustment and positive expectancy stuff where you will make notes on the pages. All of this is without Rush Limboo-Bimboo, Bill O'Really or HandNutty and Clones (Clones got fired) telling you the real story from Fox News. A personal note which very well not be true is ....that these Dudes especially LimBoo-BimBoo, hurt the rather than helped. This is my opinion only??

Vapor-ware Patriots: All three will probably run for office soon. But why do it when book deals are so good. For example, see what they all say about sports stars making mega bucks?? They are there doing that....same megabucks thing per their TV venue + books next etc. More power to them. But in my opinion they are good media people, but they are vapor-ware American patriots and very little else. Which one served anyone, except radio, TV and the Neilson ratings? If I am wrong tell me. Really no problem with them not serving anyone but themselves and the Neilson ratings.

FRUIT: KNOWING WHAT AND WHEN TO EAT FRUIT

We all think eating fruits means just buying fruits, cutting it and just popping it into our mouths. It's not as easy as you think. It's important to know how and <u>when </u>to eat.

What is the correct way of eating fruits?

IT MEANS NOT EATING FRUITS AFTER YOUR MEALS! * FRUITS SHOULD BE EATEN ON AN EMPTY STOMACH.

If you eat fruit like that, it will play a major role to detoxify your system, supplying you with a great deal of energy for weight loss and other life activities.

FRUIT IS THE MOST IMPORTANT FOOD. Let's say you eat two slices of bread and then a slice of fruit. The slice of fruit is ready to go straight through the stomach into the intestines, but it is prevented from doing so.

In the meantime the whole meal rots and ferments and turns to acid. The minute the fruit comes into contact with the food in the stomach and digestive juices, the entire mass of food begins to spoil....

So please eat your fruits on an <u>empty stomach </u>or before your meals! You have heard people complaining - every time I eat watermelon I burp, when I eat durian my stomach bloats up, when I eat a banana I feel like running to the toilet etc - actually all this will not arise if you eat the fruit on an empty stomach. The fruit mixes with the putrefying other food and produces gas and hence you will bloat!

Graying hair, balding, nervous outburst, and dark circles under the eyes all these will **NOT** happen if you take fruits on an empty stomach.

There is no such thing as some fruits, like orange and lemon are acidic, because all fruits become alkaline in our body, according to Dr. Herbert Shelton who did research on this matter. If you have mastered the correct way of eating fruits, you have the Secret of beauty, longevity, health, energy, happiness and normal weight.

When you need to drink fruit juice - drink only <u>fresh</u> fruit juice, NOT from the cans. Don't even drink juice that has been heated up. Don't eat cooked fruits because you don't get the nutrients at all. You only get to taste. Cooking destroys all the vitamins.

But eating a whole fruit is better than drinking the juice. If you should drink the juice, drink it mouthful by mouthful slowly, because you must let it mix with your saliva before swallowing it. You can go on a 3-day fruit fast to cleanse your body.. Just eat fruits and drink fruit juice throughout the 3 days and you will be surprised when your friends tell you how radiant you look!

KIWI: Tiny but mighty. This is a good source of potassium, magnesium, vitamin E & fiber. Its vitamin C content is twice that of an orange.

APPLE: An apple a day keeps the doctor away? Although an apple has a low vitamin C content, it has antioxidants & flavonoids which enhances the activity of vitamin C thereby helping to lower the risks of colon cancer, heart attack & stroke.

STRAWBERRY: Protective Fruit. Strawberries have the highest total antioxidant power among major fruits & protect the body from cancer-causing, blood vessel-clogging free radicals.

ORANGE: Sweetest medicine. Taking 2-4 oranges a day may help keep colds away, lower cholesterol, prevent & dissolve kidney stones as well as lessens the risk of colon cancer.

WATERMELON: Coolest thirst quencher.. Composed of 92% water, it is also packed with a giant dose of glutathione, which helps boost our immune system. They are also a key source of lycopene - the cancer fighting oxidant. Other nutrients found in watermelon are vitamin C & Potassium.

GUAVA & PAPAYA: Top awards for vitamin C. They are the clear winners for their high vitamin C content. Guava is also rich in fiber, which helps prevent constipation. Papaya is rich in carotene; this is good for your eyes.

Drinking Cold Water After a Meal = Cancer! Can you believe this?? For those who like to drink cold water, this article is applicable to you. It is nice to have a cup of cold drink after a meal. However, the cold water will solidify the oily stuff that you have just consumed. It will slow down the digestion. Once this 'sludge' reacts with the acid, it will break down and be absorbed by the intestine faster than the solid food. It will line the intestine. Very soon, this will turn into fats and lead to cancer. It is best to drink hot soup or warm water after a meal.

A serious note about heart attacks HEART ATTACK PROCEDURE': (THIS IS NOT A JOKE!) Women should know that not every heart attack symptom is going to be the left arm hurting. Be aware of intense pain in the jaw line.. You may never have the first chest pain during the course of a heart attack . Nausea and intense sweating are also common symptoms.. Sixty percent of people who have a heart attack while they are asleep do not wake up. Pain in the jaw can wake you from a sound sleep. Let's be careful and be aware. The more we know the better chance we could survive...

Read this again....It could save your life!!

G.

GEESE: A LEADERSHIP LESSON FROM ... GEESE!

How often do you hear people speak with envy about companies with "real heart"? Companies like Nordstrom, FedEx, Ben and Jerry's, Southwest Airlines, Starbucks, and The Container Store to name a few. Outsiders are constantly looking for their "secrets" to success. Fact is, the secret lies in the hearts of their employees. These companies create connected teams and, as a result, build dominant businesses by acting like geese. Like geese? Yes, like GEESE!

If you ever happen to see (or hear about) geese heading south for the winter – flying along in "V" formation – you might consider what science has discovered about why they fly that way. As each bird flaps its wings, it creates uplift for the bird immediately following. By flying in "V" formation, the whole flock adds at least 71% greater flying range than if each bird flew by itself. Any goose that falls out of formation suddenly feels the drag and resistance of trying to go it alone and quickly gets back into position to take advantage of the lifting power of the bird in front.

When the lead goose gets tired, it rotates back in the set and another goose moves up to fly point. And the geese in the back honk to encourage those in front to keep up their speed. Finally, when a goose gets sick or is wounded and falls out of formation, two other geese fall out with that goose and follow it down to lend help and protection. They stay with the fallen teammate until it is able to fly or it dies. Only then do they launch out on their own – or with another formation – to catch back up with their group.

The lesson: Like geese, people who share a common direction and sense of community, who take turns doing demanding jobs, and who watch out for one another, can get where they are going more quickly and easily because they are traveling on the thrust of their teammates. **Geese are defined by how they stay connected with one another. Successful teams – and excellent leaders – are defined the same way.**

GOOD MORNING GENERAL

Jim retired in his early 50's and started a second career. However, even though he loved his new job, he just couldn't seem to get to work on time.

Every day, he was 5, 10, 15 minutes late. Finally, one day, his boss called him into the office for a talk.

"Jim, I must tell you, I truly like your work ethic, you do a bang-up job, but being late for work nearly every day is quite annoying to me as well as your fellow workers."

Jim replied, "Yes, sir, I know. I'm sorry, but I am working on it."

"That's what I like to hear," his boss said. "However, the fact that you consistently come to work late does puzzle me because I understand that you retired from the United States Marine

Corps, and they have some pretty rigid rules about tardiness. Isn't that correct?"

"Yes. I did retire from the Marine Corps, and I'm mighty proud of it!" Said Jim.

"Well, what did they say when you came in late Jim?" asked his boss.

"They said, 'Good Morning, General'."

GOD NEEDS YOU:

August 14, 2009

Robert H. Schuller

"You, Lord, reward everyone according to what they have done." – Psalm 62:12

My father used to tell the story of a preacher who came to call on a farmer and noticed how all of the corn was growing in straight, clean rows. Then he looked over at the waving acres of golden wheat and said to the farmer, "Look at the corn. Look at the wheat. Isn't it beautiful what God has done with this farm?" Nodding, the farmer replied, "Yeah, but you should have seen it when the Lord had it all by himself!"

God needs you and me to do his work. In a world where so many people need help, there's no excuse to say, "I don't make a difference." Yes you do. Your life has great value.

Stop for a minute right now and make a list of the work God wants you to do for him today.

Make a difference in someone's life today.

This excerpt was taken from the

"Power for Life Daily Devotional"

GOLF BOOK: VALUABLE TIPS AND INSIDER INFORMATION

There is a new book on GOLF that gives the reader valuable playing tips and insider information. You find this a useful tool to help you enjoy your game that much more as you enjoy the great outdoors. The cost is only $9.95. It's a book of useful information and instruction. I know it's helped my game.

Chapter 1 - How to Properly Line Up Your Fourth Putt.

Chapter 2 - How to Hit a Nike from the Rough, when you Hit a Titleist from the tee.

Chapter 3 - How to Avoid the Water When You Lie 8 in a bunker.

Chapter 4 - How to Get More Distance off the Shank.

Chapter 5 - When to Give the Ranger the Finger.

Chapter 6 - Using Your Shadow on the Greens to Maximize Earnings.

Chapter 7 - When to Implement Handicap Management.

Chapter 8 - Proper Excuses for Drinking Beer Before 9:00 a.m.

Chapter 9 - How to Rationalize a 6-Hour Round.

Chapter 10 - When Does A Divot become classified as Sod.

Chapter 11 - How to Find That Ball That Everyone Else Saw Go in the water.

Chapter 12 - Why Your Spouse Doesn't Care That You Birdied the 5th.

Chapter 13 - Using Curse Words Creatively to Control Ball Flight.

Chapter 14 - When to Let a Foursome Play through Your Twosome.

Chapter 15 - How to Relax When You Are Hitting Five off the Tee.

Chapter 16 - When to Suggest Major Swing Corrections to Your Opponent.

Chapter 17 - God and the Meaning of the Birdie-to-Bogey Three-Putt.

Chapter 18 - When to Re grip Your Ball Retriever.

Chapter 19- Throwing Your Clubs: An Effective Stress-Reduction Technique.

Chapter 20 - Can You Purchase a Better Golf Game?

Chapter 21 - Why Male Golfers Will Pay $5.00 a Beer from the Cart Girl and Give a $3 Tip, but will balk beer $2.50 at the 19th Hole and stiff the Bartender.

Order Your Copy Today!

GOLF, 50 SHADES OF

Four guys have been going to the same Golfing trip to St Andrews for many years. Two days before the group is to leave, Jack's wife puts her foot down and tells him he isn't going and that she's got something else planned.

Naturally, Jack's mates are very upset that he can't go, but what can they do.

Two days later, the three get to St Andrews only to find Jack sitting at the bar with four drinks set up!

"Wow, Jack, how long you been here, and how did you talk your missus into letting you go?"

"Well, actually, I've been here since last night..

Yesterday evening, I was sitting in my living room chair and my wife came up behind me and put her hands over my eyes and asked, 'Guess who?" I pulled her hands off, and there she was, wearing only a see-through nightie.

She took my hand and pulled me into our bedroom. On her bedside table I saw the book '50 Shades of Grey'. She had lit candles and sprinkled rose petals around and on the bed she had handcuffs and ropes! Then she slipped off her nightie, laid on the bed and said, "Okay tie me up, hand-cuff me to the bed, and do whatever you want." **So, Here I am!**

GREAT STORY! THINGS HAPPEN FOR A REASON

Beautiful story.... makes you understand that things happen for a reason

The brand new pastor and his wife, newly assigned to their first ministry, to reopen a church in suburban Brooklyn, arrived in early October excited about their opportunities When they saw their church, it was very run down and needed much work. They set a goal to have everything done in time to have their first service on Christmas Eve.

They worked hard, repairing pews, plastering walls, painting, etc, and on December 18 were ahead of schedule and just about finished. On December 19 a terrible tempest - a driving rainstorm hit the area and lasted for two days.

On the 21st, the pastor went over to the church. His heart sank when he saw that the roof had leaked, causing a large area of plaster about 20 feet by 8 feet to fall off the front wall of the sanctuary just behind the pulpit, beginning about head high. The pastor cleaned up the mess on the floor, and not knowing what else to do but postpone the Christmas Eve service, headed home.

On the way he noticed that a local business was having a flea market type sale for charity so he stopped in. One of the items was a beautiful, handmade, ivory colored, crocheted tablecloth with exquisite work, fine colors and a Cross embroidered right in the center. It was just the right size to cover up the hole in the front wall. He bought it and headed back to the church.

By this time it had started to snow. An older woman running from the opposite direction was trying to catch the bus.. She missed it. The pastor invited her to wait in the warm church for the next bus 45 minutes later.

She sat in a pew and paid no attention to the pastor while he got a ladder, hangers, etc., to put up the tablecloth as a wall tapestry. The pastor could hardly believe how beautiful it looked and it covered up the entire problem area.

Then he noticed the woman walking down the center aisle. Her face was like a sheet.. "Pastor, "she asked, "where did you get that tablecloth?" The pastor explained. The woman asked him to check the lower right corner to see if the initials, EBG were crocheted into it there. They were. These were the initials of the woman, and she had made this tablecloth 35 years before, in Austria.

The woman could hardly believe it as the pastor told how he had just gotten the Tablecloth. The woman explained that before the war she and her husband were well-to-do people in Austria.

When the Nazis came, she was forced to leave. Her husband was going to follow her the next week. He was captured, sent to prison and never saw her husband or her home again.

The pastor wanted to give her the tablecloth; but she made the pastor keep it for the church. The pastor insisted on driving her home, that was the least he could do. She lived on the other side of Staten Island and was only in Brooklyn for the day for a housecleaning job.

What a wonderful service they had on Christmas Eve. The church was almost full. The music and the spirit were great. At the end of the service, the pastor and his wife greeted everyone at the door and many said that they would return.

One older man, whom the pastor recognized from the neighborhood continued to sit in one of the pews and stare, and the pastor wondered why he wasn't leaving.

The man asked him where he got the tablecloth on the front wall because it was identical to one that his wife had made years ago when they lived in Austria before the war and how could there be two tablecloths so much alike. He told the pastor how the Nazis came, how he forced his wife to flee for her safety and he was supposed to follow her, but he was arrested and put in a prison... He never saw his wife or his home again all the 35 years in between.

The pastor asked him if he would allow him to take him for a little ride. They drove to Staten Island and to the same house where the pastor had taken the woman three days earlier. He helped the man climb the three flights of stairs to the woman's apartment, knocked on the door and he saw the greatest Christmas reunion he could ever imagine.

True Story - submitted by Pastor Rob Reid Who says God does not work in mysterious ways.

I asked the Lord to bless you as I prayed for you today, to guide you and protect you as you go along your way. His love is always with you, His promises are true, and when we give Him all our cares you know He will see us through. So when the road you're traveling on seems difficult at best.. Just remember I'm here praying and God will do the rest. Pass this on to those you want God to bless and don't forget to send it back to the one who asked God to bless you first.

When there is nothing left but God that is when you find out that God is all you need. Take 60 seconds and give this a shot! All you do is simply say the following small prayer for the person who sent you this.

Father, God, bless all my friends and family in whatever it is that You know they may be needing this day! May their life be full of your peace, prosperity and power as he/she seeks to have a closer relationship with you. Amen.

GREAT TRUTHS

1. In my many years I have come to a conclusion that one useless man is a shame, two is a law firm, and three or more is a congress. -- **John Adams**

2. If you don't read the newspaper you are uninformed, if you do read the newspaper you are misinformed. -- **Mark Twain**

3. Suppose you were an idiot. And suppose you were a member of Congress. But then I repeat myself. -- **Mark Twain**

4. I contend that for a nation to try to tax itself into prosperity is like a man standing in a bucket and trying to lift himself up by the handle. --**Winston Churchill**

5. 5. A government which robs Peter to pay Paul can always depend on the support of Paul. -- **George Bernard Shaw**

6. A liberal is someone who feels a great debt to his fellow man, which debt he proposes to pay off with your money. -- **G. Gordon Liddy**

7. Democracy must be something more than two wolves and a sheep voting on what to have for dinner. --**James Bovard**, Civil Libertarian (1994)

8. Foreign aid might be defined as a transfer of money from poor people in rich countries to rich people in poor countries. -- **Douglas Case**, Classmate of Bill Clinton at Georgetown University.

9. Giving money and power to government is like giving whiskey and car keys to teenage boys. -- **P.J. O'Rourke**, Civil Libertarian

10. Government is the great fiction, through which everybody endeavors to live at the expense of everybody else. -- **Frederic Bastiat**, French economist(1801-1850)

11. Government's view of the economy could be summed up in a few short phrases: If it moves, tax it. If it keeps moving, regulate it. And if it stops moving, subsidize it. --**Ronald Reagan** (1986)

12. I don't make jokes. I just watch the government and report the facts. -- **Will Rogers**

13. If you think health care is expensive now, wait until you see what it costs when it's free! -- **P. J. O'Rourke**

14. In general, the art of government consists of taking as much money as possible from one party of the citizens to give to the other. --**Voltaire** (1764)

15. Just because you do not take an interest in politics doesn't mean politics won't take an interest in you! -- **Pericles** (430 B.C.)

16. No man's life, liberty, or property is safe while the legislature is in session. **Mark Twain** (1866)

17. Talk is cheap, except when Congress does it. -- **Anonymous**

18. The government is like a baby's alimentary canal, with a happy appetite at one end and no responsibility at the other. -- **Ronald Reagan**

19. The inherent vice of capitalism is the unequal sharing of the blessings. The inherent blessing of socialism is the equal sharing of misery. -- **Winston Churchill**

20. The only difference between a tax man and a taxidermist is that the taxidermist leaves the skin. -- **Mark Twain**

21. The ultimate result of shielding men from the effects of folly is to fill the world with fools. -- **Herbert Spencer**, English Philosopher (1820-1903)

22. There is no distinctly Native American criminal class, save Congress. -- **Mark Twain**

23. What this country needs are more unemployed politicians --**Edward Langley**, Artist (1928-1995)

24. A government big enough to give you everything you want, is strong enough to take everything you have. -- **Thomas Jefferson**

25. We hang the petty thieves and appoint the great ones to public office. -- **Aesop**

FIVE BEST SENTENCES

1. You cannot legislate the poor into prosperity, by legislating the wealthy out of prosperity.
2. What one person receives without working for, another person must work for without receiving.
3. The government cannot give to anybody anything that the government does not first take from somebody else.
4. You cannot multiply wealth by dividing it.
5. When half of the people get the idea that they do not have to work, because the other half is going to take care of them, and when the other half gets the idea that it does no good to work because somebody else is going to get what they work for, that is the beginning of the end of any nation

GUN FACTS FROM GUN HISTORY

*After reading the following historical facts, read the part about Switzerland twice_*

A LITTLE GUN HISTORY

Guess which items are used in more murders?

Column A: | Column B:

(Hint: You don't need a background check to buy one of them.)

In 1929, the Soviet Union established gun control.. From 1929 to 1953,

about 20 million dissidents, unable to defend themselves, were rounded up and exterminated.

In 1911, Turkey established gun control. From 1915 to 1917, 1..5 million Armenians, unable to defend themselves, were rounded up and exterminated.

Germany established gun control in 1938 and from 1939 to 1945, a total of 3 million Jews and others who were unable to defend themselves were rounded up and exterminated.

China established gun control in 1935. From 1948 to 1952, 20 million political dissidents, unable to defend themselves, were rounded up and exterminated

----

Guatemala established gun control in 1964.. From 1964 to 1981, 100,000

Mayan Indians, unable to defend themselves, were rounded up and exterminated..

Uganda established gun control in 1970. From 1971 to 1979, 300,000

Christians, unable to defend themselves, were rounded up and exterminated

Cambodia established gun control in 1956. From 1975 to 1977, one million

educated people, unable to defend themselves, were rounded up and exterminated.

Defenseless people rounded up and exterminated in the 20th Century because of gun control: 56 million.

You won't see this data on the US evening news, or hear politicians disseminating this information.

Guns in the hands of honest citizens save lives and property and, yes, gun-control laws adversely affect only the law-abiding citizens

Take note my fellow Americans, before it's too late!

The next time someone talks in favor of gun control, please remind them of this history lesson.

With guns, we are 'citizens.'

Without them, we are 'subjects'.

During WWII the Japanese decided not to invade America because they knew most Americans were ARMED!

If you value your freedom, please spread this anti-gun control message to all of your friends.

The purpose of fighting is to win. There is no possible victory in defense. The sword is more important than the shield, and skill is more important than either. The final weapon is the brain. All else is supplemental.

SWITZERLAND ISSUES EVERY HOUSEHOLD A GUN!

SWITZERLAND'S GOVERNMENT TRAINS EVERY ADULT THEY ISSUE A RIFLE.

SWITZERLAND HAS THE LOWEST GUN RELATED CRIME RATE OF ANY

CIVILIZED COUNTRY IN THE WORLD!!!

IT'S A NO BRAINER!

DON'T LET OUR GOVERNMENT WASTE MILLIONS OF OUR TAX DOLLARS

IN AN EFFORT TO MAKE ALL LAW ABIDING CITIZENS AN EASY TARGET.

I'm a firm believer of the 2nd Amendment!

If you are too, please forward. LEARN FROM HISTORY.

RWP2: More per Wikipedia. **Gun politics in Switzerland** are unique in Europe. The vast majority of men between the ages of 20 and 30 are conscripted into the militia and undergo military training, including weapons training. The personal weapons of the militia are kept at home as part of the military obligations, however it is not allowed to keep the ammunition. But ammunition can be easily purchased legally." Switzerland thus has one of the highest gun ownership rates in the world.[1] In recent times a minority of political opposition has expressed a desire for tighter gun regulations.[2]rejected stricter gun control

H.

HAPPY HAND BOOK 2009

Health:

1. Drink plenty of water.
2. Eat breakfast like a king, lunch like a prince and dinner like a beggar.
3. Eat more foods that grow on trees and plants and eat less food that is manufactured in plants.
4. Live with the 3 E's -- Energy, Enthusiasm, and Empathy.
5. Make time to practice meditation, yoga, and prayer.
6. Play more games.
7. Read more books than you did in 2008.
8. Sit in silence for at least 10 minutes each day.
9. Sleep for 7 hours.
10. Take a 10-30 minute walk every day. And while you walk, smile.

Personality:

11. Don't compare your life to others'. You have no idea what their journey is all about.
12. Don't have negative thoughts or things you cannot control. Instead invest your energy in the positive present moment.
13. Don't overdo. Keep your limits.
14. Don't take yourself so seriously. No one else does.
15. Don't waste your precious energy on gossip.
16. Dream more while you are awake.
17. Envy is a waste of time. You already have all you need.

18. Forget issues of the past. Don't remind your partner with his/her mistakes of the past. That will ruin your present happiness.
19. Life is too short to waste time hating anyone. Don't hate others.
20. Make peace with your past so it won't spoil the present.
21. No one is in charge of your happiness except you.
22. Realize that life is a school and you are here to learn. Problems are simply part of the curriculum that appear and fade away like algebra class but the lessons you learn will last a lifetime.
23. Smile and laugh more.
24. You don't have to win every argument. Agree to disagree.

Society:

25. Call your family often.
26. Each day give something good to others.
27. Forgive everyone for everything.
28. Spend time with people over the age of 70 & under the age of 6.
29. Try to make at least three people smile each day.
30. What other people think of you is none of your business.
31. Your job won't take care of you when you are sick. Your friends will. Stay in touch.

Life:

32. **Do the right thing!**
33. Get rid of anything that isn't useful, beautiful or joyful.
34. GOD heals everything.
35. However good or bad a situation is, it will change.
36. No matter how you feel, get up, dress up and show up.
37. The best is yet to come.
38. When you awake alive in the morning, thank GOD for it.
39. Your Inner most self is always happy. So, be happy.

Last but not the least:

40. Please Forward this to those you care about.

HASSLES: LEARNING THROUGH OUR HASSLES

November 23, 2009
By Robert H. Schuller

"...the Lord knows how to rescue the godly from trials [hassles]...." – 2 Peter 2:9

Do you remember the story of the little boy who stormed angrily home from his first day of kindergarten? "How did you like school?" his mother asked gently.

"I didn't like it," he replied sulkily. "In fact," he continued, "I not only didn't like it, I'm quitting!"

"You're quitting!" his mother exclaimed incredulously. "You *can't* do that!"

"I don't care if I can or I can't," the little boy said. "I'm quitting."

"Why do you want to quit school?" his mother questioned.

"Look, Mom," the child replied, "school is an awful place. I can't write. I don't know how to read. And they wouldn't let me talk. There's nothing to it, so I quit!"

Personal growth comes when we learn through our hassles what our potential capabilities and capacities for learning really are. Hassles show us where we need to grow.

What things most often cause you to want to quit? What do you think your heavenly Father would say to you next time you want to quit?

This excerpt was taken from the **"Power for Life Daily Devotional"**

HE SAID-SHE SAID: SURVIVE AND ADVANCE - HE SAID

Then Asa called to the LORD his God and said, "LORD, there is no one like you to help the powerless against the mighty. Help us, O LORD our God, for we rely on you, and in your name we have come against this vast army. O LORD, you are our God; do not let man prevail against you." **2 Chronicles 14:11 (NIV)**

March 11, 1983, Atlanta's Omni Arena: "After Lo hits these two free throws I want us to guard the inbound pass, but don't foul." said Jim Valvano (pictured above).The starting five for N.C. State's basketball team broke from the huddle and walked toward the free-throw lane. At the last second, Coach Jim Valvano is rumored to have pulled point guard Sidney Lowe aside and whispered, "If Lo misses these two shots I want you to..."

An unwavering belief in our abilities may be the key to our success. That Friday night in Atlanta, freshman Lorenzo Charles and N.C. State needed a confidence boost. State's chance to secure an NCAA bid rested in the hands of a freshman, a player whose free-throw average stood at 67.6%. Odds were that Charles would miss at least one of the shots. Maybe both. He'd never gone to the line with the outcome of a game resting in his hands. Valvano knew Lorenzo Charles needed a shot of confidence, so the coach told the players how to react *after* Charles made his free throws.

King Asa needed a boost of confidence too. Though he'd served God and prospered during a reign of peace, the king's men—armed only with large shields, bows, and spears—faced "a vast army and three hundred chariots." Asa knew the risk of fighting alone. He needed help. "We rely on you," he cried out to God. "You help the powerless. There is none like You. You are our God."

We're prone to think that we can win on our own strength, but our legs grow weary and our nerves fray. We squander our chances for victory, advancement, and promotion by accepting God's accolades as our own. All work is a team sport. Family, friends, and co-workers cheer us on in our profession. They remind us that we are more than the sum of our past; they believe that we can do better and that today, we will.

Charles' first attempt missed the rim—wasn't even close. But his second shot fell through the net and State advanced to the next game. The following week State was crowned ACC Champions, received an NCAA bid, and eventually won the national championship all because of Lorenzo Charles' last-second dunk.

What recent defeat prevents us from believing in God's goodness? What disease, financial setback, or broken relationship threatens to crush our confidence and causes us to cower in fear? God has placed us in His starting lineup for a reason. He expects great things of us. When no one else believes we can, God does.

Today let us advance with confidence: we play for an awesome God.

(Reprinted with permission from My Father's Business 30 Inspirational Stories for Discerning and Doing Gods Will)

Catch the premiere of **Survive and Advance**, the story of N.C. State's miraculous 1983 run and Jimmy V's fight against cancer Sunday night at 9 p.m. on ESPN

The Church will prevail!

He Will Prevail – She Said

Then Asa called to the LORD his God and said, "LORD, there is no one like you to help the powerless against the mighty. Help us, LORD our God, for we rely on you, and in your name we have come against this vast army. LORD, you are our God; do not let mere mortals prevail against you." **II Chronicles 14:11 NIV**

It's sad. Heartbreaking. Watching a congregation crumble. But I've seen it. Not once but twice. The first time when a congregation, out of greed, held so tight to a Bank CD that their church doors closed when they wouldn't pay their minister or their bills from this account. And the second time when the stubbornness of man outweighed the call of God's church.

I'm sure in both instances, Satan celebrated the demise of two churches. He'd successfully deceived God's people...won a battle.

Somehow our soldiers have managed to fall from the ranks and wander away from God's army. As straggler soldiers they're prime prey for the prince of darkness. Their armor is dented, their shields lost, the soles of their shoes worn, and the sword they once waved in Christ's name, now lays broken in the dirt.

Asa was righteous. Scripture tells us he did what was good and right. He tore down idols; smashed pagan alters and commanded Judah to seek God. His efforts brought peace and restored a weakened people back to the feet of God. When his small army faced down thousands of enemies, he called to God to not let *mere mortals prevail against Him*. With God at the helm, Asa and his army prevailed.

God's army is solid. His foothold is strong. And though a few think their way is better, nothing can destroy what God has built. No man or army is vast enough to overpower the King of Kings. So when mere mortals think they know what is best... God's army shudders, for they know when they are called into battle, those who defy will be destroyed and, from the ashes, God will raise His church.

We live in a world where absolute truths are being hidden from the eyes of men. Weak men dig into foxholes grasping hold of stubbornness and greed, refusing to unveil His righteousness. It may succeed for a time but when God raises His army and leads them into battle, His church will prevail.

Put your foothold in the army of God. When you see His people struggle, pray. Call upon the name of God and He will help the powerless against the mighty.

Eddie Jones and Cindy Sproles are friends and cofounders of ChristianDevotions.us . They co-write the popular He Said, She Said devotions and host Blog Talk Radio's **Christian Devotions SPEAK UP!** along with Scott McCausey. Eddie and Cindy travel and speak at conferences across the country and they are available to speak at your church or conference. Contact them cindy@christiandevotions.us.

HEAVEN: A TEENAGER'S VIEW OF HEAVEN

17-year-old Brian Moore had only a short time to write something for a class. The subject was what Heaven was like. 'I wowed 'em,' he later told his father, Bruce. 'It's a killer. It's the bomb. It's the best thing I ever wrote..' It also was the last.

Brian Moore died May 27, 1997, the day after Memorial Day. He was driving home from a friend's house when his car went off Bulen-Pierce Road in Pickaway County and struck a utility pole. He emerged from the wreck unharmed but stepped on a downed power line and was electrocuted.

The Moore's framed a copy of Brian's essay and hung it among the family portraits in the living room. 'I think God used him to make a point. I think we were meant to find it and make something out of it,' Mrs. Moore said of the essay. She and her husband want to share their son's vision of life after death. 'I'm happy for Brian. I know he's in heaven. I know I'll see him.'

Brian's Essay: The Room...

In that place between wakefulness and dreams, I found myself in the room. There were no distinguishing features except for the one wall covered with small index card files. They were like the ones in libraries that list titles by author or subject in alphabetical order.

But these files, which stretched from floor to ceiling and seemingly endless in either direction, had very different headings. As I drew near the wall of files, the first to catch my attention was one that read 'Girls I have liked.' I opened it and began flipping through the cards. I quickly shut it, shocked to realize that I recognized the names written on each one.

And then without being told, I knew exactly where I was. This lifeless room with its small files was a crude catalog system for my life. Here were written the actions of my every moment, big and small, in a detail my memory couldn't match. A sense of wonder and curiosity, coupled with horror, stirred within me as I began randomly opening files and exploring their content.

Some brought joy and sweet memories; others a sense of shame and regret so intense that I would look over my shoulder to see if anyone was watching.

A file named 'Friends' was next to one marked 'Friends I have betrayed.' The titles ranged from the mundane to the outright weird 'Books I Have Read,' 'Lies I Have Told,' 'Comfort I have Given,' 'Jokes I Have Laughed at.' Some were almost hilarious in their exactness: 'Things I've yelled at my brothers.' Others I couldn't laugh at: 'Things I Have Done in My Anger', 'Things I Have Muttered Under My Breath at My Parents.' I never ceased to be surprised by the contents.

Often there were many more cards than I expected. Sometimes fewer than I hoped. I was overwhelmed by the sheer volume of the life I had lived. Could it be possible that I had the time in my years to fill each of these thousands or even millions of cards? But each card confirmed this truth. Each was written in my own handwriting. Each signed with my signature.

When I pulled out the file marked 'TV Shows I have watched', I realized the files grew to contain their contents. The cards were packed tightly and yet after two or three yards, I hadn't found the end of the file. I shut it, shamed, not so much by the quality of shows but more by the vast time I knew that file represented.

When I came to a file marked 'Lustful Thoughts,' I felt a chill run through my body. I pulled the file out only an inch, not willing to test its size and drew out a card. I shuddered at its detailed content.

I felt sick to think that such a moment had been recorded. An almost animal rage broke on me. One thought dominated my mind: No one must ever see these cards! No one must ever see this room! I have to destroy them!' In insane frenzy I yanked the file out. Its size didn't matter now. I had to empty it and burn the cards. But as I took it at one end and began pounding it on the floor, I could not dislodge a single card. I became desperate and pulled out a card, only to find it as strong as steel when I tried to tear it. Defeated and utterly helpless, I returned the file to its slot. Leaning my forehead against the wall, I let out a long, self-pitying sigh.

And then I saw it. The title bore 'People I Have Shared the Gospel With.' The handle was brighter than those around it, newer, almost unused. I pulled on its handle and a small box not more than three inches long fell into my hands. I could count the cards it contained on one hand.

And then the tears came. I began to weep. Sobs so deep that they hurt. They started in my stomach and shook through me. I fell on my knees and cried. I cried out of shame, from the overwhelming shame of it all. The rows of file shelves swirled in my tear-filled eyes. No one must ever, ever know of this room. I must lock it up and hide the key. But then as I pushed away the tears, I saw Him.

No, please not Him. Not here. Oh, anyone but Jesus. I watched helplessly as He began to open the files and read the cards. I couldn't bear to watch His response. And in the moments I could bring myself to look at His face, I saw a sorrow deeper than my own.

He seemed to intuitively go to the worst boxes. Why did He have to read every one? Finally He turned and looked at me from across the room. He looked at me with pity in His eyes. But this was a pity that didn't anger me. I dropped my head, covered my face with my hands and began to cry again. He walked over and put His arm around me. He could have said so many things. But He didn't say a word. He just cried with me.

Then He got up and walked back to the wall of files. Starting at one end of the room, He took out a file and, one by one, began to sign His name over mine on each card. 'No!' I shouted rushing to Him. All I could find to say was 'No, no,' as I pulled the card from Him. His name shouldn't be on these cards. But there it was, written in red so rich, so dark, so alive. The name of Jesus covered mine. It was written with His blood. He gently took the card back. He smiled a sad smile and began to sign the cards. I don't think I'll ever understand how He did it so quickly, but the next instant it seemed I heard Him close the last file and walk back to my side.

He placed His hand on my shoulder and said, 'It is finished.' I stood up, and He led me out of the room. There was no lock on its door. There were still cards to be written.

'I CAN DO ALL THINGS THROUGH CHRIST WHO STRENGTHENS ME.'-PHIL. 4:13

'FOR GOD SO LOVED THE WORLD THAT HE GAVE HIS ONLY SON, THAT WHOEVER BELIEVES IN HIM SHALL NOT PERISH BUT HAVE ETERNAL LIFE.

HISTORY LESSON

David Kaiser is a respected historian whose published works have covered a broad range of topics, from European Warfare to American League Baseball.. Born in 1947, the son of a diplomat, Kaiser spent his childhood in three capital cities: Washington D.C, Albany , New York , and Dakar , Senegal . He attended Harvard University , graduating there in 1969 with a B.A. in history. He then spent several years more at Harvard, gaining a PhD in history, which he obtained in 1976. He served in the Army Reserve from 1970 to 1976.

He is a professor in the Strategy and Policy Department of the United States Naval War College. He has previously taught at Carnegie Mellon, Williams College and Harvard University. Kaiser's latest book, The Road to Dallas, about the Kennedy assassination, was just published by Harvard University Press.

By Dr. David Kaiser

HISTORY UNFOLDING

I am a student of history. Professionally, I have written 15 books on history that have been published in six languages, and I have studied history all my life. I have come to think there is something monumentally large afoot, and I do not believe it is simply a banking crisis, or a mortgage crisis, or a credit crisis. Yes these exist, but they are merely single facets on a very large gemstone that is only now coming into a sharper focus.

Something of historic proportions is happening. I can sense it because I know how it feels, smells, what it looks like, and how people react to it. Yes, a perfect storm may be brewing, but there is something happening within our country that has been evolving for about ten to fifteen years. The pace has dramatically quickened in the past two.

We demand and then codify into law the requirement that our banks make massive loans to people we know they can never pay back? Why?

We learned just days ago that the Federal Reserve, which has little or no real oversight by anyone, has "loaned" two trillion dollars (that is $2,000,000,000,000) over the past few months, but will not tell us to whom or why or disclose the terms. That is our money. Yours and mine. And that is three times the $700 billion we all argued about so strenuously just this past September. Who has this money? Why do they have it? Why are the terms unavailable to us? Who asked for it? Who authorized it? I thought this was a government of "we the people," who loaned our powers to our elected leaders.

Apparently not.

We have spent two or more decades intentionally de-industrializing our economy...Why?

We have intentionally dumbed down our schools, ignored our history, and no longer teach our founding documents, why we are exceptional, and why we are worth preserving. Students by and large cannot write, think critically, read, or articulate. Parents are not revolting, teachers are not picketing, school boards continue to back mediocrity.. Why?

We have now established the precedent of protesting every close election (violently in California over a proposition that is so controversial that it simply wants marriage to remain defined as between one man and one woman. Did you ever think such a thing possible just a decade ago?) We have corrupted our sacred political process by allowing unelected judges to write laws that radically change our way of life, and then mainstream Marxist groups like ACORN and others to turn our voting system into a banana republic. To what purpose?

Now our mortgage industry is collapsing, housing prices are in free fall, major industries are failing, our banking system is on the verge of collapse, social security is nearly bankrupt, as is Medicare and our entire government. Our education system is worse than a joke (I teach college and I know precisely what I am talking about) - the list is staggering in its length, breadth, and depth.. It is potentially 1929 x ten...And we are at war with an enemy we cannot even name for fear of offending people of the same religion, who, in turn, cannot wait to slit the throats of your children if they have the opportunity to do so.

And finally, we have elected a man that no one really knows anything about, who has never run so much as a Dairy Queen, let alone a town as big as Wasilla, Alaska . All of his associations and alliances are with real radicals in their chosen fields of employment, and everything we learn about him, drip by drip, is unsettling if not downright scary (Surely you have heard him speak about his idea to create and fund a mandatory civilian defense force stronger than our military for use inside our borders? No? Oh, of course. The media would never play that for you over and over and then demand he answer it. Sarah Palin's pregnant daughter and $150,000 wardrobe are more important.)

Mr. Obama's winning platform can be boiled down to one word: Change. Why?

I have never been so afraid for my country and for my children as I am now.

This man campaigned on bringing people together, something he has never, ever done in his professional life. In my assessment, Obama will divide us along philosophical lines, push us apart, and then try to realign the pieces into a new and different power structure. Change is indeed coming. And when it comes, you will never see the same nation again.

And that is only the beginning..

As a serious student of history, I thought I would never come to experience what the ordinary, moral German must have felt in the mid-1930s In those times, the "savior" was a former smooth-talking rabble-rouser from the streets, about whom the average German knew next to nothing. What they should have known was that he was associated with groups that shouted, shoved, and pushed around people with whom they disagreed; he edged his way onto the political stage through great oratory.. Conservative "losers" read it right now.

And there were the promises. Economic times were tough, people were losing jobs, and he was a great speaker. And he smiled and frowned and waved a lot. And people, even newspapers, were afraid to speak out for fear that his "brown shirts" would bully and beat them into submission. Which they did - regularly.

And then, he was duly elected to office, while a full-throttled economic crisis bloomed at hand - the Great Depression. Slowly, but surely he seized the controls of government power, person by person, department by department, bureaucracy by bureaucracy. The children of German citizens were at first, encouraged to join a Youth Movement in his name where they were taught exactly what to think. Later, they were required to do so. No Jews of course,

How did he get people on his side? He did it by promising jobs to the jobless, money to the money-less, and rewards for the military-industrial complex. He did it by indoctrinating the children, advocating gun control, health care for all, better wages, better jobs, and promising to re-instill pride once again in the country, across Europe , and across the world. He did it with a compliant media - did you know that? And he did this all in the name of justice and .... change. And the people surely got what they voted for.

If you think I am exaggerating, look it up. It's all there in the history books.

So read your history books. Many people of conscience objected in 1933 and were shouted down, called names, laughed at, and ridiculed. When Winston Churchill pointed out the obvious in the late 1930s while seated in the House of Lords in England (he was not yet Prime Minister), he was booed into his seat and called a crazy troublemaker. He was right, though. And the world came to regret that he was not listened to.

Do not forget that Germany was the most educated, the most cultured country in Europe . It was full of music, art, museums, hospitals, laboratories, and universities. And yet, in less than six years (a shorter time span than just two terms of the U. S. presidency) it was rounding up its own citizens, killing others, abrogating its laws, turning children against parents, and neighbors against neighbors. All with the best of intentions, of course. The road to Hell is paved with them.

As a practical thinker, one not overly prone to emotional decisions, I have a choice: I can either believe what the objective pieces of evidence tell me (even if they make me cringe with disgust); I can believe what history is shouting to me from across the chasm of seven decades; or I can hope I am wrong by closing my eyes, having another latte, and ignoring what is transpiring around me.

I choose to believe the evidence. No doubt some people will scoff at me, others laugh, or think I am foolish, naive, or both. To some degree, perhaps I am. But I have never been afraid to look people in the eye and tell them exactly what I believe-and why I believe it.

I pray I am wrong. I do not think I am. Perhaps the only hope is our vote in the next elections.

By David Kaiser ,Jamestown , Rhode Island

HOPE.....BOB HOPE IN HEAVEN (*IN MEMORY*)

For those of you too young to remember Bob, ask your Grandparents!!! And thanks for the memories........WHAT A WONDERFUL E-MAIL

I HOPE THIS WILL PUT A SMILE ON YOUR FACE AND IN YOUR HEART.

Tribute to a man, Bob Hope, who DID make a difference:

ON TURNING 70 - 'You still chase women, but only downhill'.

ON TURNING 80 - 'That's the time of your life when even your birthday suit needs pressing.'

ON TURNING 90 - 'You know you're getting old when the candles cost more than the cake.'

ON TURNING 100 - ' I don't feel old. In fact I don't feel anything until noon. Then it's time for my nap.'

ON GIVING UP HIS EARLY CAREER, BOXING - 'I ruined my hands in the ring. The referee kept stepping on them.'

ON NEVER WINNING AN OSCAR - 'Welcome to the Academy Awards or, as it's called at my home, 'Passover'.'

ON GOLF - 'Golf is my profession. Show business is just to pay the green fees.'

ON PRESIDENTS - 'I have performed for 12 presidents and entertained only six.'

ON WHY HE CHOSE SHOWBIZ FOR HIS CAREER - ' When I was born, the doctor said to my mother, 'Congratulations You have an eight-pound ham' ..'

ON RECEIVING THE CONGRESSIONAL GOLD MEDAL -'I feel very humble, but I think I have the strength of character to fight it.'

ON HIS FAMILY'S EARLY POVERTY - 'Four of us slept in the one bed When it got cold, mother threw on another brother.'

ON HIS SIX BROTHERS - 'That's how I learned to dance. Waiting for the bathroom.'

ON HIS EARLY FAILURES - 'I would not have had anything to eat if it wasn't for the stuff the audience threw at me.'

ON GOING TO HEAVEN - 'I've done benefits for ALL religions. I'd hate to blow the hereafter on a technicality.'

Give me a sense of humor. Lord, Give me the grace to see a joke, to get some humor out of life.

In Memory of Bob Hope

HOT AIR BALLOON

A woman in a hot air balloon realized she was lost. She lowered her altitude and spotted a man in a boat below. She shouted to him, "Excuse me, can you help me? I promised a friend I would meet him an hour ago, but I don't know where I am."

The man consulted his portable GPS and replied, "You're in a hot air balloon, approximately 30 feet above a ground elevation of 2,346 feet above sea level. You are at 31 degrees, 14.97 minutes north latitude and 100 degrees, 49.09 minutes west longitude."

She rolled her eyes and said, "You must be a republican."

"I am," replied the man. "How did you know?"

"Well," answered the balloonist, "everything you told me is technically correct. But I have no idea what to do with your information, and I'm still lost. Frankly, you've not been much help to me."

The man smiled and responded, "You must be an Obama Democrat."

"I am," replied the balloonist. "How did you know?"

"Well," said the man, "you don't know where you are or where you are going. You've risen to where you are, due to a large quantity of hot air. You made a promise you have no idea how to keep, and you expect me to solve your problem. You're in exactly the same position you were in before we met, but somehow, now it's my fault.

HOW LONG DO WE HAVE?- "I'M 63 AND I'M TIRED"

by Robert A. Hall

Robert A. Hall is an actor. He played the coroner on CSI if you watched that show. He also is a Marine Vietnam War veteran, but does not mention that he had his legs blown off in that war.

This should be required reading for every man, woman and child in the United States of America .

I'm 63. Except for one semester in college when jobs were scarce and a six-month period when I was between jobs, but job-hunting every day, I've worked hard since I was 18. Despite some health challenges, I still put in 50-hour weeks, and haven't called in sick in seven or eight years. I make a good salary, but I didn't inherit my job or my income, and I worked to get where I am. Given the economy, there's no retirement in sight, and I'm tired. Very tired.

I'm tired of being told that I have to "spread the wealth" to people who don't have my work ethic. I'm tired of being told the government will take the money I earned, by force if necessary, and give it to people too lazy to earn it.

I'm tired of being told that I have to pay more taxes to "keep people in their homes." Sure, if they lost their jobs or got sick, I'm willing to help. But if they bought Mc Mansions at three times the price of our paid-off, $250,000 condo, on one-third of my salary, then let the left-wing Congress-critters who passed Fannie and Freddie and the Community Reinvestment Act that created the bubble use their own money to help them.

I'm tired of being told how bad America is by left-wing millionaires like Michael Moore, George Soros and Hollywood Entertainers who live in luxury because of the opportunities

America provided to them. In thirty years, if they get their way, the United States will have:

1. the economy of Zimbabwe,
2. the freedom of the press of China
3. the crime and violence of Mexico,
4. the tolerance for Christian people of Iran
5. the freedom of speech of Venezuela

I'm tired of being told that Islam is a "Religion of Peace," when every day I can read stories of Muslim men killing their sisters, wives and daughters for their family "honor"; of Muslims rioting over some slight offense; of Muslims murdering Christian and Jews because they aren't "believers"; of Muslims burning schools for girls; of Muslims stoning teenage rape victims to death for "adultery"; of Muslims mutilating the genitals of little girls; all in the name of Allah, because the Qur'an and Sharia's law tells them to.

I'm tired of being told that "race doesn't matter" in the post-racial world of Obama, when it's all that matters in affirmative action jobs, lower college admission and graduation standards for minorities (harming them the most), government contract set-asides, tolerance for the ghetto culture of violence and fatherless children that hurts minorities more than anyone, and in the appointment of U.S. Senators from Illinois.

I think it's very cool that we have a black president and that a black child is doing her homework at the desk where Lincoln wrote the Emancipation Proclamation. I just wish the black president was Condi Rice, or someone who believes more in freedom and the individual and less arrogantly in an all-knowing government.

I'm tired of being told that out of "tolerance for other cultures" we must not complain when Saudi Arabia uses the money we pay for their oil to fund mosques and madras Islamic schools to preach hate in America, while no American group is allowed to fund a church, synagogue or religious school in Saudi Arabia to teach love and tolerance.

I'm tired of being told I must lower my living standard to fight global warming, which no one is allowed to debate. My wife and I live in a two-bedroom apartment and carpool together five miles to our jobs. We also own a three-bedroom condo where our daughter and granddaughter live. Our carbon footprint is about 5% of Al Gore's, and if you're greener than Gore, you're green enough.

I'm tired of being told that drug addicts have a disease, and I must help support and treat them, and pay for the damage they do. Did a giant germ rush out of a dark alley, grab them, and stuff white powder up their noses while they tried to fight it off? I don't think gay people choose to be gay, but I #@*# sure think druggies chose to take drugs. And I'm tired of harassment from "cool" people treating me like a freak when I tell them I never tried marijuana.

I'm tired of illegal aliens being called "undocumented workers," especially those who aren't working, but living on welfare or crime. What's next? Calling drug dealers, "Undocumented Pharmacists"? And, no, I'm not against Hispanics. Most of them are Catholic, and it's been a few hundred years since Catholics wanted to kill me for my religion.. I'm willing to fast track citizenship for any Hispanic who can speak English, doesn't have a criminal record and who is self-supporting without family on welfare, or who serves honorably for three years in our military. Those are the kind of citizens we need.

I'm tired of the trashing of our military by latte liberals and journalists, who would never wear the uniform of the Republic themselves, or let their entitlement-handicapped kids near a recruiting station. They and their kids can sit at home, never having to make split-second decisions under life and death circumstances, and bad mouth better people than themselves. Do bad things happen in war? You bet. Do our troops sometimes misbehave? Sure. Does this compare with the atrocities that were the policy of our enemies for the last fifty years and still are? Not even close. So here's a deal for those folks. I'll let myself be subjected to all the humiliation and abuse that was heaped on terrorists at Abu Ghraib or Gitmo, while the critics of our military can be subject to captivity by the Muslims, who tortured and beheaded Daniel Pearl in Pakistan, or the Muslims who tortured and murdered Marine Lt. Col. William Higgins in Lebanon, or the Muslims who ran the blood-spattered Al Qaeda torture rooms our troops found in Iraq, or the Muslims who cut off the heads of schoolgirls in Indonesia because the girls were Christian -- then we'll compare notes. British and American soldiers are the only troops in history that civilians came to for help and handouts, instead of hiding from in fear.

I'm tired of people telling me that their party has a corner on virtue and the other party has a corner on corruption. Read the papers; bums are bipartisan. And I'm tired of people telling me we need bipartisanship. I live in Illinois , where the "Illinois Combine" of Democrats has looted the public treasury for years. Not to mention the tax cheats in Obama's cabinet.

I'm tired of hearing wealthy athletes, entertainers and politicians of both parties talking about "innocent" mistakes, "stupid" mistakes or "youthful" mistakes, when all of us know they think their only mistake was getting caught.

Speaking of poor, I'm tired of people with a sense of entitlement who have air-conditioned homes, color TVs and two cars called poor. The majority of Americans didn't have that in 1970, but we didn't know we were "poor." The poverty pimps have to keep changing the definition of poor to keep the dollars flowing.

I'm real tired of people, rich or poor, who don't take responsibility for their lives and actions. I'm tired of hearing them blame the government, or discrimination or big-whatever for their problems.

Yes, I'm tired, but I'm also glad to be 63, mostly because I'm not going to have to see the world these people are making. I'm just sorry for my granddaughter.

Robert A. Hall is a Marine Vietnam veteran who served five terms in the Massachusetts State Senate. There is no way this will be widely publicized, unless each of us sends it

I.

INDIAN WANTING COFFEE:

An Indian walks into a cafe with a shotgun in one hand and pulling a male buffalo with the other. He says to the waiter:

"Want coffee."

The waiter says, "Sure Chief. Coming right up."

He gets the Indian a tall mug of coffee. The Indian drinks the coffee down in one gulp, turns and blasts the buffalo with the shotgun, causing parts of the animal to splatter everywhere and then just walks out.

The next morning the Indian returns.

He has his shotgun in one hand, pulling another male buffalo with the other.

He walks up to the counter and says to the waiter:

"Want coffee."

"Whoa, Tonto!" says the waiter. We're still cleaning up your mess from yesterday. What was all that about, anyway?"

The Indian smiles and proudly says,

"Me training for position in United States Congress. Come in, drink coffee, shoot the bull, leave mess for others to clean up and disappear for rest of day."

4 NOVEMBER 2014--- DID YOU VOTE WISELY?

INSPIRING LIFE LESSONS FROM BRUCE LEE

Many people know of Bruce Lee from his wide achievements in film and martial arts. Born in the United States, Bruce Lee's family hailed from Hong Kong. Bruce Lee lived in both countries throughout his life, and was a student of nearly ten different styles of martial arts. Bruce Lee became a master martial artist, and even founded his own branch, named Jeet Kune Do.

While this may be a lesser known area of martial arts, notable Jeet Kune Do students include Chuck Norris and Kareem Abdul-Jabbar. His talents don't stop there. Bruce Lee is often credited with changing the way Asians were portrayed in Western cinema. Not someone who only cultivated an air of high achievement, Bruce Lee really lived the lessons he sought to impart. The following quotes are some of the most mind blowing examples of this man's true wisdom.

Keep Pushing Yourself

"There are no limits. There are plateaus, but you must not stay there, you must go beyond them. If it kills you, it kills you. A man must constantly exceed his level." In order to be successful, you must constantly challenge yourself and set new goals. In order to overcome some obstacles in life you must be determined enough to keep going no matter what.

Stay Positive

"Choose the positive. — You have choice — you are master of your attitude — choose the POSITIVE, the CONSTRUCTIVE. Optimism is a faith that leads to success." Be as optimistic as possible and you'll find you can do more than you thought you could.

Be True To Yourself

"In life, what more can you ask for than to be real? To fulfill one's potential instead of wasting energy on [attempting to] actualize one's dissipating image, which is not real and an expenditure of one's vital energy. We have great work ahead of us, and it needs devotion and much, much energy. To grow, to discover, we need involvement, which is something I experience every day — sometimes good, sometimes frustrating. No matter what, you must let your inner light guide you out of the darkness." All of us must put effort into growing a more functional society, whether in a distant country, or in our own communities.

Cultivate Determination

"You must have complete determination. The worst opponent you can come across is one whose aim has become an obsession. For instance, if a man has decided that he is going to bite off your nose no matter what happens to him in the process, the chances are he will succeed in doing it. He may be severely beaten up, too, but that will not stop him from carrying out his objective. That is the real fighter." Determination is a crucial skill on the road to success. Complete perseverance is sometimes required to reach them.

Always Keep Growing

"There is no such thing as maturity. There is instead an ever-evolving process of maturing. Because when there is a maturity, there is a conclusion and a cessation. That's the end. That's when the coffin is closed." A rich life is one that's constantly open to new information and experiences. Once you cut yourself off to growth, you might as will be dead.

Never Stop Educating Yourself

"Faith makes it possible to achieve that which man's mind can conceive and believe. Even today, I dare not say that I have reached a state of achievement. I'm still learning, for learning is boundless." In order to stay successful, one must always challenge themselves.

Time Is Precious

"We all have time to spend or waste, and it is our decision what to do with it. But once passed, it is gone forever." The time we have on this earth is limited, and each of us should want to make the most of it. We can achieve great things if we seize the day and jump in.

Live In The Moment

"What is more important than what should be." It is critical to accept your current circumstance in order to move on from them. If you obsess over what you should or would have done, you only waste time that could be used to find solutions.

Be The Best Version Of Yourself

"Knowledge will give you power, but character respect." Most effective people in life are those who "walk the walk."

Failures Are Steps To Success

"Don't fear failure. — Not failure, but low aim, is the crime. In great attempts it is glorious even to fail." Failures are inevitable when trying new things. Failures are not permanent however, and failures should encourage you, because they show that you are in new territory.

Always Move Forward

"Walk on." You must keep challenging yourself and moving forward to truly reach your full potential.

There Are No Limits

"Life is wide, limitless. There is no border, no frontier." Societal stigmas or popular opinions don't really have any true power. Everyone deserves to have a chance to explore and discover what makes them happy.

Life Should Be Enjoyed

"The meaning of life is that it is to be lived, and it is not to be traded and conceptualized and squeezed into a pattern of systems." If you don't fit into other people's expectations, don't be afraid. You can go after things that make you feel truly alive.

Reflect On Your Experiences

"Life itself is your teacher, and you are in a state of constant learning." Always try to learn from your experiences in life.

Be Proactive

"Balance your thoughts with action. — If you spend too much time thinking about a thing, you'll never get it done." We need goals to achieve anything, however thinking about an idea too long prevents us from taking time to achieve it.

Be Flexible

"Be like water making its way through cracks. Do not be assertive, but adjust to the object, and you shall find a way around or through it. If nothing within you stays rigid, outward things will disclose themselves." Sometimes the path to where you want to go isn't the way you imagined it. However, if you remain flexible, you will always be able to move towards your goal.

Change Starts On The Inside

"The change is from inner to outer. — We start by dissolving our attitude not by altering outer conditions." Change starts from the inside, and we must utterly believe we can do something before we do it.

Negativity Is Toxic

"Pessimism blunts the tools you need to succeed." On the other hand, approaching life in a negative light makes it easy to walk away from challenges.

Live Your Life

"The key to immortality is first living a life worth remembering." Don't be afraid to pursue your real goals. Our time here is short, and living a fulfilling life is a better reward than anything else.

ITALY TRIP? A young New York woman was so depressed that she decided to end her life by throwing herself into the ocean; but just before she could throw herself from the docks, a handsome young man stopped her.

"You have so much to live for," said the man. "I'm a sailor, and we are off to Italy tomorrow. I can stow you away on my ship. I'll take care of you, bring you food every day, and keep you happy."

With nothing to lose, combined with the fact that she had always wanted to go to Italy, the woman accepted.

That night the sailor brought her aboard and hid her in a small but comfortable compartment in the ships hold.

From then on every night he would bring her three sandwiches, a bottle of red wine, and make love to her until dawn.

Three weeks later she was discovered by the captain during a routine inspection.

"What are you doing here?" asked the captain.

"I have an arrangement with one of the sailors," she replied. "He brings me food and I get a free trip to Italy ."

"I see," the captain says.

Her conscience got the best of her, and she added, "Plus, he's screwing me."

"He certainly is," replied the captain. "This is the Staten Island Ferry."

J.

JANUARY 3RD, 2007: THE DAY THE DEMOCRATS TOOK OVER THE SENATE AND THE CONGRESS:

At the time:

1. The DOW Jones closed at 12,621.77
2. The GDP for the previous quarter was 3.5%
3. The Unemployment rate was 4.6%
4. George Bush's Economic policies SET A RECORD of 52 STRAIGHT MONTHS of JOB CREATION!

Remember the day...

1. January 3rd, 2007 was the day that Barney Frank took over the House Financial Services Committee and Chris Dodd took over the Senate Banking Committee.
2. The economic meltdown that happened 15 months later was in what part of the economy? BANKING AND FINANCIAL SERVICES!
3. Thank Congress for taking us from 13,000 DOW, 3.5 GDP and 4.6% Unemployment to this CRISIS by dumping 5-6 TRILLION Dollars of toxic loans on the economy from YOUR Fannie Mae and Freddie fiasco's!

   (BTW: Bush asked Congress **17 TIMES** to stop Fannie & Freddie - starting in 2001, because it was financially risky for the U.S. economy, but no one was listening).

And who took the THIRD highest pay-off from Fannie Mae AND Freddie Mac?

OBAMA.

And who fought against reform of Fannie and Freddie??? OBAMA and the Democratic Congress.

So when someone tries to blame Bush...

REMEMBER JANUARY 3rd, 2007.... THE DAY THE DEMOCRATS TOOK OVER!" Bush may have been in the car, but the Democrats were in charge of the gas pedal and steering wheel they were driving. Set the record straight on Bush!

So, as you listen to all the commercials and media from the Democrats who are now distancing themselves from their voting record and their party, remember how they didn't listen to you when you said you didn't want all the bailouts, you didn't want the health care bill, you didn't want cap and trade, you didn't want them to continue spending money we don't have.

I'm not forgetting their complicity in getting us into this mess, and I'll be marking my vote accordingly!

"It's not that liberals aren't smart, it's just that so much of what they know isn't so" -Ronald Reagan

JANUARY 3, 2015- THE DAY AMERICA CAN BEGIN TO CHANGE

RWP2: What will change between January 3, 2015 to January 3, 2017, during the final two years of Barack Obama? WOW! Midterm elections on November 4, 2014 created a wave of change across America and possible change to the deadlock between the Senate and House to what now may be real change.

My title of *AMERICA: Once the United State?* was partially a direct correlation to what has gone on in our Congress. A divided US government has occurred many times since WWII, but nothing like what has existed with the Republican House and Democratic Senate now soon to end in January 3, 2015, seven years after 2007. The current Senate has done nothing as Senator McConnell said today in his first speech to the press on November 5, 2015. The House passed many good bills that were stopped dead in their tracks in the Senate creating total gridlock. He also said the American people can have more confidence in Congress, if Congress can actually get House bills through the Senate which can start on January 3, 2015.

He stated also that there is really only one Democrat that counts and that is President Obama. The gridlock and dysfunction can stop now if the new Senate and Congress can work together. One thing now is that a simple majority of the Senate can now have a budget for America which the Democrats failed to pass in the last 4 years. "Now we have the opportunity to pass the budget," said Senator McConnell. But still the veto pen can be used by Obama to keep his "democratic socialist agenda in view", stalled by a veto. What will Obama do now; go more to the center from his far left views. Time will tell and the FOX stars and their mud wrestling team FOX Five will now have much to talk about.

JESUS KNOWS YOU'RE HERE

A burglar broke into a house one night. He shined his flashlight around, looking for valuables when a voice in the dark said, **'Jesus knows you're here.'** He nearly jumped out of his skin, clicked his flashlight off, and froze. When he heard nothing more, after a bit, he shook his head and continued.

Just as he pulled the stereo out so he could disconnect the wires, clear as a bell he heard **'Jesus is watching you.'**

Freaked out, he shined his light around frantically, looking for the source of the voice.

Finally, in the corner of the room, his flashlight beam came to rest on a parrot.

'Did you say that?' he hissed at the parrot.

'Yep', the parrot confessed, then squawked, **'I'm just trying to warn you that he is watching you.'**

The burglar relaxed. **'Warn me, huh? Who in the world are you?**

'Moses,' replied the bird.

'**Moses?**' the burglar laughed.

'**What kind of people would name a bird Moses?"** The same kind of people that would name a **Rottweiler-Jesus.**' said the parrot .

RWP2: Or have a dog with speed of a bullet named Bullitt with night vision eyes!!

K.

KEYS TO SUCCESS

The key to success is to keep growing in all areas of life - mental, emotional, spiritual, as well as physical. **Julius Erving**

Before anything else, preparation is the key to success. **Alexander Graham Bell**

Focused, hard work is the real key to success. Keep your eyes on the goal, and just keep taking the next step towards completing it. If you aren't sure which way to do something, do it both ways and see which works better. **John Carmack**

Honesty and loyalty are key. If two people can be honest with each other about everything, that's probably the biggest key to success. **Taylor Lautner**

Even if you're on the right track, you'll get run over if you just sit there. **Will Rogers**

The fear of death follows from the fear of life. A man who lives fully is prepared to die at any time. **Mark Twain**

It is better to keep your mouth closed and let people think you are a fool than to open it and remove all doubt. **Mark Twain**

KINDLY REMEMBER THE 26TH REGIMENT NC CIVIL WAR TROOPS

From http://www.26nc.org/ Welcome to the home of the 26th Regiment North Carolina Troops past and present. We hope that you will take the time to review the pages of this site to learn more of the gallant men of the original regiment as well as the endeavors of the modern day Reactivated 26th NC reenacting unit.

The 26th North Carolina was the largest regiment in the Army of Northern Virginia and one of North Carolina's most famous units. The 26th NC served with distinction throughout the war from the coastal plains of North Carolina, to the defense of Richmond, to the invasion into Pennsylvania, throughout the siege of Petersburg, and finally at Appomattox Court House. The regiment would find its way into the epic tale of the battle of Gettysburg after its climatic clash with the Iron Brigade on the first day of that battle as well as its tenacity in pushing to the forefront in the Pettigrew-Pickett-Trimble assault. The memory of this regiment and the story of Confederate soldier from North Carolina is what we are all about.

Since 1981 the "Society for the Historical Preservation of the 26th Regiment North Carolina Troops" has grown from humble beginning into the largest single re-enactment unit in the state of North Carolina and one of the largest in the nation. With over 275 members in all regions of the state, from the coast to the mountains as well as members in other states and even a few in other countries, the 26th NC "Reactivated" has much to offer. We have many facets as a unit including components representing not only infantry but also field music, medical, commissary, artillery, cavalry, and civilians.

Anyone interested in preserving the history of the 26th NC and North Carolina's pivotal role in the Confederacy is encouraged to become a member of our organization either as a military member or as a supporting member. Help us remember the over 36,000 North Carolinians who gave their lives for their state, their homes, and their beliefs.

The 26th Regiment - North Carolina Troops was organized from companies raised from the middle and western portions of the "Old North State". Originally commanded by Zebulon Baird Vance, who later became North Carolina's wartime governor, the regiment first saw action at New Bern, N.C. in March 1862. Here they attempted to resist an assault by forces of Union General Ambrose Burnside. After this action, the regiment went north to Virginia and soon distinguished itself in battle. During a portion of the Seven Days' Battle, at Malvern Hill, the 26th charged to within 25 five yards of the Federal positions, further encouraging McClellan's departure from the York-James Peninsula. Upon returning to eastern North Carolina, the unit helped keep Union forces located there in check, protecting the "back door" to Richmond and the vital supplies coming from Wilmington to the Confederate capital.

Returning to service in Virginia again in 1863, the regiment was attached to Robert E. Lee's Army of Northern Virginia. Moving into Pennsylvania with the ANV, the gallant 26th saw action at Gettysburg in Pettigrew's Brigade, Heth's Division, Hill's Corps. On 1 July 1863, the 26th would forever etch its name in history.

On this first day of the Battle of Gettysburg, the regiment was called upon to assault Federal troops of the Iron Brigade (specifically the 24th Michigan) posted in Herbst's woods on McPherson's Ridge. After brutal fighting, which saw the 26th break through three separate lines of resistance, the regiment forced Union troops to withdraw from the position of strength which they had held. Though the 26th achieved its goal, it was at a tremendous cost. The regimental colors were shot down fourteen times; the regimental commander Colonel Henry King Burgwyn, Jr., was killed; and his second-in-command, Lt. Col. John R. Lane, was seriously wounded. Out of 800 muskets taken into the fight by the 26th on that bloody day, 588 men were killed, wounded, or missing. Sidelined to regroup and tend their significant number of wounded, the regiment rested on July 2nd on the slopes of Seminary Ridge.

On July 3rd, the 26th participated in the Pettigrew-Trimble-Pickett Assault against the center of the Federal line on Cemetery Hill. Having the colors shot down eight more times, the regiment planted its colors on the Federal works -- The Angle -- achieving the farthest advance of any Confederate unit during this epic struggle. On 3 July, the unit lost an additional 120 men. The regiment suffered greatly during this three-day bloodletting. Company F, The Hibriten Guards, suffered a 100 percent loss with all of its ninety one men and officers being killed or wounded. The 26th holds the tragic distinction of suffering the highest casualties of any unit, Confederate or Union, during the Battle of Gettysburg.

The Wilderness was the next major battle in which the regiment saw action. Again, the regiment was with the corps commanded by A.P. Hill, and it figured prominently in the outcome of the contest. With the battle wavering on the Confederate right, the 26th was thrown into the fight with the remainder of Hill's Corps to save the day.

The regiment next participated in the defense of Petersburg. For nearly one and one half years, the 26th bolstered the Confederate forces in the area and stalled the Union forces under Grant around Richmond and Petersburg. The result of this stubborn resistance was that the Southern Nation continued to live on and struggle to survive despite the constant and vicious frontal assaults of the north.

With the War Between the States drawing to a close, the regiment continued its service with the Army of Northern Virginia and surrendered with Gen. Lee at Appomattox Courthouse on 9 April 1865.

KINDNESS

Kindness is the language which the deaf can hear and the blind can see. **Mark Twain**

L.

LAWS OF LIFE:

* Murphy's First Law for Wives: If you ask your husband to pick up five items at the store and then you add one more as an afterthought, he will forget two of the first five.

* Kauffman's Paradox of the Corporation: The less important you are to the corporation, the more your tardiness or absence is noticed.

* The Salary Axiom: The pay raise is just large enough to increase your taxes and just small enough to have no effect on your take-home pay.

* Miller's Law of Insurance: Insurance covers everything except what happens.

* First Law of Living: As soon as you start doing what you always wanted to be doing, you'll want to be doing some-thing else.

* Weiner's Law of Libraries: There are no answers, only cross-references.

* The Grocery Bag Law: The candy bar you planned to eat on the way home from the market is hidden at the bottom of the grocery bag.

* Lampner's Law of Employment: When leaving work late, you will go unnoticed. When you leave work early, you will meet the boss in the parking lot.

LEROY

A woman walks into the downtown Shelby County welfare office, trailed by 15 kids.

'WOW,' the social worker exclaims, 'are they all yours?"

'Yep, they are all mine,' the flustered momma sighs, having heard that question a thousand times before.

She says, 'Sit down Leroy.' All the children rush to find seats.

'Well,' says the social worker, 'then you must be here to sign up. I'll need all your children's names.'

'Well, to keep it simple, the boys are all named Leroy and the girls are all named Leighroy.'

In disbelief, the case worker says, 'Are you serious? They're ALL named Leroy?' Their momma replied, 'Well, yes-it makes it easier. When it's time to get them out of bed and ready for school, I yell, 'Leroy!' An' when it's time for dinner, I just yell 'Leroy!' An they all comes a runnin. An' if I need to stop the kid who's running into the street, I just yell Leroy' and all of them stop. It's the smartest idea I ever had, naming 'them all Leroy.'

The social worker thinks this over for a bit, then wrinkles her forehead and says tentatively, 'But what if you just want ONE kid to come, and not the whole bunch?'

'Then I call them by their last names.'

LIFE: 40 THINGS FOR A BETTER LIFE

Take a 10-30 minute walk every day. And while you walk, smile. It is the ultimate anti-depressant.

1. Sit in silence for at least 10 minutes each day. Buy a lock if you have to.
2. Buy a DVR and tape your late night shows and get more sleep.
3. When you wake up in the morning complete the following statement, 'My purpose is to _____ today.'
4. Live with the 3 E's -- Energy, Enthusiasm, and Empathy.

5. Play more games and read more books than you did in 2007.

6. Make time to practice meditation, yoga, tai chi, and prayer. They provide us with daily fuel for our busy lives.

7. Spend time with people over the age of 70 and under the age of 6.

8. Dream more while you are awake.

9. Eat more foods that grow on trees and plants and eat less food that is manufactured in plants.

10. Drink green tea and plenty of water.. Eat blueberries, wild Alaskan salmon, broccoli, almonds & walnuts.

11. Try to make e at least three people smile each day.

12. Clear clutter from your house, your car, your desk and let new and flowing energy into your life.

13. Don't waste your precious energy on gossip, energy vampires, issues of the past, negative thoughts or things you cannot control. Instead invest your energy in the positive present moment.

14. Realize that life is a school and you are here to learn . Problems are simply part of the curriculum that appear and fade away like algebra class but the lessons you learn will last a lifetime.

15. Eat breakfast like a king, lunch like a prince and dinner like a college kid with a maxed out charge card.

16. Smile and laugh more. It will keep the energy vampires away.

17. Life isn't fair, but it's still good.

18. Life is too short to waste time hating anyone.

19. Don't take yourself so seriously. No one else does.

20. You don't have to win every argument. Agree to disagree.

21. Make peace with your past so it won't spoil the present.

22. Don't compare your life to others'. You have no idea what their journey is all about.

23. No one is in charge of your happiness except you.

24. Frame every so-called disaster with these words: 'In five years, will this matter?'

25. Forgive everyone for everything.
26. What other people think of you is none of your business.
27. GOD heals almost everything.
28. However good or bad a situation is, it will change.
29. Your job won't take care of you when you are sick. Your friends will.
30. Stay in touch.
31. Get rid of anything that isn't useful, beautiful or joyful.
32. Envy is a waste of time. You already have all you need.
33. The best is yet to come.
34. No matter how you feel, get up, dress up and show up.
35. Do the right thing!
36. Call your family often.
37. Each night before you go to bed complete the following statements: I am thankful for _____. Today I accomplished _____ _____.
38. Remember that you are too blessed to be stressed.
39. Enjoy the ride. Remember this is not Disney World and you certainly don't want a fast pass. You only have one ride through life so make the most of it and enjoy the ride.

Please Forward this to everyone you care about.

May your troubles be less, May your blessings be more,

May nothing but happiness come through your door!

LOU PRITCHETT'S OPEN LETTER TO PRESIDENT OBAMA

Lou Pritchett is one of corporate America's true living legends- an acclaimed author, dynamic teacher and one of the world's highest rated speakers. Successful corporate executives everywhere recognize him as the foremost leader in change management. Lou changed the way America does business by creating an audacious concept that came to be known as "partnering." Pritchett rose from soap salesman to Vice-President, Sales and Customer Development for Procter and Gamble and over the course of 36 years, made corporate history.

AN OPEN LETTER TO PRESIDENT OBAMA

Dear President Obama,:

You are the thirteenth President under whom I have lived and unlike any of the others, you truly scare me.

You scare me because after months of exposure, I know nothing about you.

You scare me because I do not know how you paid for your expensive Ivy League education and your upscale lifestyle and housing with no visible signs of support.

You scare me because you did not spend the formative years of youth growing up in America and culturally you are not an American.

You scare me because you have never run a company or met a payroll.

You scare me because you have never had military experience, thus don't understand it at its core.

You scare me because you lack humility and 'class', always blaming others.

You scare me because for over half your life you have aligned yourself with radical extremists who hate America and you refuse to publicly denounce these radicals who wish to see America fail.

You scare me because you are a cheerleader for the 'blame America ' crowd and deliver this message abroad.

You scare me because you want to change America to a European style country where the government sector dominates instead of the private sector.

You scare me because you want to replace our health care system with a government controlled one.

You scare me because you prefer 'wind mills' to responsibly capitalizing on our own vast oil, coal and shale reserves.

You scare me because you want to kill the American capitalist goose that lays the golden egg which provides the highest standard of living in the world.

You scare me because you have begun to use 'extortion' tactics against certain banks and corporations.

You scare me because your own political party shrinks from challenging you on your wild and irresponsible spending proposals.

You scare me because you will not openly listen to or even consider opposing points of view from intelligent people.

You scare me because you falsely believe that you are both omnipotent and omniscient.

You scare me because the media gives you a free pass on everything you do.

You scare me because you demonize and want to silence the Limbaughs, Hannitys, O'Riellys and Becks who offer opposing, conservative points of view.

You scare me because you prefer controlling over governing.

Finally, you scare me because if you serve a second term I will probably not feel safe in writing a similar letter in 8 years.

Lou Pritchett

TRUE - CHECK: http://www.snopes.com/politics/soapbox/youscareme.asp

This letter was sent to the NY Times but they never acknowledged it. Big surprise. Since it hit the Internet, however, it has had over 500,000 hits. Keep it going. All that is necessary for evil to succeed is that good men do nothing. It's happening right now.

M.

MOON COMMUNION BY BUZZ ALDRIN THAT NASA DIDN'T WANT TO BROADCAST

The Huffington Post | By Yasmine Hafiz

45 years ago, Man Landed on the Moon.

As Neil Armstrong and Buzz Aldrin prepared to take "one small step for man," Aldrin wanted to commemorate the moment in a way he found most personally meaningful -- by taking communion.

Aldrin, a church elder at **Webster Presbyterian Church** in Webster, Texas, at the time, spoke to his pastor Dean Woodruff to try to find a way to symbolize the wonder and awe of the moon landing a few weeks before lift-off. Aldrin said, "We wanted to express our feeling that what man was doing in this mission transcended electronics and computers and rockets."

The communion bread and wine, symbols of everyday life, seemed to be a fitting way to commemorate the extraordinary moment. Woodruff equipped Aldrin with a piece of communion bread, a sip of wine, and a tiny silver chalice which he brought aboard as part of the few personal items each astronaut is allowed.

Aldrin wrote about the experience a year later, for *Guideposts* magazine:

In a little while after our scheduled meal period, Neil would give the signal to step down the ladder onto the powdery surface of the moon. Now was the moment for communion.

Neil wrote; "So I unstowed the elements in their flight packets. I put them and the scripture reading on the little table in front of the abort guidance system computer.

Then I called back to Houston.

"Houston, this is Eagle. This is the LM Pilot speaking. I would like to request a few moments of silence. I would like to invite each person listening in, wherever and whomever he may be, to contemplate for a moment the events of the past few hours and to invite each person listening, wherever and whomever he may be, to contemplate for a moment the events of the past few hours and to give thanks in his own individual way.

In the radio blackout I opened the little plastic packages which contained bread and wine.

I poured the wine into the chalice our church had given me. In the one-sixth gravity of the moon the wine curled slowly and gracefully up the side of the cup. It was interesting to think that the very first liquid ever poured on the moon, and the first <u>food</u> eaten there, were communion elements."

Before taking communion, Aldrin silently read a passage from the Bible, which he had hand written on a piece of paper: "I am the vine, you are the branches. Whoever remains in me, and I in him, will bear much fruit; for you can do nothing without me" (John 15:5).

Astronaut Buzz Aldrin planned to broadcast back to Earth the lunar Holy Communion service. He originally wanted for the experience to be broadcast with the rest of his comments, but was discouraged by NASA, which was at the time fighting a lawsuit brought by atheist activist Madalyn Murray O'Hair. She sued them over the public reading of Genesis by the crew of Apollo 8, citing the status of astronauts as government employees and the separation of church and state to support her case.

Looking back on that moment, Aldrin reflected in his memoir that perhaps he should have chosen a more universal way of commemorating the achievement, a first for all humankind." Perhaps if I had it to do over again, I would not choose to celebrate communion," he wrote. "Although it was a deeply meaningful experience for me, it was a Christian sacrament, and we had come to the moon in the name of all mankind—be they Christians, Jews, Muslims, animists, agnostics, or atheists. But at the time I could think of no better way to acknowledge the enormity of the Apollo 11 experience than by giving thanks to God.

N.

NEXT TIME

RWP2: Next time around I would like to do the following;

1. I really was late in accepting JESUS CHRIST As My Lord and Savior and was in my forties.
2. I realize that my life has been good the closer I am to GOD and our Savior JESUS CHRIST.
3. I would have not quit during Norm Sloan's first year at NC State just before the RED & WHITE Game. That year Press Maravich left NCSU to LSU so he could coach his son "PISTOL Pete Maraivich. As a head coach Press knew I only wanted for play and go NCSU to study industrial engineering. I passed up offers to Furman and D2 schools throughout the state
4. I should have taken my father-in-law's (Bill Bristow) suggestion that should have play football in college rather than basketball.... Likewise I wanted to go to STATE after Brevard College.
5. I regret not being a better husband to my wife Joyce in our early years and in our vintage years. I will do better in the 75+ range.
6. I do not regret avoided drugs completely (even weed) and never ever I smoked.
7. I would have tried Bob Gaskin's favorite saying..."Work Smarter-Not Harder".
8. I would have worked out with weight more than I did. They said it was not ideal for basketball players. The only weights we have in junior & high school were various sized cans in concrete.

9. I would not have grown into a pro-sized left tackle before gaining 325 pounds

O.

OBAMA# 1: GETTING A PARKING TICKET

The other day I went downtown to run a few errands. I went into the local coffee shop for a snack.

I was only there for about 5 minutes, and when I came out, there was this cop writing out a parking ticket. I said to him, 'Come on, man, how about giving a retired person a break'?

He ignored me and continued writing the ticket. His insensitivity annoyed me, so I called him a 'Nazi.'

He glared at me and then wrote out another ticket for having worn tires.

So I proceeded to call him a 'doughnut eating Gestapo.' He finished the second ticket and put it on the windshield with the first.

Then he wrote a third ticket when I called him a moron in blue.

This went on for about 20 minutes. The more I talked back to him the more tickets he wrote.

Personally, I didn't really care. I came downtown on the bus, and the car that he was putting the tickets on had one of those bumper stickers that said, ' Obama '08.'

I try to have a little fun each day now that I'm retired.

The doctor tells me that it's important for my health.

OBAMA #2: OBAMACARE AND ME

August 06, 2009
By Zane F Pollard, MD

I have been sitting quietly on the sidelines watching all of this national debate on healthcare. It is time for me to bring some clarity to the table by explaining many of the problems from the perspective of a doctor.

First off, the government has involved very few of us physicians in the healthcare debate. While the American Medical Association has come out in favor of the plan, it is vital to remember that the AMA only represents 17% of the American physician workforce.

I have taken care of Medicaid patients for 35 years while representing the only pediatric ophthalmology group left in Atlanta, Georgia, that accepts Medicaid. For example, in the past 6 months I have cared for three young children on Medicaid who had corneal ulcers. This is a potentially blinding situation because if the cornea perforates from the infection, almost surely blindness will occur. In all three cases the antibiotic needed for the eradication of the infection was not on the approved Medicaid list.

Each time I was told to fax Medicaid for the approval forms, which I did. Within 48 hours the form came back to me which was sent in immediately via fax, and I was told that I would have my answer in 10 days. Of course by then each child would have been blind in the eye.

Each time the request came back denied. All three times I personally provided the antibiotic for each patient which was not on the Medicaid approved list. Get the point -- rationing of care.

Over the past 35 years I have cared for over 1,000 children born with congenital cataracts. In older children and in adults the vision is rehabilitated with an intraocular lens. In newborns we use contact lenses which are very expensive. It takes Medicaid over one year to approve a contact lens post cataract surgery. By that time a successful anatomical operation is wasted as the child will be close to blind from a lack of focusing for so long a period of time.

Again, extreme rationing. Solution: I have a foundation here in Atlanta supported 100% by private funds which supplies all of these contact lenses for my Medicaid and illegal immigrants children for free. Again, waiting for the government would be disastrous.

Last week I had a lady bring her child to me. They are Americans but live in Sweden, as the father has a job with a big corporation. The child had the onset of double vision 3 months ago and has been unable to function normally because of this. They are people of means, but are waiting 8 months to see the ophthalmologist in Sweden. Then if the child needed surgery, they would be put on a 6-month waiting list. She called me and I saw her that day. Again, rationing of care.

Last month I operated on a 70 year old lady with double vision present for 3 years. She responded quite nicely to her surgery and now is symptom free. I also operated on a 69 year old judge with vertical double vision. His surgery went very well and now he is happy as a lark. I have been told -- but of course there is no healthcare bill that has been passed yet -- that these 2 people because of their age would have been denied surgery and just told to wear a patch over one eye to alleviate the symptoms of double vision. Obviously cheaper than surgery.

I spent two years in the US Navy during the Viet Nam war and was well treated by the military. There was tremendous rationing of care and we were told specifically what things the military personnel and their dependents could have and which things they could not have. While I was in Viet Nam, my wife Nancy got sick and got essentially no care at the Naval Hospital in Oakland, California. She went home and went to her family's private internist in Beverly Hills. While it was expensive, she received an immediate work up. Again rationing of care.

For those of you who are over 65, this bill in its present form might be lethal for you. People in England over 59 cannot receive stents for their coronary arteries. The government wants to mimic the British plan. For those of you younger, it will still mean restriction of the care that you and your children receive.

While 99% of physicians went into medicine because of the love of medicine and the challenge of helping our fellow man, economics are still important. My rent goes up 2% each year and the salaries of my employees go up 2% each year. Twenty years ago, ophthalmologists were paid $1,800 for a cataract surgery and today $500. This is a 73% decrease in our fees. I do not know of many jobs in America that have seen this sort of lowering of fees.

But there is more to the story than just the lower fees. When I came to Atlanta, there was a well-known ophthalmologist that charged $2,500 for a cataract surgery as he felt he was the best. He had a terrific reputation and in fact I had my mother's bilateral cataracts operated on by him with a wonderful result. She is now 94 and has 20/20 vision in both eyes. People would pay his $2,500 fee.

However, then the government came in and said that any doctor that does Medicare work cannot accept more than the going rate (now $500) or he or she would be severely fined. This put an end to his charging $2,500. The government said it was illegal to accept more than the government-allowed rate. What I am driving at is that those of you well off will not be able to go to the head of the line under this new healthcare plan, just because you have money, as no physician will be willing to go against the law to treat you.

I am a pediatric ophthalmologist and trained for 10 years post-college to become a pediatric ophthalmologist (add two years of my service in the Navy and that comes to 12 years). A neurosurgeon spends 14 years post-college, and if he or she has to do the military that would be 16 years. I am not entitled to make what a neurosurgeon makes, but the new plan calls for all physicians to make the same amount of payment. I assure you that medical students will not go into neurosurgery and we will have a tremendous shortage of neurosurgeons. Already, the top neurosurgeon at my hospital, who is in good health and only 52 years old, has just quit because he can't stand working with the government anymore.. Forty-nine percent of children under the age of 16 in the state of Georgia are on Medicaid, so he felt he just could not stand working with the bureaucracy anymore.

We are being lied to about the uninsured. They are getting care. I operate on at least 2 illegal immigrants each month who pay me nothing, and the children's hospital at which I operate charges them nothing also. This is true not only of Atlanta, but of every community in America.

The bottom-line is that I urge all of you to contact your congresswomen and congressmen and senators to defeat this bill. I promise you that you will not like rationing of your own health.

Furthermore, how can you trust a physician that works under these conditions knowing that he is controlled by the state? I certainly could not trust any doctor that would work under these draconian conditions.

One last thing: with this new healthcare plan there will be a tremendous shortage of physicians. It has been estimated that approximately 5% of the current physician work force will quit under this new system. Also, it is estimated that another 5% shortage will occur because of the decreased number of men and women wanting to go into medicine.

At the present time the US government has mandated gender equity in admissions to medical schools. That means that for the past 15 years somewhere between 49 and 51% of each entering class are females. This is true of private schools also, because all private schools receive federal funding.

The average career of a woman in medicine now is only 8-10 years and the average work week for a female in medicine is only 3-4 days. I have now trained 35 fellows in pediatric ophthalmology. Hands down the best was a female that I trained 4 years ago -- she was head and heels above all others I have trained. She now practices only 3 days a week.

Page Printed from:
http://www.americanthinker.com/2009/08/obamacare_and_
me.html at August 06, 2009 - 02:19:06 AM EDT

OBAMA # 3: MOST TRANSPARENT PRESIDENT IN HISTORY?

Obama Admin Official Defends Obama as 'the Most Transparent President in History'

It's no secret that Americans are souring on the notion of President Obama's promises of "hope" and "change." Just as Fidel Castro rode to power promising a radical departure from the previous regime, Obama ignited a hysteria wherever he went in 2007 and 2008 as he promised to fix the problems that faced America by operating differently than other presidents who came before him. Just like Castro, the radical departure promised led the populace from bad to worse in short order.

By now, it's no secret that this administration operates with a level of secrecy seldom seen outside the Soviet-era Kremlin. With one scandal emerging after another, the go-to response from this administration has been to simply deny, deny, deny and when confronted with evidence of a cover-up, claim complete ignorance. This textbook evasion can be seen in virtually every scandal that plagues this horrid, abusive administration.

White House Press secretary Josh Earnest had the audacity to defend the indefensible: he defended President Obama as operating as the most transparent president in history.

On CNN's "Reliable Sources," Earnest claimed, "I have a responsibility in this job to try to help the president live up to his commitment to be the most transparent president in history."

Host Brian Stelter was dumbfounded. "I am surprised you still said that line, 'the most transparent president in history,'" Stelter stated. "He has been criticized so many times for saying that, given the prosecution of whistleblowers and other steps. You all still stick by that line?"

Earnest boldly replied, "Absolutely."

Of course, none of this jibes with reality as this administration, with even a cursory review, would receive an "F" for transparency.

The NSA has been monitoring the electronic communications of hundreds of millions of Americans and doing so without any justifiable legal authority. Though the FISA court has allowed this, obscure bureaucracies within despotic regimes often rubberstamp the orders of tyrannical dictators.

After all, China, North Korea and Cuba all cite some sort of dubious legal justification for the heinous abuses the regimes carry out. Obama cites the FISA court.

Further, can an administration really get credit for "transparency" when it took the work of a dedicated whistleblower to sound the alarm bells about a secretive program occurring without the knowledge of hundreds of millions of Americans being monitored?

What follows is just a brief list of some of the more outrageous and secretive abuses inflicted upon the American people by "the most transparent president in history":

- This administration spent years working quietly to squash political dissent by targeting Tea Party groups, using the IRS as a cudgel to pound them into submission;

- This administration repeatedly lied to the American people, telling them that they could keep their healthcare insurance plans and their doctors when Obamacare was implemented- a whopper that politifact dubbed the "Lie of the Year." They blasted all critics who pointed out that this was not true as being conservative fear-mongers;

- This administration conducted in secret a DOJ operation that pumped thousands of firearms into the hands of Mexican drug cartels while blaming border violence on irresponsible American gun owners and sellers. When Attorney General Eric Holder was to be held to account for his crimes, the president cloaked him in executive privilege;

- This administration disregarded repeated requests for security at our consulate in Benghazi, Libya, and after they had left four of our fellow Americans to be murdered by terrorists, concocted an absurd story surrounding a YouTube video;

- This administration monitored and bullied employees of the Associated Press under flimsy pretenses concerning national security;

- This administration has maintained a shockingly closed-off relationship with the press and has even taken to, more and more, prohibiting media outlet photographers at events but instead, issuing "official" photos to be used by media outlets;

-This administration surveilled and bullied Fox News' James Rosen and even threatened to indict him as a co-conspirator in an intelligence leak for having done nothing more than simply reporting what a source told him;

- This administration, in secret, negotiated with Haqqani terrorists to release five terrorists in exchange for one American Army deserter and did so without any congressional approval;

- As one of the first acts of this administration, the DOJ quietly dropped the charges against Black Panthers who stood outside a Philadelphia voting station, thumping billy clubs and hurling racial slurs at white voters in an effort to intimidate white voters.

It appears clear that Earnest is either incredibly naïve or, more likely, a proponent of the "say it 'till it's true" mindset that has come to define this regime.

With two more years of this disastrous presidency, it's likely we will witness only a worsening of the adversarial and secretive relationship this regime maintains with the American people.

OBITUARY OF THE UNITED STATES? PLUS

In 1887 Alexander Tyler, a Scottish history professor at the University of Edinburgh, had this to say about the fall of the Athenian Republic some 2,000 years prior: "A democracy is always temporary in nature; it simply cannot exist as a permanent form of government. A democracy will continue to exist up until the time that voters discover that they can vote themselves generous gifts from the public treasury. From that moment on, the majority always votes for the candidates who promise the most benefits from the public treasury, with the result that every democracy will finally collapse over loose fiscal policy, (which is) always followed by a dictatorship."

"The average age of the world's greatest civilizations from the beginning of history, has been about 200 years. During those 200 years, these nations always progressed through the following sequence:

From bondage to spiritual faith;
From spiritual faith to great courage;
From courage to liberty;
From liberty to abundance;
From abundance to complacency;
From complacency to apathy;
From apathy to dependence;
From dependence back into bondage."

The Obituary follows:

Born 1776, Died 2012

It doesn't hurt to read this several times.

Professor Joseph Olson of Hamline University School of Law in St. Paul, Minnesota, points out some interesting facts concerning the last Presidential election:

Number of States won by: Obama: 19 Romney: 29

Square miles of land won by: Obama: 580,000 Romney: 2,427,000

Population of counties won by: Obama: 127 million Romney: 143 million Murder rate per 100,000 residents in counties won by: Obama: 13.2 Romney: 2.1

Professor Olson adds: "In aggregate, the map of the territory

Romney won was mostly the land owned by the taxpaying citizens of the country.

Obama territory mostly encompassed those citizens living in low income tenements and living off various forms of government welfare..."

Olson believes the United States is now somewhere between the "complacency and apathy" phase of Professor Tyler's definition of democracy, with some forty percent of the nation's population already having reached the "governmental dependency" phase.

If Congress grants amnesty and citizenship to twenty million criminal invaders called illegals and they vote - then we can say goodbye to the USA in fewer than five years.

If you are in favor of this, then by all means, delete this message.

If you are not, then pass this along to help everyone realize just how much is at stake, knowing that apathy is the greatest danger to our freedom.

RWP2: You Cannot Believe All from the Internet; check this out.

Origins of the item cited above began circulating on the Internet since shortly after the 2000 U.S. presidential election, reappeared briefly after the 2004 presidential election, saw a strong resurgence in a modified form which replaced the names "Bush" and "Gore" with "McCain and "Obama" after the 2008 presidential election, and was circulated again after the 2012 election in a shortened version with the names "Obama" and Romney" replacing the original's "Bush" and "Gore":

Professor Joseph Olson of Hamline University School of Law in St. Paul, Minnesota, points out some interesting facts concerning the last Presidential election:

Number of States won by: Obama: 19 Romney: 29

Square miles of land won by: Obama: 580,000 Romney: 2,427,000

Population of counties won by: Obama: 127 million Romney: 143 million

Murder rate per 100,000 residents in counties won by: Obama: 13.2 Romney: 2.1

Professor Olson adds: "In aggregate, the map of the territory Romney won was mostly the land owned by the taxpaying citizens of the country.

Obama territory mostly encompassed those citizens living in low income tenements and living off various forms of government welfare..."

Olson believes the United States is now somewhere between the "complacency and apathy" phase of Professor Tyler's definition of democracy, with some forty percent of the nation's population

Already having reached the "governmental dependency" phase..

If Congress grants amnesty and citizenship to twenty million criminal invaders called illegal's - and they vote - then we can say goodbye to the USA in fewer than five years.

If you are in favor of this, then by all means, delete this message.

If you are not, then pass this along to help everyone realize just how much is at stake, knowing that apathy is the greatest danger to our freedom.

What follows is our analysis of the statements included in the original piece as it initially appeared in 2000:

- Professor Joseph Olson of Hamline University was not the source of any of the statistics or the text attributed to him above. When contacted via e-mail, Professor Olson confirmed that he had no authorship or involvement in this matter, and as Fayette Citizen editor Dave Hamrick wrote in January 2001:

  I really enjoyed one recent message that was circulated extremely widely, at least among conservatives. It gave several interesting "facts" supposedly compiled by statisticians and political scientists about the counties across the nation that voted for George Bush and the ones that voted for Al Gore in the recent election.

  Supposedly, the people in the counties for Bush had more education, more income, ad infinitum, than the counties for Gore.

  I didn't have time to check them all out, but I was curious about one item in particular... the contention that the murder rate in the Gore counties was about a billion times higher than in the Bush counties.

This was attributed to a Professor Joseph Olson at the Hamline University School of Law. I never heard of such a university, but went online and found it. And Prof. Olson does exist.

"Now I'm getting somewhere," I thought.

But in response to my e-mail, Olson said the "research" was attributed to him erroneously. He said it came from a Sheriff Jay Printz in Montana. I e-mailed Sheriff Printz, and guess what? He didn't do the research either, and didn't remember who had e-mailed it to him.

In other words, he got the same legend e-mailed to him and passed it on to Olson without checking it out, and when Olson passed it on, someone thought it sounded better if a law professor had done the research, and so it grew.

Who knows where it originally came from, but it's just not true.

- The "Alexander Tyler" quoted at the head of the article is actually Lord Woodhouselee, Alexander Fraser Tytler, a Scottish historian/professor who wrote several books in the late 1700s and early 1800s. However, there is no record of a Tytler's having authored a work entitled *The Fall of the Athenian Republic* (or *The Decline and Fall of the Athenian Republic*), and the quoted material attributed to him above is likely apocryphal.

- The population of the counties and square miles of area won by each Bush and Gore are reasonably accurate. They are close to figures in an election result map published by *USA Today* on 20 November 2000.

- The number of states won by each candidate is inaccurate. The numbers given (29 and 19) imply that the piece was written before the results of the Florida and New Mexico vote counts were determined. The final tallies were 30 states for Bush and 20 for Gore.

- The county-by-county murder-rate comparison presented in this piece appears to be flawed. According to the U.S. Department of Justice (DoJ), in the year 2000 the national murder rate was about 5.5 per 100,000 residents. Homicide data by county for 1999 and 2000 was downloaded from the National Archive of Criminal Justice Data (NAJCD), and the counties won by Gore and Bush were identified using the county-by-county election results made available by CNN. (The NACJD provided not only the number of reported murders for each county, but also the population for each.) The average murder rate in the counties won by Gore versus the rate in the counties won by Bush was determined from this data.

By calculating the murder rate for each county and then taking the averages, we found a murder rate (defined as number of murders per 100,000 residents) of about 5.2 for the average Gore county and 3.3 for the average Bush county. But since people, rather than counties, commit murders, a more appropriate approach was to calculate the total number of murders in the counties won by each candidate and divide that figure by the total number of residents in those counties. This more appropriate method yielded the following average murder rates in counties won by each candidate:

Gore: 6.5

Bush: 4.1

There is a distinct difference between these two numbers, but it is nowhere near as large as the quoted e-mail message states (i.e., 13.2 for Gore vs. 2.1 for Bush).

- The tagline to the piece maintains that "The map of the territory Bush won was mostly the land owned by the taxpaying citizens of this great country. Gore's territory mostly encompassed those citizens living in government-owned tenements and living off government welfare." However, according to an analysis of federal spending and electoral votes in the 2000 election prepared by Dean Lacy of Ohio State University:

In the 2000 U.S. presidential election, George W. Bush won most of the states that are net beneficiaries of federal spending programs, while Al Gore won most of the states that are net contributors to federal spending.

The information in that study corresponds to a chart prepared by the Tax Foundation for fiscal year 2005 that ranks states according to federal spending per dollar of taxes paid.

Last updated: 24 June 2014

Hamrick, Dave. "Don't Believe, Or Pass On, All You Read." *The [Fayette] Citizen.* 17 January 2001.

Lacy, Dean. "A Curious Paradox of the Red States and Blue States." 2 March 2002.

Tax Foundation. "Federal Spending Received Per Dollar of Taxes Paid by State, 2005."

9 October 2007.

OLD FARTS

I'm passing this on as I did not want to be the only old fart receiving it.

Actually, it's not a bad thing to be called, as you will see. Old Farts are easy to spot at sporting events; during the playing of the Star Spangled Banner. Old Farts remove their caps and stand at attention and sing without embarrassment. They know the words and believe in them.

Old Farts remember World War II, Pearl Harbor, Guadalcanal, Normandy and Hitler. They remember the Atomic Age, the Korean War, The Cold War , the Jet Age and the Moon Landing. They remember the 50 plus Peacekeeping Missions from 1945 to 2005, not to mention Vietnam .

If you bump into an Old Fart on the sidewalk he will apologize. If you pass an Old Fart on the street, he will nod or tip his cap to a lady. Old Farts trust strangers and are courtly to women.

Old Farts hold the door for the next person and always, when walking, make certain the lady is on the inside for protection.

Old Farts get embarrassed if someone curses in front of women and children and they don't like any filth or dirty language on TV or in movies.

Old Farts have moral courage and personal integrity. They seldom brag unless it's about their children or grandchildren.

It's the Old Farts who know our great country is protected, not by politician's, but by the young men and women in the military serving their country.

This country needs Old Farts with their work ethic, sense of responsibility, pride in their country and decent values.

We need them now more than ever.

Thank God for Old Farts!

Pass this on to all the Old Farts you know.

I was taught to respect my elders. It's just getting harder to find them.

ONLY IN AMERICA

Only in America.....do drugstores make the sick walk all the way to the back of the store to get their prescriptions while healthy people can buy cigarettes at the front.

Only in America......do people order double cheeseburgers, large fries, and a diet coke. !

Only in America......do banks leave both doors open and then chain the pens to the counters.

Only in America......do we leave cars worth thousands of dollars in the driveway and put our useless junk in the garage.

Only in America......do we buy hot dogs in packages of ten and buns in packages of eight.

Only in America......do we use the word 'politics' to describe the process so well: 'Poli' in Latin meaning 'many' and 'tics' meaning 'bloodsucking creatures'.

Only in America......do they have drive-up ATM machines with Braille lettering.

EVER WONDER...

Why the sun lightens our hair, but darkens our skin?

Why women can't put on mascara with their mouth closed?

Why don't you ever see the headline "Psychic Wins Lottery"?

Why is "abbreviated" such a long word?

Why is it that doctors call what they do "practice"?

Why is lemon juice made with artificial flavor, and dishwashing liquid made with real lemons?

Why is the man who invests all your money called a broker?

Why is the time of day with the slowest traffic called rush hour?

Why isn't there mouse-flavored cat food?

Why didn't Noah swat those two mosquitoes?

Why do they sterilize the needle for lethal injections?

You know that indestructible black box that is used on airplanes? Why don't they make the whole plane out of that stuff?!

Why don't sheep shrink when it rains?

Why are they called apartments when they are all stuck together?

If con is the opposite of pro, is Congress the opposite of progress?

If flying is so safe, why do they call the airport the terminal?

Now that you've smiled at least once, it's your turn to spread the stupidity and send this to someone you want to bring a smile to (maybe even a chuckle)...in other words, send it to everyone. We all need to smile every once in a while.

P.

PENTAGON: FRIDAY MORNINGS AT THE PENTAGON

Subject: Friday Morning at the Pentagon

Friday Mornings at the Pentagon
By JOSEPH L. GALLOWAY
McClatchy Newspapers

Over the last 12 months, 1,042 soldiers, Marines, sailors and Air Force personnel have given their lives in the terrible duty that is war. Thousands more have come home on stretchers, horribly wounded and facing months or years in military hospitals.

This week, I'm turning my space over to a good friend and former roommate, Army Lt. Col. Robert Bateman, who recently completed a yearlong tour of duty in Iraq and is now back at the Pentagon.

Here's Lt. Col. Bateman's account of a little-known ceremony that fills the halls of the Army corridor of the Pentagon with cheers, applause and many tears every Friday morning. It first appeared on May 17 on the Weblog of media critic and pundit Eric Alterman at the Media Matters for America Website.

"It is 110 yards from the "E" ring to the "A" ring of the Pentagon. This section of the Pentagon is newly renovated; the floors shine, the hallway is broad, and the lighting is bright. At this instant the entire length of the corridor is packed with officers, a few sergeants and some civilians, all crammed tightly three and four deep against the walls. There are thousands here.

This hallway, more than any other, is the `Army' hallway. The G3 offices line one side, G2 the other, G8 is around the corner. All Army. Moderate conversations flow in a low buzz. Friends who may not have seen each other for a few weeks, or a few years, spot each other, cross the way and renew.

Everyone shifts to ensure an open path remains down the center. The air conditioning system was not designed for this press of bodies in this area.

The temperature is rising already. Nobody cares. "10:36 hours: The clapping starts at the E-Ring. That is the outermost of the five rings of the Pentagon and it is closest to the entrance to the building. This clapping is low, sustained, hearty. It is applause with a deep emotion behind it as it moves forward in a wave down the length of the hallway.

"A steady rolling wave of sound it is, moving at the pace of the soldier in the wheelchair who marks the forward edge with his presence. He is the first. He is missing the greater part of one leg, and some of his wounds are still suppurating. By his age I expect that he is a private, or perhaps a private first class.

"Captains, majors, lieutenant colonels and colonels meet his gaze and nod as they applaud, soldier to soldier. Three years ago when I described one of these events, those lining the hallways were somewhat different. The applause a little wilder, perhaps in private guilt for not having shared in the burden ... yet.

"Now almost everyone lining the hallway is, like the man in the wheelchair, also a combat veteran. This steadies the applause, but I think deepens the sentiment. We have all been there now. The soldier's chair is pushed by, I believe, a full colonel.

"Behind him, and stretching the length from Rings E to A, come more of his peers, each private, corporal, or sergeant assisted as need be by a field grade officer.

"11:00 hours: Twenty-four minutes of steady applause. My hands hurt, and I laugh to myself at how stupid that sounds in my own head. My hands hurt. Please! Shut up and clap. For twenty-four minutes, soldier after soldier has come down this hallway - 20, 25, 30... Fifty-three legs come with them, and perhaps only 52 hands or arms, but down this hall came 30 solid hearts.

They pass down this corridor of officers and applause, and then meet for a private lunch, at which they are the guests of honor, hosted by the generals. Some are wheeled along. Some insist upon getting out of their chairs, to march as best they can with their chin held up, down this hallway, through this most unique audience. Some are catching handshakes and smiling like a politician at a Fourth of July parade. More than a couple of them seem amazed and are smiling shyly.

"There are families with them as well: the 18-year-old war-bride pushing her 19-year-old husband's wheelchair and not quite understanding why her husband is so affected by this, the boy she grew up with, now a man, who had never shed a tear is crying; the older immigrant Latino parents who have, perhaps more than their wounded mid-20s son, an appreciation for the emotion given on their son's behalf. No man in that hallway, walking or clapping, is ashamed by the silent tears on more than a few cheeks. An Airborne Ranger wipes his eyes only to better see. A couple of the officers in this crowd have themselves been a part of this parade in the past.

These are our men, broken in body they may be, but they are our brothers, and we welcome them home. This parade has gone on, every single Friday, all year long, for more than four years."Did you know that? The media haven't yet told the story

PREDICTIONS AND PAINS

As much as it pains me to say this, I have to admit it - my Democrat friends were right. They told me if I voted for McCain, the nation's hope would deteriorate, & sure enough there has been a 20 point drop in the Consumer Confidence Index since the election, reaching a lower point than any time under Bush administration.

They told me if I voted for McCain, the US would become more deeply embroiled in the Middle East, and now, tens of thousands of additional troops are scheduled to be deployed into Afghanistan My Democrat Party friends told me if I voted for McCain, that the economy would get worse and sure enough unemployment is at 9.4%.

They told me if I voted for McCain, we would see more "crooks" in high ranking positions in Federal government and sure enough, several recent cabinet nominees and Senate appointments revealed resumes of scandal, bribery and tax fraud.

They told me if I voted for McCain, we would see more "Pork at the trough" in Federal government and sure enough, 17,500 "Pork Bills" showed up in Congress since January 2009.

I was also told by my Democrat friends that if I voted for McCain, we would see more deficit pending in Washington D.C. and sure enough, Obama has spent more in just 120 days than all other Presidents together - in the entire history of the good ole USA !!

Well, I voted for McCain in November and my Democrat friends were right... all of their predictions have come true!

PRO-CHOICE IS PRO-DEATH!!

RWP2: Politically, I am a Rightly Moderate to a Right Wing Conservative bordering upon being or becoming a vintage Right Wing Extremist. No but not really! But one example that takes me to the edge! When I hear and see Pro-Death/Pro-Choice people protecting salamanders, milk cows & gorillas I am alarmed. More alarmed and very sad when they advocate mutilating and then killing real people in the womb. I am really very sad. I am also sad for *America: Once the United States?*

FYI, I grew up and lived on a dairy farm from 1945 to 1975 and I love cows, Chick-Filet and chickens. I love nature, salamanders and gorillas too!! It is hard for me to comprehend the reasoning of Pro-Choice advocates. Many are Pro-Life for cold blooded mass murderers, yet Pro-Death for people still in the womb. What?

Pro-Death for people in the womb and Pro-Life for convicted murderers, salamanders and other endangered species like pandas and polar bears. This does not make sense from any perspective! Especially in *America: Once the United States?*

Would a pro-life gorilla, polar bear and panda advocate spend the time to eliminate or lessen the pro-death movement for humans in the womb? Not many that we know or read about?

Remember that Pro-Choice is Pro-Death! A very simple fact now in America & with no explanation needed. The horrible facts are there as facts in America. Some will demonstrate & fight to save murderers outside Central Prison here in Raleigh, NC. But they will fight much harder to murder babies in the womb? Pro-

Choice is Pro-Death for those Americans awaiting legal entry to the United States of America.

Can all of this really be true and happening in America? Or is it a bad dream? And it may never change back where America tries to protect unborn Americans.

DOES THIS MAKE SENSE? Pro-Choice Advocates Are;

1. Pro-life for cold blooded mass murderers,
2. Yet they are pro-death for people still in the womb.
3. What a sad contrast but often true belief!
4. This does not make sense from any perspective?

ALWAYS...REMEMBER THAT PRO-CHOICE IS PRO-DEATH!! The unborn person has No-Choice at all! It is very simple. Again Pro Choice is Pro Death with no explanations needed. The facts are available for America since the 1973 passing of Roe vs. Wade to show what has tragically happened with Pro Death. Over 57,000,000 deaths of unborn American have occurred since 1973. Go to http://www.numberofabortions.com/ to see the current count of abortions in *AMERICA: Once the United States?* and around the world. You can watch the count continue via a live update and running total.

One note from "The Communist" is that the founder of Planned Parenthood, Margaret Sanger was a true communist. She advocated in a 1926 speech to a Ku Klux Klan leadership conference in New Jersey for abortion of as many black babies as possible. She was a racial eugenicist with a **"Negro Project"**. Basically her intent was to rid America what she termed **"human weeds"** and **"morons"** and **"imbeciles"** and she wanted birth control for what she openly called **"race improvement"**. This was back in the Frank Marshal Davis era where she too was a documented Communist and she actually visited Russia to see the model cities of communism as millions were starving. And where mass killings occurred under Communist regimes during the twentieth century had an estimated death toll numbering between 85 and 100 million.

Total Abortion Since Roe vs. Wade Passed in 1973	57, 355,381
Total Black Babies Since Roe vs. Wade passed in 1973	17,206,616 (30% of Total) and 12.6% of US population
Total 2014 Abortions in USA as of Nov 14, 2014	942,625
Total Capital Punishments Since 1976	1,3049
Total on Death Row for Capital Punishment	3,049
Average USA Abortions Per Day (300 days in 2014)	2,993

Go to http://www.numberofabortions.com/
to see the current count of abortions.

Conclusions:

1. There is basically the same number of abortion deaths per day (2993) in the USA as there are murderers on Death Row (3,049) who are still alive.

2. Some Americans will mob up, demonstrate & fight to save murderers outside of Central Prison here in Raleigh, NC and across America.

3. **Margaret Sanger's "Negro Project" is Going Strong in 2014**: Thirty percent US totals were black babies (17,000,000+) and victims of the Pro Death movement since 1973. Currently African-Americans make up only 13.6% of U.S. population per the 2010 U.S. Census of America's total population. So Margaret Sanger, a true communist, got her wish to abort as many black babies as possible with her racial eugenicist with her "Negro Project" that continues strong in 2014.

4. And Pro Deather's will fight even harder to allow doctors to murder babies and future Americans in the womb?
5. More recently the actual sale of human baby had been a big business until it was declared illegal.

Can this really be true in America where there demographics are shifting to the point that in 30-50 years the make –up of America could see less doers and contributors and more takers and therefore a movement closer to a socialistic environment ?

PRICELESS PRICES!

All these examples do NOT imply that gasoline is cheap; it just illustrates how outrageous some prices are. You will be really shocked by the last one *(at least, I was)!!!*

Think a gallon of gas is expensive?

This makes one think, and also puts things into perspective.

Diet Snapple, 16 oz., $1.29 ... $10.32 per gallon!

Lipton Ice Tea, 16 oz., $1.19 ... $9.52 per gallon!

Gatorade, 20 oz., $1.59 ... $10.17 per gallon!

Ocean Spray, 16 oz., $1.25 ... $10.00 per gallon!

Brake Fluid, 12 oz., $3.15 ... $33.60 per gallon!

Vick's Nyquil, 6 oz., $8.35 ... $178.13 per gallon!

Pepto Bismol, 4 oz. $3.85 ... $123.20 per gallon!

Whiteout, 7 oz., $1.39 ... $25.42 per gallon!

Scope, 1.5 oz., $0.99 ... $84.48 per gallon!

And this is the REAL KICKER.

Evian water, 9 oz., $1.49 .... $21.19 per gallon! $21.19 for a gallon of WATER!!

and the buyers don't even know the source *(Evian spelled backwards is Naive.)*

Ever wonder why computer printers are so cheap? So they can hook you for the ink.

Someone calculated the cost of the ink at, you won't believe it but it's true; $5,200 a gal. $5200 A GALLON!!!

So, the next time you're at the pump, be glad your car doesn't run on water , Scope,

Whiteout, Pepto Bismol, Nyquil or, God forbid, Printer Ink!!!!!

And - If you don't pass this along to at least one person, your muffler will fall off!!

PROFILING: DO IT AND SAVE LIVES; MAYBE YOUR OWN

Prohibit profiling: you may be the next victim and friend of Obama and you wouldn't have hurt any murderer's feelings!!!

This is all factually (and historically) correct - and verifiable.

If you even go back further from November 2014 you find these facts;

... **In 732 AD** the Muslim Army which was moving on Paris was defeated and turned back at Tours, France, by Charles Martell.

...**in 1571 AD** the Muslim Army/Navy was defeated by the Italians and Austrians as they tried to cross the Mediterranean to attack Southern Europe in the Battle of Lapanto.

....**in 1683 AD** the Turkish Muslim Army, attacking Eastern Europe, was finally defeated in the Battle of Vienna by German and Polish Christian Armies.

....**this crap has been going on for 1,400 years and half of these damn politicians don't even know it !!!**

If these battles had not been won we might be speaking Arabic and Christianity could be non - existent;

Judaism certainly would be! And let us not forget that Hitler was an admirer of Islam and that the Mufti of Jerusalem was Hitler's guest in Berlin and praised Bosnian Muslim SS Divisions: the 13th and 21st Waffen SS Divisions who killed Jews, Russians, Gypsies, and any other "sub-human's".

Reflecting A lot of Americans have become so insulated from reality that they imagine that America can suffer defeat without any inconvenience to themselves.

Pause a moment, reflect back. These events are actual events from history. They really happened!!!

Do you remember?

1. **In 1968**, Bobby Kennedy was shot and killed by a **Muslim male.**
2. **In 1972** at the Munich Olympics, athletes were kidnapped and massacred by **Muslim males.**

3. **In 1972** a Pan Am 747 was hijacked and eventually diverted to Cairo where a fuse was lit on final approach, it was blown up shortly after landing by **Muslim males.**
4. **In 1973** a Pan Am 707 was destroyed in Rome, with 33 people killed, when it was attacked with grenades by **Muslim males.**
5. **In 1979**, the US embassy in Iran was taken over by **Muslim males.**
6. **During the 1980's** a number of Americans were kidnapped in Lebanon by **Muslim males.**
7. **In 1983,** the US Marine barracks in Beirut was blown up by **Muslim males.**
8. **In 1985,** the Cruise Ship Achilles Lauro was hijacked and a 70 year old American passenger was murdered and thrown overboard in his wheelchair by **Muslim males.**
9. **In 1985,** TWA flight 847 was hijacked at Athens, and a US Navy diver trying to rescue passengers was murdered by **Muslim males.**
10. **In 1988**, Pan Am Flight 103 was bombed by **Muslim males.**
11. **In 1993**, the World Trade Center was bombed the first time by **Muslim males.**
12. **In 1998**, the US embassies in Kenya and Tanzania were bombed by **Muslim males.**
13. **On 9/11/01**, four airliners were hijacked; two were used as missiles to take down the World Trade Centers and of the remaining two, one crashed into the US Pentagon and the other was diverted and crashed by the passengers. Thousands of people were killed by **Muslim males.**
14. **In 2002**, the United States fought a war in Afghanistan against **Muslim males.**
15. **In 2002**, reporter Daniel Pearl was kidnapped and beheaded by---you guessed it was a--- **Muslim male.**
16. **In 2013**, Boston Marathon Bombing 4 Innocent people including a child killed, 264 injured by **Muslim males.**
17. **Now as of November 4, 2014,** the ISIS organization, is made up of mostly **Muslim males** has taken back most

of Iraq and is murdering western captives and innocent Iraqi citizens.

No, I really don't see a pattern here to justify profiling, do you?

So, to ensure <u>we Americans never offend anyone</u>, particularly fanatics intent on killing us, airport security screeners will no longer be allowed to profile certain people. <u>**So, ask yourself , "Just how stupid are we???"**</u>

<u>**Absolutely No Profiling??**</u>

NO!!They must conduct random searches of 80-year-old women, little kids, airline pilots with proper identification, secret agents who are members of the President's security detail, 85-year old, Congressmen with metal hips, and Medal of Honor winner and former Governor Joe Foss, <u>**but leave Muslim Males, alone lest they be guilty of profiling. Ask yourself "Just how stupid are we?"**</u>

<u>**Have the American people completely lost their Minds, or just their Power of Reason???**</u>

Let's send this to as many people as we can so that the Gloria Aldreds and other stupid attorneys along with Federal Justices that want to thwart common sense, feel ashamed of themselves -- if they have any such sense. As the writer of the award winning story 'Forrest Gump' so aptly put it, 'Stupid Is As Stupid Does'. Each opportunity that you have to send this to a friend or media outlet...

DO IT! OR SIT BACK, JUST KEEP GRIPING, AND
DO-NOTHING.

PUPPIES-THE RUNT IN THE LITTER HAS VALUE TOO!

A farmer had some puppies he needed to sell.

He painted a sign advertising the 4 pups and set about nailing it to a post on the edge of his yard.

As he was driving the last nail into the post, he felt a tug on his overalls. He looked down into the eyes of a little boy.

"Mister," he said, "I want to buy one of your puppies."

"Well," said the farmer, as he rubbed the sweat off the back of his neck, "These puppies come from fine parents and cost a good deal of money."

The boy dropped his head for a moment. Then reaching deep into his pocket, he pulled out a handful of change and held it up to the farmer.

"I've got thirty-nine cents. Is that enough to take a look?"

"Sure," said the farmer. And with that he let out a whistle. "Here, Dolly!" he called.

Out from the doghouse and down the ramp ran Dolly followed by four little balls of fur.

The little boy pressed his face against the chain link fence. His eyes danced with delight. As the dogs made their way to the fence, the little boy noticed something else stirring inside the doghouse.

Slowly another little ball appeared this one noticeably smaller. Down the ramp it slid. Then in a somewhat awkward manner, the little pup began hobbling toward the others, doing its best to catch up...

"I want that one," the little boy said, pointing to the runt. The farmer knelt down at the boy's side and said, "Son, you don't want that puppy. He will never be able to run and play with you like these other dogs would."

With that the little boy stepped back from the fence, reached down, and began rolling up one leg of his trousers.

In doing so he revealed a steel brace running down both sides of his leg attaching itself to a specially made shoe.

Looking back up at the farmer, he said, "You see sir, I don't run too well myself, and he will need someone who understands."

With tears in his eyes, the farmer reached down and picked up the little pup.

Holding it carefully he handed it to the little boy.

"How much?" asked the little boy... "No charge," answered the farmer, "There's no charge for love."

The world is full of people who need someone who understands...

Q

QUICK AND MORE

I know there are some of you that are Democratic, and love Obama, but this is for Christians first, politics later. I do pray that it doesn't offend anybody with the truth of the message, but it has to be sent. If you love your Lord first and your politics later, then you will appreciate this message. If you don't, I'm sorry I judged you wrong.

When we get 100,000,000, that's one hundred million willing Christians to BOND together, voice their concerns and vote, we can take back America with God's help. Become one of the one hundred million.

Then let's get 200 million. It can be done by sending this email to your friends. Do the math. It only takes a willing heart and a fed up soul. *God Bless America and Shine your light on Her!*

In 1952 President Truman established one day a year as a "National Day of Prayer."

In 1988 President Reagan designated the First Thursday in May of each year as The National Day of Prayer.

In June 2007 (then) Presidential Candidate Barack Obama declared that the USA "Was no longer a Christian nation."

This year (2009) President Obama canceled the 21st annual National Day of Prayer ceremony at the White House under the ruse of "not wanting to offend anyone". President George W. Bush had a White House ceremony during all 8 years while he was in office.

BUT on September 25, 2009 from 4 AM until 7 PM, A National Day of Prayer FOR THE MUSLIM RELIGION was held on Capitol Hill, beside the White House. There were over 50,000 Muslims in D.C. that day.

HE PRAYS WITH THE MUSLIMS! I guess it doesn't matter if "Christians" are offended by this event . We obviously don 't count as "anyone" anymore.

Now he is encouraging schools to teach the qua-ran for extra credit in schools, while they cannot even talk about the bible, God or salute the American Flag.

The direction this country is headed should strike fear in the heart of every Christian, especially knowing that the Muslim religion believes that if Christians cannot be Converted, they should be annihilated.

Send this to ten people And the person who sent it to you!... To let them know that indeed, it was sent out to many more.

AMEN!

RWP2: Well some important things changed politically on November 4, 2014. A new Congress will take over on January 3, 2015 and we will have a new President in January 2017. But for now, a bit of history. In 1982 a conservative evangelical Christian organization called the "National Prayer Committee" was formed to coordinate and implement a fixed annual day of prayer for the purpose of organizing evangelical Christian prayer events with local, state, and federal government entities.

]In his 1983 declaration, Ronald Reagan said, "From General Washington's struggle at Valley Forge to the present, this Nation has fervently sought and received divine guidance as it pursued the course of history. This occasion provides our Nation with an opportunity to further recognize the source of our blessings, and to seek His help for the challenges we face today and in the future."

In 1988, the law was amended so that the National Day of Prayer would be held on the first Thursday of May. Two stated intentions of the National Day of Prayer were that it would be a day when adherents of all great religions could unite in prayer and that it may one day bring renewed respect for God to all the peoples of the world.

Presidents <u>Ronald Reagan</u> and <u>George H. W. Bush</u> each hosted special National Day of Prayer events held at the <u>White House</u> only once during their administrations, President <u>Bill Clinton</u> did not hold any such events during his time in office, though he issued proclamations annually.

President <u>George W. Bush</u> made his first presidential act be the announcement of a National Day of Prayer[j] and *he held events at the White House in each year of his presidency.*

President <u>Barack Obama</u> did not hold any public events at the White House though he has issued presidential proclamations regularly each year.

RWP2: Well...... Obama still has two May dates available before he is part of history. Maybe he goes into history just like President Bill Clinton, who was 0 for 8 in not hosting a White House event on National Day of Prayer!!

R

<u>RWP2:</u> This next R somewhat sums up my title of this collection of ****THINGS**** that I have negatively called: *America: Once the United States?* But is it far from my personal beliefs about the future and maybe the title of my sequel should be called **America -The Journey Back!** I see a more positive future if we do not give up and listen to all the negatives listed in A-Q and R to ZZ. When we hear something like the above 6-7 times, the "principle of spaced repetition" makes it something we remember and often it becomes a part of our psychic and influences our actions. So for the positives in A to ZZ, read them over and over and make some changes in your life.

READ, WEEP, PRINT AND KEEP!

Charley Reese's Final Column for the Orlando Sentinel!

A very interesting column. COMPLETELY NEUTRAL.

Be sure to Read the Poem at the end.

Charley Reese's final column for the Orlando Sentinel... He has been a journalist for 49 years. He is retiring and this is HIS LAST COLUMN.

Be sure to read the Tax List at the end.

This is about as clear and easy to understand as it can be. The article below is completely neutral, neither anti-republican or democrat. Charlie Reese, a retired reporter for the Orlando Sentinel, has hit the nail directly on the head, defining clearly who it is that in the final analysis must assume responsibility for the judgments made that impact each one of us every day. It's a short but good read. Worth the time. Worth remembering!

545 vs. 300,000,000 People

Politicians are the only people in the world who create problems and then campaign against them.

Have you ever wondered, if both the Democrats and the Republicans are against deficits, WHY do we have deficits? **RWP2:** Now at $17,500,000,000 or $17.5 trillion dollars total.

Have you ever wondered, if all the politicians are against inflation and high taxes, WHY do we have inflation and high taxes?

You and I don't propose a federal budget. The President does.

You and I don't have the Constitutional authority to vote on appropriations. The House of Representatives does.

You and I don't write the tax code, Congress does.

You and I don't set fiscal policy, Congress does.

You and I don't control monetary policy, the Federal Reserve Bank does.

One hundred senators, 435 congressmen, one President, and nine Supreme Court justices equates to 545 human beings out of the 300 million are directly, legally, morally, and individually responsible for the domestic problems that plague this country.

I excluded the members of the Federal Reserve Board because that problem was created by the Congress. In 1913, Congress delegated its Constitutional duty to provide a sound currency to a federally chartered, but private, central bank.

I excluded all the special interests and lobbyists for a sound reason. They have no legal authority. They have no ability to coerce a senator, a congressman, or a President to do one cotton-picking thing. I don't care if they offer a politician $1 million dollars in cash. The politician has the power to accept or reject it. No matter what the lobbyist promises, it is the legislator's responsibility to determine how he votes.

Those 545 human beings spend much of their energy convincing you that what they did is not their fault. They cooperate in this common con regardless of party.

What separates a politician from a normal human being is an excessive amount of gall. No normal human being would have the gall of a Speaker, who stood up and criticized the President for creating deficits. (The President can only propose a budget. He cannot force the Congress to accept it.)

The Constitution, which is the supreme law of the land, gives sole responsibility to the House of Representatives for originating and approving appropriations and taxes. Who is the speaker of the House? (John Boehner). He is the leader of the majority party. He and fellow House members, not the President, can approve any budget they want xxx;;;.) If the President vetoes it, they can pass it over his veto if they agree to. [The House has passed a budget but the Senate has not approved a budget in over three years. The President's proposed budgets have gotten almost unanimous rejections in the Senate in that time.]

It seems inconceivable to me that a nation of 300 million cannot replace 545 people who stand convicted -- by present facts -- of incompetence and irresponsibility. I can't think of a single domestic problem that is not traceable directly to those 545 people. When you fully grasp the plain truth that 545 people exercise the power of the federal government, then it must follow that what exists is what they want to exist.

If the tax code is unfair, it's because they want it unfair.

If the budget is in the red, it's because they want it in the red.

If the Army & Marines are in Iraq and Afghanistan it's because they want them in Iraq and Afghanistan.

If they do not receive social security but are on an elite retirement plan not available to the people, it's because they want it that way.

There are no insoluble government problems.

Do not let these 545 people shift the blame to bureaucrats, whom they hire and whose jobs they can abolish; to lobbyists, whose gifts and advice they can reject; to regulators, to whom they give the power to regulate and from whom they can take this power. Above all, do not let them con you into the belief that there exists disembodied mystical forces like "the economy," "inflation," or "politics" that prevent them from doing what they take an oath to do.

Those 545 people, and they alone, are responsible. They, and they alone, have the power.

They, and they alone, should be held accountable by the people who are their bosses. Provided the voters have the gumption to manage their own employees... We should vote all of them out of office and clean up their mess!

Charlie Reese is a former columnist of the Orlando Sentinel Newspaper.

What you do with this article now that you have read it... is up to you.

This might be funny if it weren't so true.

Be sure to read all the way to the end; 88 different taxes:

1. Tax his land,
2. Tax his bed,
3. Tax the table, at which he's fed.
4. Tax his tractor,
5. Tax his mule,
6. Teach him taxes are the rule.
7. Tax his work,
8. Tax his pay,
9. He works for peanuts anyway!
10. Tax his cow,

11. Tax his goat,
12. Tax his pants,
13. Tax his coat.
14. Tax his ties,
15. Tax his shirt,
16. Tax his work,
17. Tax his dirt.
18. Tax his tobacco,
19. Tax his drink,
20. Tax him if he
21. Tries to think.
22. Tax his cigars,
23. Tax his beers,
24. If he cries tax his tears.
25. Tax his car,
26. Tax his gas,
27. Find other ways to tax his ass.
28. Tax all he has
29. Then let him know
30. That you won't be done
31. Till he has no dough.
32. When he screams and hollers;
33. Then tax him some more,
34. Tax him till he's good and sore.
35. Then tax his coffin,
36. Tax his grave,
37. Tax the sod in which he's laid...
38. Put these words
39. Upon his tomb, 'taxes drove me to my doom...'
40. When he's gone,
41. Do not relax,
42. It's time to apply the inheritance tax.
43. Accounts Receivable Tax
44. Building Permit Tax
45. CDL license Tax
46. Cigarette Tax

47. Corporate Income Tax
48. Dog License Tax
49. Excise Taxes
50. Federal Income Tax
51. Federal Unemployment Tax (FUTA)
52. Fishing License Tax
53. Food License Tax
54. Fuel Permit Tax
55. Gasoline Tax (currently 44.75 cents per gallon)
56. Gross Receipts Tax
57. Hunting License Tax
58. Inheritance Tax
59. Inventory Tax
60. IRS Interest Charges IRS Penalties (tax on top of tax)
61. Liquor Tax
62. Luxury Taxes
63. Marriage License Tax
64. Medicare Tax
65. Personal Property Tax
66. Property Tax
67. Real Estate Tax
68. Service Charge Tax
69. Social Security Tax
70. Road Usage Tax
71. Recreational Vehicle Tax
72. Sales Tax
73. School Tax
74. State Income Tax
75. State Unemployment Tax (SUTA)
76. Telephone Federal Excise Tax
77. Telephone Federal Universal Service Fee Tax
78. Telephone Federal, State and Local Surcharge Taxes
79. Telephone Minimum Usage Surcharge Tax
80. Telephone Recurring and Nonrecurring Charges Tax
81. Telephone State and Local Tax
82. Telephone Usage Charge Tax

83. Utility Taxes
84. Vehicle License Registration Tax
85. Vehicle Sales Tax
86. Watercraft Registration Tax
87. Well Permit Tax
88. Workers Compensation Tax

STILL THINK THIS IS FUNNY?

Few these taxes existed 100 years ago, & our nation was the most prosperous in the world. We had absolutely no national debt, had the largest middle class in the world, and Mom stayed home to raise the kids.

What in the heck happened? Can you spell 'politicians?' I hope this goes around THE USA at least 545 times!!! YOU can help it get there!!! GO AHEAD. . . BE AN AMERICAN!!!

REFORM: A CONGRESSIONAL REFORM PROPOSAL

This needs to grow legs and move across America thru everyone's email friends.

The proposal is to promote a "Congressional Reform Act of 2009." It would contain eight provisions, all of which would probably be strongly endorsed by those who drafted the Constitution and the Bill of Rights.

I know many of you will say, "this is impossible." Remember, Congress has the lowest approval of any entity in Government, now is the time when Americans will join together to reform Congress - the entity that represents us.

We need a Senator to introduce this bill in the US Senate and a Representative to introduce a similar bill in the US House. Please add any ideas on how to get this done.

If all else fails, something like this needs to be added to the ballot for the next election. After what's been going on for the past few years, I'm certain the American public will vote for these changes

****

Congressional Reform Act of 2009

1. **Term Limits:** 12 years only, one of the possible options below.

    A. Two Six-year Senate terms
    B. Six Two-year House terms
    C. One Six-year Senate term and three Two-Year House terms

Serving in Congress is an honor, not a career. The Founding Fathers envisioned citizen legislators, serve your term(s), then go home and back to work.

2. **No Tenure / No Pension:** A congressman collects a salary while in office and receives no pay when they are out of office. Serving in Congress is an honor, not a career. The Founding Fathers envisioned citizen legislators, serve your term(s), then go home and back to work.

3. **Congress (past, present & future) participates in Social Security:** All funds in the Congressional retirement fund moves to the Social Security system immediately. All future funds flow into the Social Security system, Congress participates with the American people. Serving in Congress is an honor, not a career. The Founding Fathers envisioned citizen legislators, server your term(s), then go home and back to work.

4. Congress can purchase their own retirement plan just as all Americans...

Serving in Congress is an honor, not a career. The Founding Fathers envisioned citizen legislators, serve your term(s), then go home and back to work.

5. Congress will no longer vote themselves a pay raise. Congressional pay will rise by the lower of CPI or 3%: Serving in Congress is an honor, not a career. The Founding Fathers envisioned citizen legislators, serve your term(s), then go home and back to work.

6. Congress loses their current health care system and participates in the same health care system as the American people. Serving in Congress is an honor, not a career. The Founding Fathers envisioned citizen legislators, serve your term(s), then go home and back to work.

7. Congress must equally abide in all laws they impose on the American people. Serving in Congress is an honor, not a career. The Founding Fathers envisioned citizen legislators, serve your term(s), then go home and back to work.

8. All contracts with past and present congressmen are void effective 1/1/10.

<u>**PLEASE REMEMBER:**</u> **The American people did not give all these perks to congressmen; congressmen gave all these sweetheart deals to themselves.   We need to take back the Congress.**

<u>**They all seem to have forgotten:**</u>

Serving in Congress is an honor, not a career. The Founding Fathers envisioned citizen legislators, serve your term(s), then go home and back to work.

ROBIN WILLIAMS-(IN MEMORY)

YOU HAVE TO LOVE HIM. A MUST READ!...READ THIS! HE MADE THIS SPEECH IN NEW YORK

The Plan!

Robin Williams, wearing a shirt that says 'I love New York ' in Arabic.

You gotta love Robin Williams........Even if he's nuts! Leave it to Robin Williams to come up with the perfect plan. What we need now is for our UN Ambassador to stand up and repeat this message. Robin Williams' plan...(Hard to argue with this logic!)

'I see a lot of people yelling for peace but I have not heard of a plan for peace.. So, here's one plan.'

1) 'The US, UK , CANADA and AUSTRALIA will apologize to the world for our 'interference' in their affairs, past & present. You know, Hitler, Mussolini, Stalin, Tojo, Noriega, Milosevic, Hussein, and the rest of those 'good 'ole' boys', we will never 'interfere' again.

2) We will withdraw our troops from all over the world, starting with Germany , South Korea , the Middle East , and the Philippines . They don't want us there. We would station troops at our borders. No one allowed sneaking through holes in the fence.

3) All illegal aliens have 90 days to get their affairs together and leave We'll give them a free trip home. After 90 days the remainder will be gathered up and deported immediately, regardless of whom or where they are from. They're illegal!!! France will welcome them.

4) All future visitors will be thoroughly checked and limited to 90 days unless given a special permit!!!! No one from a terrorist nation will be allowed in. If you don't like it there, change it yourself and don't hide here. Asylum would never be available to anyone. We don't need any more cab drivers or 7-11 cashiers...

5) No foreign 'students' over age 21. The older ones are the bombers. If they don't attend classes, they get a 'D' and it's back home baby.

6) The US, UK, CANADA and AUSTRALIA will make a strong effort to become self-sufficient energy wise. This will include developing nonpolluting sources of energy but will require a temporary drilling of oil in the Alaskan wilderness. The caribou will have to cope for a while.

7) Offer Saudi Arabia and other oil producing countries $10 a barrel for their oil. If they don't like it, we go someplace else. They can go somewhere else to sell their production. (About a week of the wells filling up the storage sites would be enough.)

8) If there is a famine or other natural catastrophe in the world, we will not 'interfere.' They can pray to Allah or whomever, for seeds, rain, cement or whatever they need. Besides most of what we give them is stolen or given to the army. The people who need it most get very little, if anything.

9) Ship the UN Headquarters to an isolated island someplace. We don't need the spies and fair weather friends here. Besides,

the building would make a good homeless shelter or lockup for illegal aliens.

10) All Americans must go to charm and beauty school. That way, no one can call us 'Ugly Americans' any longer. The Language we speak is ENGLISH.....learn it...or LEAVE...Now, isn't that a winner of a plan?

'The Statue of Liberty is no longer saying 'Give me your tired, your poor, your huddled masses.' She's got a baseball bat and she's yelling, 'you want a piece of me?'

RULES, MORE NEW ONES BY GEORGE CARLEN

New Rule: No more gift registries. You know, it used to be just for weddings. Now it's for babies and new homes, graduations, and releases from jail. Picking out the stuff you want and having other people buy it for you isn't gift giving, it's the white people version of looting.

New Rule: Stop giving me that pop-up ad for classmates. com! There's a reason you don't talk to people for 25 years. Because you don't particularly like them!? Besides, I already know what the captain of the football team is doing these days--mowing my lawn.

New Rule: Stop saying that teenage boys who have sex with their hot, blonde teachers are permanently damaged. I have a better description for these kids: LUCKY BASTARDS!

New Rule: If you need to shave and you still collect baseball cards, you're gay. If you're a kid, the cards are keepsakes of your idols. If you're a grown man, they're pictures of men.

New Rule: Don't eat anything that's served to you out a window unless you're a seagull. People are acting all shocked that a human finger was found in a bowl of Wendy's chili. Hey, it cost less than a dollar. What did you expect it to contain?? Trout?

New Rule: Ladies, leave your eyebrows alone. Here's how much men care about your eyebrows: do you have two of them? Okay, we're done.

New Rule: There's no such thing as flavored water. There's a whole aisle of this crap at the supermarket, water, but without that watery taste. Sorry, but flavored water is called a soft drink. You want flavored water? Pour some scotch over ice and let it melt. That's your flavored water.

New Rule: Stop screwing with old people. Target is introducing a redesigned pill bottle that's square, with a bigger label. And the top is now the bottom. And by the time grandpa figures out how to open it, his ass will be in the morgue. Congratulations, Target, you just solved the Social Security crisis.

New Rule: The more complicated the Starbucks order, the bigger the axxhole. If you walk into a Starbucks and order a "decaf grande half-soy, half-low fat, iced vanilla, double-shot, gingerbread cappuccino, extra dry, light ice, with one sweet-n'-Low, and one NutraSweet," ooh, you're a huge axxhole.

New Rule: I'm not the cashier! By the time I look up from sliding my card, entering my PIN number, pressing "Enter," verifying the amount, deciding no, I don't want cash back, and pressing "Enter" again, the kid who is supposed to be ringing me up is standing there eating my Almond Joy.

New Rule: Just because your tattoo has Chinese characters in it doesn't make you spiritual. It's right above the crack of your ass. And it translates to "beef with broccoli." The last time you did anything spiritual, you were praying to God you weren't pregnant. You're not spiritual. You're just high.

New Rule: Competitive eating isn't a sport. It's one of the seven deadly sins. ESPN recently televised the U.S. Open of Competitive Eating, because watching those athletes at the poker table was just too damned exciting. What's next, competitive farting??? Oh wait!? They're already doing that. It's called "The Howard Stern Show."

New Rule: I don't need a bigger mega M&Ms. If I'm extra hungry for M&Ms, I'll go nuts and eat two.

New Rule: and this one is long overdue: No more bathroom attendants. After I zip up, some guy is offering me a towel and a mint like I just had sex with George Michael. I can't even tell if he's supposed to be there, or just some freak with a fetish. I don't want to be on your web cam, dude. I just want to wash my hands.

New Rule: When I ask how old your toddler is, I don't need to know in months. "27 Months" "He's two," will do just fine. He's not a cheese. And I didn't really care in the first place.

New Rule: If you ever hope to be a credible adult and want a job that pays better than minimum wage, then for God's sake don't pierce or tattoo every available piece of flesh. If so, then plan your future around saying, "Do you want fries with that?"

New Rule: If you're going to insist on making movies based on crappy, old television shows, then you have to give everyone in the Cineplex a remote so we can see what's playing on the other screens. Let's remember the reason something was a television show in the first place is that the idea wasn't good enough to be a movie.

RUN, FORREST, RUN!   10 LIFE LESSONS WE CAN LEARN FROM FORREST GUMP

By Kayla Matthews

Science Has It: You Should Stop Doing These 10 Things to Be More Productive Want to master the 24 hours you have in each day? Use these scientifically-backed strategies to be more productive:

1. Stop ignoring your ultradium rhythm! Every person experiences a natural lull in productivity after doing an activity for about 90-120 minutes. This period is called the ultradium rhythm, and you shouldn't ignore its power. Instead of trying to "push through" mental fatigue, it's better to take a break when your ultradium rhythm cycles. Get up, walk around and do something different for up to 20 minutes.

You may even want to take a nap, especially if you work for a company that has a napping room or policy as do NASA, AOL and – not surprisingly – Google. After your break or some power shut-eye, come back to your original activity with more energy, creativity and focus.

2. Stop checking your social media accounts every hour! Are you one of the millions of people who keeps his or her social media account live and active on your smart phone, tablet, and laptop or desktop? Doing so presents an attractive nuisance, and you'll end up wasting tons of minutes per day watching cat videos and finding out your second-cousin once remove's neighbor's boss saw a penguin at the zoo. Make a pact with yourself to relegate checking your social media accounts once or twice per day instead of allowing them to suck your time.

Spending time with people as people – and not avatars on a screen – was very useful for one Citrix vice president. He discovered that relationships made in the "real world" were not only more satisfying than those made in social media, but that they produced a stronger sense of supportiveness.

3. Stop saying "yes" to everything and everyone. Are you a "yes" man or woman? It's time to rethink the way you're responding when you're asked to do something. While you can't always say "no" to your boss, your spouse or your friends, you are allowed to pick and choose most decisions you make during the day. By saying "no," you can avail yourself of the scientifically-based Pareto Principle. The Pareto Principle claims that 20 percent of efforts produce 80 percent of results. Conversely, 20 percent of results consume 80 percent of efforts. Spend your 80 percent doing what matters, not what doesn't.

If this is a difficult principle for you to adapt, don't worry – you can always schedule one day a week to say "yes". That's what TED Talks' guest speaker Tania Luna does.

4. Stop checking your email incessantly. Most of us habitually check our email on an unstructured basis. That is, we look whenever we feel like it. This turns into a problem because emails can sap time that is better spent elsewhere. Get off the email train by making it a point to only check emails at specific points during your day. For instance, you may want to check yours at lunchtime, and then again in the evening.

Tim Ferris, author of *The 4-Hour Work Week*, recommends picking two specific times each day for maximum productivity.

5. Stop doing everything yourself. Sure, it can be thrilling to tell everyone that you are "doing it all," but there's no reason to try and be superhuman. Eventually, you'll fail – miserably – without help. If delegating is tough for you, just remind yourself that the old adage "many hands make lighter work" holds true in all aspects of life.

Need a little help? Buy or borrow the Harvard Business School Press book Hidden Value: How Great Companies Achieve Extraordinary Results with Ordinary People. In it, author Charles O'Reilly gives tips on how to begin the process if you're uncomfortable with or unaccustomed to delegation.

Reach out and get the assistance you need; in fact, you may want to start looking at areas where others can do the tasks you're doing now. Free up your time to work on other things, and start really being productive.

6. Stop trying to be perfect. Let's get this on the table right now: You're not perfect and you shouldn't try to be. A research study published by University Affairs illustrates this point. The study showed that professors who were perfectionists had lower productivity levels than those who accepted the fact that they were only human. The moral of the story is that, on most occasions, being good is good enough.

Besides, Google has had incredible success fostering leaders who weren't top students from universities. That says something.

7. Stop being busy all the time. A Harvard study and scientific evidence has shown that spending downtime by oneself is more important than we might have otherwise thought. Dubbed "The Power of Lonely" by a Boston Globe writer, the principle suggests that people have stronger memories of moments they spend by themselves. In other words, it's time for a little introspection to get to the heart of who you honestly are, as well as what you want to do "when you grow up."

When Brigid Schulte slowed down, she found the time to pen Overwhelmed: Work, Love and Play When No One Has the Time. Schulte shows how doing less can be freeing, and recommends this to anyone who truly wants to be a success.

8. Stop saying "I can't." Want to kick a habit or keep yourself from overeating? Don't tell yourself "I can't," because it just sets you up for failure. Instead, replace "I can't" with "I don't." For example, those who say they "don't" do something actually do it in half the cases of those who say, "I can't." If you want to give up smoking, tell yourself you "don't" smoke rather than you "can't" smoke; you'll find that you have a better chance of quitting.

Exercise guru Joe English talks about the power of "I can" in this blog post on Running Advice. While Joe's discussion of "I can" applies mainly to exercise and working out, he touches on some universal strategies all of us can use to be more productive. Rather than thinking, "I can't do this" or "I don't know if I can do this," Joe says he thinks to himself, "You can and you will." Changing the way you think about the obstacles in front of you can have a huge impact on your daily productivity.

9. Stop multitasking. It seems like multitasking is embraced in our culture as a "given," but it isn't exactly efficient. Researchers examined the skills of multi-taskers and were shocked to discover that they didn't do well on any of the tasks to which they were assigned. Focus on single tasks, and leave the multitasking to those who haven't read this article yet. You'll be in good company – the CBS Evening News started discouraging multitasking in their offices and had fascinating results.

10. Stop being so negative. Are you someone for whom the glass is always half-empty... or just empty? While a little negativity can be understandable, a lot of it will only cramp your style and keep you from achieving your goals. According to scientists from Japan, when we think negative thoughts, we color our world with pessimism and make it harder to attain success.

So start looking at the glass a different way and enjoy your newfound outlook on life, business and everything under the sun. As sales guru Zig Ziglar said: "Winners evaluate themselves in a positive manner and look for their strengths as they work to overcome weaknesses."

As you can see, being productive means "stopping." If that's tough for you to do, just practice. Changing behaviors takes time. However, doing something for about 21 days usually makes it easier to continue with the routine. Make this day one, and in three weeks your productivity level should be much higher.

S.

SEEDS: HOW SEEDS WERE USED TO SELECT A NEW CEO

A successful business man was growing old and knew it was time to choose a successor to take over the business. Instead of choosing one of his Directors or his children, he decided to do something different.. He called all the young executives in his company together.

He said, "It is time for me to step down and choose the next CEO. I have decided to choose one of you. "The young executives were Shocked, but the boss continued". I am going to give each one of you a SEED today - one very special SEED. I want you to plant the seed, water it, and come back here one year from today with what you have grown from the seed I have given you. I will then judge the plants that you bring, and the one I choose will be the next CEO."

One man, named Jim, was there that day and he, like the others, received a seed. He went home and excitedly, told his wife the story. She helped him get a pot, soil and compost and he planted the seed. Every day, he would water it and watch to see if it had grown.. After about three weeks, some of the other executives began to talk about their seeds and the plants that were beginning to grow.

Jim kept checking his seed, but nothing ever grew. Three weeks, four weeks, five weeks went by, still nothing. By now, others were talking about their plants, but Jim didn't have a plant and he felt like a failure. Six months went by -- still nothing in Jim's pot. He just knew he had killed his seed. Everyone else had trees and tall plants, but he had nothing.

Jim didn't say anything to his colleagues, however... He just kept watering and fertilizing the soil - He so wanted the seed to grow. A year finally went by and all the young executives of the company brought their plants to the CEO for inspection. Jim told his wife that he wasn't going to take an empty pot. But she asked him to be honest about what happened.

Jim felt sick to his stomach, it was going to be the most embarrassing moment of his life, but he knew his wife was right. He took his empty pot to the board room. When Jim arrived, he was amazed at the variety of plants grown by the other executives. They were beautiful -- in all shapes and sizes.

Jim put his empty pot on the floor and many of his colleagues laughed, a few felt sorry for him! When the CEO arrived, he surveyed the room and greeted his young executives. Jim just tried to hide in the back.

"My, what great plants, trees, and flowers you have grown," said the CEO. "Today one of you will be appointed the next CEO!" All of a sudden, the CEO spotted Jim at the back of the room with his empty pot.

The CEO ordered the Financial Director to bring JIM to the front. And Jim was terrified. He thought, "The CEO knows I'm a failure! Maybe he will have me fired! When Jim got to the front, the CEO asked him what had happened to his seed - Jim told him the story. The CEO asked everyone to sit down except Jim.

The CEO looked at Jim, and then announced to the young executives, "Behold your next Chief Executive Officer! His name is Jim!" Jim couldn't believe it. Jim couldn't even grow his seed. "How could he be the new CEO?" the others said.

Then the CEO said, "One year ago today, I gave everyone in this room a seed. I told you to take the seed, plant it, water it, and bring it back to me today.

But I gave you all boiled seeds; they were dead - it was not possible for them to grow.

All of you, except Jim, have brought me trees and plants and flowers. When you found that the seed would not grow, you substituted another seed for the one I gave you. Jim was the only one with the courage and honesty to bring me a pot with my seed in it.

Therefore, Jim is the one who will be the new Chief Executive Officer!" Why...because;

If you plant honesty, you will reap trust.
If you plant goodness, you will reap friends.
If you plant humility, you will reap greatness.
If you plant perseverance, you will reap contentment
If you plant consideration, you will reap perspective
 If you plant hard work, you will reap success
If you plant forgiveness, you will reap reconciliation
If you plant faith in God , you will reap a harvest,

So, be careful what you plant now!...It will determine what you will reap later...And....."Whatever You Give To Life, Life Gives You Back"

SERVICE-STIMULUS SERMON AT VIRGINIA CHURCH

Genesis 47:13-27

I would love to give the Pastor of this predominantly black church in Virginia a hug and a high five. This guy is obviously a leader. Perhaps we should each decide who our real leader is.... It is amazing to see that very little has changed in 4,000 years.

Good morning, brothers and sisters; it's always a delight to see the pews crowded on Sunday morning, and so eager to get into God's Word. Turn with me in your Bibles, if you will to the 47th chapter of Genesis, we'll begin our reading at verse 13, and go through verse 27.

Brother Ray, would you stand and read that great passage for us? ... (Reading)...

Thank you for that fine reading, Brother Ray... So we see that economic hard times fell upon Egypt, and the people turned to the government of Pharaoh to deal with this for them. And Pharaoh nationalized the grain harvest, and placed the grain in great storehouses that he had built. So the people brought their money to Pharaoh, like a great tax increase, and gave it all to him willingly in return for grain. And this went on until their money ran out, and they were hungry again.

So when they went to Pharaoh after that, they brought their livestock -their cattle, their horses, their sheep, and their donkey - to barter for grain, and verse 17 says that only took them through the end of that year.

But the famine wasn't over, was it? So the next year, the people came before Pharaoh and admitted they had nothing left, except their land and their own lives. "There is nothing left in the sight of my lord but our bodies and our land. Why should we die before your eyes, both we and our land? Buy us and our land for food, and we with our land will be servants to Pharaoh." So they surrendered their homes, their land, and their real estate to Pharaoh's government, and then sold themselves into slavery to him, in return for grain.

What can we learn from this, brothers and sisters? That turning to the government instead of to God to be our provider in hard times only leads to slavery? Yes. That the only reason government wants to be our provider is to also become our master? Yes.

But look how that passage ends, brothers and sisters! Thus Israel settled in the land of Egypt, in the land of Goshen. And they gained possessions in it, and were fruitful and multiplied greatly." God provided for His people, just as He always has! They didn't end up giving all their possessions to government, no, it says they gained possessions! But I also tell you a great truth today, and an ominous one.

We see the same thing happening today - the government today wants to "share the wealth "once again, to take it from us and redistribute it back to us. It wants to take control of health-care, just as it has taken control of education, and ration it back to us, and when government rations it, then government decides who gets it, and how much, and what kind. And if we go along with it, and do it willingly, then we will wind up no differently than the people of Egypt did four thousand years ago - as slaves to the government, and as slaves to our leaders.

What Mr. Obama's government is doing now is no different from what Pharaoh's government did then, and it will end the same. And a lot of people like to call Mr. Obama a "Messiah," don't them? Is he a Messiah?

A savior? Didn't the Egyptians say, after Pharaoh made them his slaves, "You have saved our lives; may it please my lord, we will be servants to Pharaoh"?

> Well, I tell you this - I know the Messiah; the Messiah is a friend of mine; and Mr. Obama is no Messiah! No, brothers and sisters, **if Mr. Obama is a character from the Bible, then he is Pharaoh.**
>
> **Bow with me in prayer, if you will.**
>
> Lord, You alone are worthy to be served, and we rely on You, and You alone.
>
> We confess that the government is not our deliverer, and never rightly will be.

We read in the eighth chapter of 1 Samuel, when Samuel warned the people of what a ruler would do, where it says **"And in that day you will cry out because of your king, whom you have chosen for yourselves, but the LORD will not answer you in that day."** And Lord, we acknowledge that day has come. We cry out to you because of the ruler that we have chosen for ourselves as a nation. Lord, we pray for this nation. We pray for revival, and we pray for deliverance from those who would be our masters.

Give us hearts to seek You and hands to serve You, and protect Your people from the atrocities of Pharaoh's government. In God We Trust...

You may consider sharing this with others.

If you don't agree ... just delete.
Have a nice day.

T.

TEXAS CHILI

If you can read this whole story without laughing, then there's no hope for you. I was crying by the end. This is an actual account as relayed to paramedics at a chili cook-off in Texas.

Note: Please take time to read this slowly. If you pay attention to the first two judges, the reaction of the third judge is even better. For those of you who have lived in Texas, you know how true this is. They actually have a Chili Cook-off about the time Halloween comes around. It takes up a major portion of a parking lot at the San Antonio City Park.

Judge #3 was an inexperienced Chili taster named Frank, who was visiting from Springfield, IL.

Frank: "Recently, I was honored to be selected as a judge at a chili cook-off. The original person called in sick at the last moment and I happened to be standing there at the judge's table, asking for directions to the Coors Light truck, when the call came in. I was assured by the other two judges (Native Texans) that the chili wouldn't be all that spicy; and, besides, they told me I could have free beer during the tasting, so I accepted and became Judge 3."

Here are the scorecard notes from the event:

CHILI # 1 - MIKE'S MANIAC MONSTER CHILI

Judge # 1 -- A little too heavy on the tomato. Amusing kick.

Judge # 2 -- Nice, smooth tomato flavor. Very mild.

Judge # 3 (Frank) -- Holy crap, what the hell is this stuff? You could remove dried paint from your driveway. Took me two beers to put the flames out. I hope that's the worst one. These Texans are crazy.

CHILI # 2 - AUSTIN'S AFTERBURNER CHILI

Judge # 1 -- Smoky, with a hint of pork. Slight jalapeno tang.

Judge # 2 -- Exciting BBQ flavor, needs more peppers to be taken seriously.

Judge # 3 -- Keep this out of the reach of children. I'm not sure what I'm supposed to taste besides pain. I had to wave off two people who wanted to give me the Heimlich maneuver. They had to rush in more beer when they saw the look on my face.

CHILI # 3 - FRED'S FAMOUS BURN DOWN THE BARN CHILI

Judge # 1 -- Excellent firehouse chili. Great kick.

Judge # 2 -- A bit salty, good use of peppers.

Judge # 3 -- Call the EPA. I've located a uranium spill. My nose feels like I have been snorting Drano. Everyone knows the routine by now. Get me more beer before I ignite. Barmaid pounded me on the back, now my backbone is in the front part of my chest. I'm getting shxx-faced from all of the beer.

CHILI # 4 - BUBBA'S BLACK MAGIC

Judge # 1 -- Black bean chili with almost no spice. Disappointing.

Judge # 2 -- Hint of lime in the black beans. Good side dish for fish or other mild foods, not much of a chili.

Judge # 3 -- I felt something scraping across my tongue, but was unable to taste it. Is it possible to burn out taste buds? Sally, the beer maid, was standing behind me with fresh refills. This 300 lb. woman is starting to look HOT ... just like this nuclear waste I'm eating! Is chili an aphrodisiac?

CHILI # 5 - LISA'S LEGAL LIP REMOVER

Judge # 1 -- Meaty, strong chili. Cayenne peppers freshly ground, adding considerable kick. Very impressive.

Judge # 2 -- Chili using shredded beef, could use more tomato. Must admit the cayenne peppers make a strong statement.

Judge # 3 -- My ears are ringing, sweat is pouring off my forehead and I can no longer focus my eyes. I farted, and four people behind me needed paramedics. The contestant seemed offended when I told her that her chili had given me brain damage. Sally saved my tongue from bleeding by pouring beer directly on it from the pitcher. I wonder if I'm burning my lips off. It really ticks me off that the other judges asked me to stop screaming. Screw them.

CHILI # 6 - VERA'S VERY VEGETARIAN VARIETY

Judge # 1 -- Thin yet bold vegetarian variety chili. Good balance of spices and peppers.

Judge # 2 -- The best yet. Aggressive use of peppers, onions, garlic. Superb.

Judge # 3 -- My intestines are now a straight pipe filled with gaseous, sulfuric flames. I crapped on myself when I farted, and I'm worried it will eat through the chair. No one seems inclined to stand behind me except that Sally. Can't feel my lips anymore. I need to wipe my butt with a snow cone.

CHILI # 7 - SUSAN'S SCREAMING SENSATION CHILI

Judge # 1 -- A mediocre chili with too much reliance on canned peppers.

Judge # 2 -- Ho hum, tastes as if the chef literally threw in a can of chili peppers at the last moment. **I should take note that I am worried about Judge # 3. He appears to be a bit of distress as he is cursing uncontrollably.

Judge # 3 -- You could put a grenade in my mouth, pull the pin, and I wouldn't feel a thing. I've lost sight in one eye, and the world sounds like it is made of rushing water. My shirt is covered with chili, which slid unnoticed out of my mouth. My pants are full of lava to match my shirt.

At least during the autopsy, they'll know what killed me. I've decided to stop breathing it's too painful. Screw it; I'm not getting any oxygen anyway. If I need air, I'll just suck it in through the 4-inch hole in my stomach.

CHILI # 8 - BIG TOM'S TOENAIL CURLING CHILI

Judge # 1 -- The perfect ending, this is a nice blend chili. Not too bold but spicy enough to declare its existence.

Judge # 2 -- This final entry is a good, balanced chili. Neither mild nor hot. Sorry to see that most of it was lost when Judge #3 farted, passed out, fell over and pulled the chili pot down on top of himself.

Not sure if he's going to make it. Poor feller, wonder how he'd have reacted to really hot chili?

Judge # 3 - No Report

THE MUSIC STOPPED

(For those who are unaware: At all military base theaters, the National Anthem is played before the movie begins.) This is written from a Chaplain in Iraq:

I recently attended a showing of 'Superman 3' here at LSA Anaconda. We have a large auditorium we use for movies, as well as memorial services and other large gatherings. As is the custom at all military bases, we stood to attention when the National Anthem began before the main feature. All was going well until three-quarters of the way through The National Anthem, the music stopped.

Now, what would happen if this occurred with 1,000 18-22 year-olds back in the States? I imagine there would be hoots, catcalls, laughter, a few rude comments, and everyone would sit down and yell for the movie to begin. Of course, that is, if they had stood for the National Anthem in the first place.

Here in Iraq, 1,000 Soldiers continued to stand at attention, eyes fixed forward. The music started again and the Soldiers continued to quietly stand at attention. But again, at the same point, the music stopped. What would you expect 1000 Soldiers standing at attention to do ?? Frankly, I expected some laughter, and everyone would eventually sit down and wait for the movie to start.

But No!!... You could have heard a pin drop, while every Soldier continued to stand at attention. Suddenly, there was a lone voice from the front of the auditorium, then a dozen voices, and soon the room was filled with the voices of a thousand soldiers, finishing where the recording left off: "And the rockets' red glare, the bombs bursting in air, gave proof through the night that our flag was still there. Oh, say does that Star Spangled Banner yet wave, o'er the land of the free, and the home of the brave."

It was the most inspiring moment I have had in Iraq and I wanted you to know what kind of Soldiers are serving you. Remember them as they fight for us!

Written by Chaplain Jim Higgins LSA

Anaconda is at the Ballad Airport in Iraq , north of Baghdad

THE TOUCH OF THE MASTER

By Jim Coleman

"I am with you always." -Matthew 28:20

On Memorial Day and Independence Day weekends, we open up the Crystal Cathedral's choir and orchestra to all church members and young musicians from the community who want to volunteer to sing and play. Ever since I played drums in junior and senior high school (45 years ago), I have LOVED to play snare drum to the Sousa marches that are featured on these patriotic Sundays. I do, however, need and find comfort in the assurance of a more experienced drummer beside me.

On July 4, 2010, I showed up in the Crystal Cathedral at 6:45 a.m. for rehearsal. Several new drumming volunteers showed up, too - young persons that I had not yet met. I scanned the faces wondering who might provide the assurance I was hoping for. A nice young girl stood next to me on another snare drum. Before we began, I had a chance to ask her, "Do you go to school locally?" She looked to be about 17 or 18 years old. At my age, anyone younger than 30 looks high-school age to me. She answered by telling me that she had just completed her master's degree in orchestra conducting and percussion performance. I was impressed. And, as she played, I knew why. She sight-read all eight of the numbers superbly...didn't miss a beat...she did it with ease. It was wonderful to see and hear. Her every stroke was snappy and crisp. She provided the support and the leadership that this rusty old drummer-boy needed.

At first sight, I had not imagined the capabilities that were hers. She truly brought "the touch of the master" to our percussion section that morning. To me, what was most important was the confidence her expertise provided for my soul.

There are "masters" at all of life's levels. A child, for instance, may perceive his or her teacher, coach, or parent as a master. Our perceptions of "masters" change and grow as each of us develops in our own mastering of a discipline, endeavor, or field of knowledge. Each area of human interest and activity presents its masters...the arts, the trades, teachers, moms, dads, etc. All of us have known when we were in the presence of a master. And, believe it or not, someone around you is looking up to you as a master in some way, today.

Jesus Christ is Master of the Universe. He created it. He, alone, is Master of all. He tells you and He tells me, "I am with you ALWAYS." What incredible assurance we have in Him.

Prayer:

Lord God, blessed Savior, thank You that Your Master's touch and presence is always there. Lord, give me the confidence to take the first step knowing that You step with me...and, at times, carry me. I love You, Lord...I trust You, Master. Amen.

* * *

Who has provided the "master's touch" in your life? Are there people who look up to you? How will you use their confidence in you to direct them to Jesus?

THE SHANTY'- (WHAT WE CALLED AND OUT HOUSE)

RWP2: I really do remember this type of outdoor human waste storage facility as a child visiting Grandma (Blanche) and Granddad (James Owen Peters) in Rock Oak, WV. Back then we also had no lights or even running water but were very happy...yes they provided a happy and loving home for Mom and I in 1945 right after I was born on 01/23/45. Thereafter we visited them every year from wherever we lived; Siler City, NC, Mullins, SC, Chattanooga, TN or Durham, NC.

My Mom and I lived in WV after I was born on 01/23/45 in Winston-Salem, NC. She stayed in WV while my Dad (Ralph Sr.) served in WWII where he was reported "Missing in Action". This was after being wounded in his left arm trying to cross the Elbe River heading to Berlin before General Eisenhower decided to stop at the Elbe River and let the Russians go into Berlin first. This later was considered by historians as a mistake and was one reason for the resulting "Cold War".

Dad survived his wound from a machine gunner firing from the other side that ripped his raincoat off and could have cut him in two. But here God saw fit for him to live, return home after he was taken as a Prisoner of War for several months at the end of the war. The recollection below is not my words but it is about what we simply called an Out House. Ours was not very fancy and was only a one holer, so as a small child you had to hang on tight and not fall through the large hole.

**Here is a great recollection of a bygone era from......
someone else.**

> One of my bygone recollections
> As I recall the days of yore
> Is the little house, behind the house,
> With the crescent over the door.
> Twas a place to sit and ponder
> With your head bowed down low;
> Knowing that you wouldn't be there,
> If you didn't have to go.
> Ours was a three-holer,
> With a size for everyone.
> You left there feeling better,
> After your usual job was done.
> You had to make these frequent trips
> Whether snow, rain, sleet, or fog-
> To the little house where you usually
> Found the Sears-Roebuck catalog.
> Oft times in dead of winter,
> The seat was covered with snow.
> Twas then with much reluctance,
> To the little house you'd go.
> With a swish you'd clear the seat,
> Bend low, with dreadful fear
> You'd blink your eyes and grit your teeth
> As you settled on your rear.
> I recall the day that Grandpa,

who stayed with us one summer
Made a trip to the shanty
Which proved to be a hummer.
Twas the same day my Dad
Finished painting the kitchen green
He'd just cleaned up the mess he made
With rags and gasoline.
He tossed the rags in the shanty hole
And went on his usual way
Not knowing that by doing so
He would eventually rue the day.
Now Grandpa had an urgent call,
I never will forget!!!
This trip he made to the little house
Lingers in my memory yet.
He sat down on the shanty seat,
With both feet on the floor.
Then filled his pipe with tobacco
And struck a match on the outhouse door.
After the Tobacco began to glow,
 He slowly raised his rear:
Tossed the flaming match in the open hole,
with no sign of fear.
The Blast that followed, I am sure
Was heard for miles around;
And there was poor ol' Grandpa
just sitting on the ground.
The smoldering pipe was still in his mouth,
His suspenders he held tight;
The celebrated three-holer
Was blown clear out of sight.
When we asked him what had happened,
His answer I'll never forget.
He thought it must be something
That he had recently et!
Next day we had a new one

Which my Dad built with ease.
With a sign on the entrance door
Which read: No Smoking, Please!
Now that's the end of the story,
With memories of long ago,
Of the little house, behind the house
Where we went cause we had to go!

THINGS THAT I FOUND HELPFUL BY LIVING THIS LONG

The purpose of fighting is to win.

The sword is more important than the shield, and skill is more important than either.

The final weapon is the brain. All else is supplemental.

Don't pick a fight with an old man. If he is too old to fight, he'll just kill you.

If you find yourself in a fair fight, your tactics suck.

I carry a gun because a cop is too heavy.

When seconds count, the cops are just minutes away.

A reporter doing a human-interest piece on the Texas Rangers recognized the Colt Model 1911 the Ranger was carrying and asked him, "Why do you carry a 45?" The Ranger responded, "Because they don't make a 46"

The old sheriff was attending an awards dinner when a lady commented on his wearing his sidearm. "Sheriff, I see you have your pistol. Are you expecting trouble?" "No Ma'am. If I were expecting trouble, I would have brought my shotgun."

Beware the man who only carries one gun: HE PROBABLY KNOWS HOW TO USE IT!!! I was once asked by a lady visiting if I had a gun in the house. I said I did. She said "Well I certainly hope it isn't loaded!" To which I said, "Of course it is loaded, it can't work without bullets!" She then asked, "Are you that afraid of someone evil coming into your house?"

My reply was, "No not at all. I am not afraid of the house catching fire either, but I have fire extinguishers around, and they are all loaded too".

THOMAS JEFFERSON QUOTES:

Here are some examples of current situations in the USA in 2010 that clearly shows that Thomas Jefferson could very well be called a prophet:

When we get piled upon one another in large cities, as in Europe, we shall become as corrupt as Europe.** ** ** * Thomas Jefferson*

The democracy will cease to exist when you take away from those who are willing to work and give to those who would not.** * *Thomas Jefferson*

It is incumbent on every generation to pay its own debts as it goes. A principle which if acted on would save one-half the wars of the world.** * *Thomas Jefferson*

I predict future happiness for Americans if they can prevent the government from wasting the labors of the people under the pretense of taking care of them.****Thomas Jefferson*

My reading of history convinces me that most bad government results from too much government.* * *Thomas Jefferson*

No free man shall ever be debarred the use of arms.****Thomas Jefferson*

The strongest reason for the people to retain the right to keep and bear arms is, as a last resort, to protect themselves against tyranny in government. ****Thomas Jefferson*

The tree of liberty must be refreshed from time to time with the blood of patriots and tyrants.****Thomas Jefferson*

To compel a man to subsidize with his taxes the propagation of ideas which he disbelieves and abhors is sinful and tyrannical.*** *Thomas Jefferson**

Very Interesting Quote

In light of the present financial crisis, it's interesting to read what Thomas Jefferson said in **1802:** *

"'I believe that banking institutions are more dangerous to our liberties than standing armies. If the American people ever allow private banks to control the issue of their currency, first by inflation, then by deflation, the banks and corporations that will grow up around the banks will deprive the people of all property until their children wake-up homeless on the continent their fathers conquered."

TOMATOES AND CHEAP LABOR

This should make everyone think, be you Democrat, Republican or Independent

From a California school teacher - - -

"As you listen to the news about the student protests over illegal immigration, there are some things that you should be **aware** of:

I am in charge of the English-as-a-second-language department at a large southern California high school which is designated a Title 1 school, meaning that its students average lower socioeconomic and income levels

Most of the schools you are hearing about, South Gate High, Bell Gardens , Huntington Park , etc., where these students are protesting, are also Title 1 schools.

Title 1 schools are on the free breakfast and free lunch program. When I say free breakfast, I'm not talking a glass of milk and roll -- but a full breakfast and cereal bar with fruits and juices that would make a Marriott proud. The **waste** of this food is **monumental**, with trays and trays of it being **dumped in the trash uneaten.**

I estimate that well over 50% of these students are obese or at least moderately overweight. About 75% or more DO have cell phones. The school also provides day care centers for the unwed teenage pregnant girls (some as young as 13) so they can attend class without the inconvenience of having to arrange for babysitters or having family watch their kids.

I was ordered to spend $700,000 on my department or risk losing funding for the upcoming year even though there was little need for anything; my budget was already substantial. I ended up buying new computers for the computer learning center, half of which, one month later, have been carved with graffiti by the appreciative students who obviously feel humbled and grateful to have a free education in America ..

I have had to intervene several times for young and substitute teachers whose classes consist of many illegal immigrant students, here in the country less than 3 months, who raised so much hell with the female teachers, calling them "Putas" (whores) and throwing things, that the teachers were in tears.

Free medical, free education, free food, free day care etc., etc, etc. Is it **any** wonder they feel entitled to not only be in this country but to demand rights, privileges and entitlements?

To those who want to point out how much these illegal immigrants contribute to our society because they LIKE their gardener and housekeeper and they like to pay less for tomatoes: spend some time in the real world of illegal immigration and see the TRUE costs.

Higher insurance, medical facilities closing, higher medical costs, more crime, lower standards of education in our schools, overcrowding, new diseases. For me, I'll pay more for tomatoes.

Americans, We need to wake up.

It does, however, have everything to do with culture: It involves an American third-world culture that does not value education, that accepts children getting pregnant and dropping out of school by 15 and that refuses to assimilate, and an American culture that has become so weak and worried about "political correctness" that we don't have the will to do anything about it.

If this makes your blood boil, as it did mine, forward this to everyone you know.

CHEAP LABOR? Isn't that what the whole immigration issue is about?

Business doesn't want to pay a decent wage.

Consumers don't want expensive produce.

Government will tell you Americans don't want the jobs.

But the bottom-line is cheap labor. The phrase "cheap labor" is a myth, a farce, and a lie. There is no such thing as "cheap labor."

Take, for example, an illegal alien with a wife and five children. He takes a job for $5.00 or 6.00/hour. At that wage, with six dependents, he pays no income tax, yet at the end of the year, if he files an Income Tax Return, he gets an "earned income credit" of up to $3,200 free.

He qualifies for Section 8 housing and subsidized rent.

He qualifies for food stamps.

He qualifies for free (no deductible, no co-pay) health care.

His children get free breakfasts and lunches at school.

He requires bilingual teachers and books.

He qualifies for relief from high energy bills.

If they are, or become, aged, blind or disabled, they qualify for SSI. If qualified for SSI they can qualify for Medicaid. All of this is at (our) taxpayer's expense.

He doesn't worry about car insurance, life insurance, or homeowners insurance.

Taxpayers provide Spanish language signs, bulletins and printed material.

He and his family receive the equivalent of $20.00 to $30.00/hour in benefits.

Working Americans are lucky to have $5.00 or $6..00/hour left after paying their bills and his.

Cheap labor? YEAH RIGHT!

These Are The Questions We Should Be Addressing To The Congressional Members Of Either Party. 'And When They Lie To Us And Don't Do As They Say, We Should Replace Them.

Please pass this on to as many as possible. Immigration legislation is to be considered in 2010. This is important to working Americans, our economy and our American culture and heritage.

TIFFANYS AND FARTS

A lady walks into Tiffanys. She looks around, spots a beautiful diamond bracelet and walks over to inspect it.

As she bends over to look more closely, she unexpectedly farts. Very embarrassed, she nervously prays that a sales person was not anywhere near.

As she turns around, her worst nightmare materializes in the form of a salesman standing right behind her. Cool as a cucumber, he displays all of the qualities one would expect of a Tiffanys professional. Politely he greets the lady with,

Good day, Madam. How may we help you today?'

Blushing and uncomfortable, but still hoping that the salesman somehow missed her little 'incident', she asks, 'How much is this lovely bracelet?'

'Madam - if you farted just looking at it - you're going to sh-t when I tell you the price".

TIME- WE ALL HAVE THE SAME NUMBER HOURS EACH DAY ON EARTH

RWP2: I could have said this and really resemble the message below as I used to say: 68 and Still Great! Now 69 and Still Fine. That is almost as vain as Bill O'Rielly at Fox News? Now the other Ralph Peters from Warrenton, VA is a regular military analysis on Fox News and has written more books than I have fingers and toes. If I somehow got on Fox with O'Rielly's show, I have a plan. Just keep talking until the producer has to pull the plug on me.

You know... Time has a way of moving quickly and catching you unaware of the passing years. It seems just yesterday that I was young, just married and embarking on my new life with my mate. Yet in a way, it seems like eons ago, and I wonder where all the years went. I know that I lived them all. I have glimpses of how it was back then and of all my hopes and dreams.

But, here it is... The winter of my life and it catches me by surprise... How did I get here so fast? Where did the years go and where did my youth go? I remember well seeing older people through the years and thinking that those older people were years away from me and that winter was so far off that I could not fathom it or imagine fully what it would be like.

But, here it is... My friends are retired and getting grey... They move slower and I see an older person now. Some are in better and some worse shape than me... But, I see the great change... Not like the ones that I remember who were young and vibrant... But, like me, their age is beginning to show and we are now those older folks that we used to see and never thought we'd be. Each day now, I find that just getting a shower is a real target for the day! And taking a nap is not a treat anymore... it's mandatory! Cause if I don't on my own free will... I just fall asleep where I sit!

And so... Now I enter into this new season of my life unprepared for all the aches and pains and the loss of strength and ability to go and do things that I wish I had done but never did!! But, at least I know, that though the winter has come, and I'm not sure how long it will last...

This I know, that when it's over on this earth... It's over. A new adventure will begin!

Yes, I have regrets. There are things I wish I hadn't done... Things I should have done, but indeed, there are many things I'm happy to have done. It's all in a lifetime.

So, if you're not in your winter yet... Let me remind you, that it will be here faster than you think. So, whatever you would like to accomplish in your life please do it quickly! Don't put things off too long!! Life goes by quickly. So, do what you can today, as you can never be sure whether this is your winter or not! You have no promise that you will see all the seasons of your life... So, live for today and say all the things that you want your loved ones to remember... And hope that they appreciate and love you for all the things that you have done for them in all the years past!! "Life" is a gift to you. The way you live it is your gift to those who come after. Make it a fantastic one.

LIVE IT WELL! ENJOY TODAY! DO SOMETHING FUN! BE HAPPY! HAVE A GREAT DAY! Remember: "It is health that is real wealth and not pieces of gold and silver.

LIVE HAPPY IN 2013!:::::>2020

LASTLY, CONSIDER THE FOLLOWING: TODAY IS THE OLDEST YOU'VE EVER BEEN, YET THE YOUNGEST YOU'LL EVER BE, SO ENJOY THIS DAY WHILE IT LASTS.

~Your kids are becoming you...... But your grandchildren are perfect!

~Going out is good... Coming home is better!

~You forget names.... But it's OK because other people forgot they even knew you!!!

~You realize you're never going to be really good at anything... especially golf.

~The things you used to care to do, you no longer care to do, but you really do care that you don't care to do them anymore.

~You sleep better on a lounge chair with the TV blaring than in bed. It's called "pre-sleep".

~You miss the days when everything worked with just an "ON" and "OFF" switch..

~You tend to use more 4 letter words ... "what?"..."when?"... ???

~Now that you can afford expensive jewelry, it's not safe to wear it anywhere.

~You notice everything they sell in stores is "sleeveless"?!!!

~What used to be freckles are now liver spots.

~Everybody whispers.

~You have 3 sizes of clothes in your closet.... Two of which you'll never wear.

~But Old is good in some things: Old Songs, Old movies, and best of all, OLD FRIENDS!!

Stay well, "OLD FRIEND!" Send this on to other "Old Friends!" and let them laugh in AGREEMENT!!!

It's Not What You Gather, But What You Scatter That Tells What Kind Of Life You Have Lived.

TEN THINGS HIGHLY PRODUCTIVE PEOPLE DON'T DO

1. They don't wait till they feel motivated, they just do it

"Amateurs sit and wait for inspiration, the rest of us just get up and go to work." Stephen King

Your ability to do things when you don't feel like it defines how much you get paid at the end of the week/month.

Life is not always a great experience. Many times bad moods are uncontrollable. That's why the skill of neglecting your bad mood, and putting your feelings aside while working is an important skill if you want to be super productive and get a lot of tasks done in a short period of time.

2. They don't run without a plan

Knowing where you're heading is half the way there. Productive people know this well and that's why they plan almost everything.

They are clear about what they want and how they can reach it which leaves them with a sense of relaxation and confidence in their ability to achieve what they want.

3. They don't sabotage themselves

Even when they wake up late, procrastinate or feel lazy (they're humans too), they don't beat themselves up. They just work hard and in the end they feel good about themselves.

4. They are not realistic when it comes to their abilities

When it comes to your own skills and expectations; it's better to be an illusionist than being modest or realistic. Successful people and high achievers are overconfident of their abilities. They believe that they can achieve anything and expect the very best to come. This is very important in order to be productive.

Holding such beliefs about yourself will make you (even if you are the laziest person on earth) tend to take actions in order to justify your own beliefs. It will lower your resistance against hard work.

If you feel incompetent, simply ask yourself if holding such a belief has ever helped you. If not get rid of it and get a new belief because at the end of the day a wrong belief that makes you feel good is far better than a more realistic one that makes you feel incompetent.

5. They don't leave the biggest tasks till the end

Super productive people have the habit of starting with their most important/hardest task which makes their life easier for the rest of the day and gives them an extra boost of confidence.

High productive people tend to let go of being control freaks and accept the idea that they don't have to do everything on their own. They do what nobody else can do for them but they outsource or **delegate the rest to people** who can manage these tasks. Thus they have extra time to focus on their life and personal growth.

6. They avoid all kinds of interruptions

It's hard to be productive when you keep getting distracted. To be productive, you must avoid anything that gets you out of your mental flow and focus more on getting things done fast. Turn off your phone, close your internet browser and your bedroom/office door that's the best way to concentrate and be more effective and productive.

7. They don't start without a deadline

A deadline will make you run faster and gives you a sense of urgency. Try setting even shorter ones. This alone could double up your productivity.

8. They don't change their routine

Why change a winning plan?

9. They don't multitask

It has been said,: **"Your brain, my brain and everyone's brain is not designed for multitasking"**. Focus on one thing at a time and you will get things done faster and be more effective.

U.

U.S. ON ALERT FOR NUCLEAR BLAST OVERHEAD: PRAY THIS NOT ACCURATE!

'Space launch vehicle' could put kill electric grid, devastate nation.

WASHINGTON – U.S. officials quietly are expressing concern that North Korea could use its "space launch vehicle" to explode a high-altitude nuclear device over the United States, creating an electromagnetic pulse that would destroy major portions of the U.S. electrical grid system as well as the nation's critical infrastructures.

The concern is so great that U.S. officials who watch North Korea closely are continually monitoring the status of the North Korean "space launch vehicle," whose status could suggest a pre-emptive nuclear strike against the United States.

Want to know the full impact of an EMP? Click here to read more about WND's newest book: "A Nation Forsaken – EMP: The Escalating Threat of an American Catastrophe."

They are aware of the three-stage missile North Korea launched last December that also orbited a "package," which experts say could be a test to orbit a nuclear weapon that then would be deorbited on command anywhere over the U.S. and exploded at a high altitude, creating an EMP effect.

This concern is in addition to North Korea's latest threat to strike targets in Hawaii and the continental U.S., as well as possible attacks against U.S. bases in South Korea and Japan.

The 28-year-old North Korean leader, Kim Jong-un, has signed an order for North Korea's strategic rocket forces to be on standby to fire at U.S. targets.

The signing was against a photo backdrop following an emergency meeting of his senior military leaders showing large maps that were labeled "U.S. mainland strike plan, specifically at Hawaii, Washington, D.C., Los Angeles and Austin, Texas."

One WND reader who traced the targeting to Texas said that it really was aimed at the Dallas/Fort Worth area.

THIS is how an EMP event could bring the world's remaining superpower to its knees. Read it in "A Nation Forsaken".

The latest North Korean threats occurred after the U.S. sent two B-2 stealth bombers to strike targets with inert bombs during joint U.S.-South Korean military exercises, which Kim considered a major provocation.

"He finally signed the plan on technical preparations of strategic rockets, ordering them to be on standby to fire so that they may strike any time the U.S. mainland, its military bases in the operational theaters in the Pacific, including Hawaii and Guam, and those in South Korea," according to a statement by the North Korean news agency, KCNA.

The statement added that the B-2 flights showed Washington's "hostile" intent, and the "reckless" act had gone "beyond the phase of threat and blackmail."

In response, U.S. Secretary of Defense Chuck Hagel condemned North Korea's actions which to date have included dissolving the 1953 armistice between North and South Korea, severing the military hotline with South Korea and putting its artillery forces on high alert and threatening, once again, nuclear strikes against the U.S. In recent weeks, North Korea also had released three videos showing a nuclear strike on the U.S.

"We've made very clear that we have the capability and willingness to protect our interests and our allies in the region," according to deputy White House press secretary Josh Earnest. He said that the U.S. military exercises with South Korea should offer "pretty clear evidence" that the U.S. can defend its interests and those of its allies in the region.

Sources say that sending the B-2s was in response to the recent North Korean threats to send a message – a message which Russia and China called a "provocative act." Russia and China have asked the U.S. to continue talking to North Korea and not to take military action against North Korea.

In response to North Korea's initial bellicose rhetoric, Hagel ordered the deployment of additional Aegis anti-missile systems for the U.S. West Coast. They originally were destined for Europe. And a second anti-ballistic missile radar is to be installed in Japan. However, the Aegis anti-missile systems won't be operational until 2017, although there are some systems already deployed along the West Coast.

North Korea's continuing threats of a pre-emptive nuclear strike against U.S. targets suggest to U.S. officials that its military is confident in the capability of its missiles and that its recent nuclear testing for miniaturization of a warhead to be placed on a missile similarly was successful. These officials are looking at the prospect that upon launch of the missile and a potential nuclear payload, it would take a polar path, clearly out of range of U.S. Aegis anti-missile systems.

The fact that U.S. military officials are expressing quiet but increasing concern that North Korea could launch an EMP attack has raised alarms over the preservation of the U.S. national grid and such critical infrastructures as communications, energy, food and water delivery and space systems. This concern recently has been reinforced by a little-publicized study by the U.S. Army War College that said a nuclear detonation at altitude above a U.S. city could wipe out the electrical grid for hundreds, possibly thousands of miles around.

The impact would be catastrophic. "Preparing for months without a commercial source of clean water (city water pressure is often dependent on electric pumping to storage towers) and stoppage of sewage treatment facilities will require net methods of survival particularly in populated areas," the military study said. The May 2011 study, titled, "In the Dark: Military Planning for a Catastrophic Critical Infrastructure Event," concluded that there is "very little" in the way of backup capability to the electric grid upon which the communications infrastructure is vitally dependent.

Analysts say that it is apparent that Kim has ignored any advice from its closest friend, China, to stop any further missile or nuclear testing suggesting, as one official described Kim, as a "loose cannon." Kim also has been defiant of any United Nations Security Council resolutions similarly condemning the recent missile and nuclear tests. China had joined in approving those resolutions. "The time has come to settle accounts with the U.S.," the KCNA agency declared.

"The Obama administration is either clueless or deceiving the American people with false assurances that North Korea's recent threats to destroy the United States are merely 'empty rhetoric' because they allegedly 'lack the capability,'" one former U.S. official told WND. Some regional analysts, however, believe that Kim is seeking to leverage the U.S. for further concessions while attempting to win favor with his own military to show how tough he can be.

These analysts say that until now Kim has not had the support from the military that his father, Kim Jong-Il, had. His war-like tone may be indicative of attempts to solidify military support within his country. At the moment, experts are looking at efforts for preparations at known long-range missile launch sites. Those signs may be appearing.

"North Korea's launch sites to fire off mid- and long-range missiles have recently shown increased movement of vehicles and forces," according to one South Korean official who described the activity at the sites as "brisk." "We are closely watching possibilities of missile launches," the official said. In this connection, officials have seen several vehicles moving to the Tongchang-ri missile site on the western coast, in what appeared to them to be preparations for testing its long-range missiles. Some observers, however, believe the latest threats of a pre-emptive nuclear strike against the U.S. remain for now just domestic posturing and efforts to establish military credentials on Kim's part to show that he is more forceful than his father.

In other efforts to determine warnings and indications of an attack, analysts are looking for major troop movements, although none has been detected to date. Late last week, a North Korean Mig-21 fighter jet flew near South Korea's front line airspace, known as the Tactical Action Line, but returned to base, according to a South Korean military official. In response, the South Koreans scrambled a KF-16 fighter. The TAL is the point between 20 and 50 kilometers north of South Korean airspace that will prompt the South Korea to scramble its fighter jets.

V.

VERSE

DAILY VERSE
When pride comes, then comes disgrace,
but with humility comes wisdom.
Proverbs 11:2
DAILY QUOTE
If you are humble, nothing will touch you, neither praise nor
disgrace, because you know what you are. **Mother Teresa**
DAILY THOUGHT

The sin of pride can be hard to define. Arrogance can be part of
it, yes; but it's possible to have both pride and poor self-image
at work in one's life at the same time. God doesn't want us to
lack self-respect, either. Maybe it's best simply to be ever aware
that all of us are vulnerable to vain pride and that it can find us
at anytime, anywhere.

Pride says, "I can do what I want," "I'm better than others," and
"I'm looking out for number one." Above all, pride says, "I don't
need God or anyone—I can make it on my own." But of course
we do need God. And when we resist surrendering to Him,
depending on Him, we experience damage to our souls.

Fortunately, we can resist our pride by simply praying and
asking God to heal us from a prideful attitude and help us think
rightly about ourselves, God, and others. When that happens,
we can rest content in God's will and at peace with ourselves
and those around us.

*Lord, please heal me of a vain pride and set me in right relationship
with You. Amen.*

VETERANS ARE THE REAL "1 PERCENTERS"

RWP2: III Percenters in the Revolutionary War were the 3% of the population that actually took up arms against the British.

Commentary By: Bruce Klingner, a senior research fellow for Northeast Asia at The Heritage Foundation's Asian Studies Center, spent 20 years in the intelligence community working at the CIA and Defense Intelligence Agency. Read his research

Mentioning "1 percenters" conjures up images of protest and class warfare. But there is another 1 percent who is beyond politics: the men and women who serve in America's armed forces, as well as the veterans who served before them. Despite over a decade of ceaseless war against terrorism, less than 1 percent of the U.S. population has been on active duty.

A smaller share of Americans now serves in the military than at any point since the era between World Wars I and II, according to a Pew Research study. In 1975, 70 percent of members of

Congress had military service. Today, only 20 percent do. Thankfully, we live in a time where we at least have a culture that appreciates our veterans.

After Desert Storm, it became fashionable again to appreciate and praise the U.S. military. Gone was the stigma of Vietnam, when returning service members didn't wear uniforms in public lest they be spit on or called baby-killers? No longer would our service members suffer the disparagement that Rudyard Kipling wrote of, "For its Tommy this, and Tommy that, and 'Chuck him out, the brute!'" But it's "'Savior of his country' when the guns begin to shoot."

The heinous attacks on 9/11 resurrected the flame of patriotism that had faded in the hearts of so many Americans. Flags resting dormant in closets came back out to be displayed proudly and demand for new flags skyrocketed. The nation came together in a way not seen since Pearl Harbor—first in grief, then in resolve.

We saw acts of selfless courage, first by firefighters and police officers risking their lives to give aid, then by service members who sallied forth into harm's way to impose retribution for the attack. Even when people criticized the wars in Iraq and Afghanistan, they still praised the men and women who volunteered to serve in the military.

"Thank you for your service" seems such a pitifully inadequate acknowledgement of gratitude and respect for someone who spends months away from their loved ones, who endure hardships and dangers that ordinary people shirk from. And what can one offer to the families of those who gave the last full measure of devotion by sacrificing their lives to defend us?

We who benefit from their service should honor it by urging our government to provide the funding to enable the military to carry out its missions. And provide the medical care for those returning home wounded in body and spirit. From the old veterans bent with age to the young men now hunched over in a cold, dark foxhole, perhaps you can stand a little straighter today, knowing our nation is forever indebted to you. As George Orwell wrote, "People sleep peaceably in their beds at night only because rough men stand ready to do violence on their behalf."

So to my father and my son—both U.S. Marines—and to all the other men and women who ever put on our country's uniform, I humbly and respectfully thank you for unfailingly standing your post on the ramparts in order to keep us safe.

W.

WE WILL NOT FORGET: YOU MUST READ THIS ONE!

Subject: Fwd: From a Major Airline Captain...YES YOU MUST READ THIS ONE..!!

My lead flight attendant came to me and said, "We have an H.R. on this flight." (H.R. stands for human remains.)

"Are they military?" I asked.

'Yes', she said.

'Is there an escort?' I asked.

'Yes, I've already assigned him a seat'.

'Would you please tell him to come to the Flight Deck. You can board him early," I said...

A short while later a young army sergeant entered the flight deck. He was the image of the perfectly dressed soldier. He introduced himself and I asked him about his soldier.

The escorts of these fallen soldiers talk about them as if they are still alive and still with us. 'My soldier is on his way back to Virginia ,' he said. He proceeded to answer my questions, but offered no words.

I asked him if there was anything I could do for him and he said no. I told him that he had the toughest job in the military, and that I appreciated the work that he does for the families of our fallen soldiers. The first officer and I got up out of our seats to shake his hand. He left the Flight Deck to find his seat.

We completed our preflight checks, pushed back and performed an uneventful departure. About 30 minutes into our flight, I received a call from the lead flight attendant in the cabin.

'I just found out the family of the soldier we are carrying, is also on board', she said. She then proceeded to tell me that the father, mother, wife and 2-year old daughter were escorting their son, husband, and father home. The family was upset because they were unable to see the container that the soldier was in before we left.

We were on our way to a major hub at which the family was going to wait four hours for the connecting flight home to Virginia . The father of the soldier told the flight attendant that knowing his son was below him in the cargo compartment and being unable to see him was too much for him and the family to bear. He had asked the flight attendant if there was anything that could be done to allow them to see him upon our arrival. The family wanted to be outside by the cargo door to watch the soldier being taken off the airplane.

I could hear the desperation in the flight attendants voice when she asked me if there was anything I could do. 'I'm on it', I said. I told her that I would get back to her.

Airborne communication with my company normally occurs in the form of e-mail like messages. I decided to bypass this system and contact my flight dispatcher directly on a secondary radio. There is a radio operator in the operations control center who connects you to the telephone of the dispatcher. I was in direct contact with the dispatcher. I explained the situation I had on board with the family and what it was the family wanted. He said he understood and that he would get back to me.

Two hours went by and I had not heard from the dispatcher. We were going to get busy soon and I needed to know what to tell the family. I sent a text message asking for an update. I saved the return message from the dispatcher and the following is the text:

'Captain, sorry it has taken so long to get back to you. There is policy on this now, and I had to check on a few things. Upon your arrival a dedicated escort team will meet the aircraft. The team will escort the family to the ramp and plane side. A van will be used to load the remains with a secondary van for the family.

The family will be taken to their departure area and escorted into the terminal, where the remains can be seen on the ramp. It is a private area for the family only. When the connecting aircraft arrives, the family will be escorted onto the ramp and plane side to watch the remains being loaded for the final leg home.

Captain, most of us here in flight control are veterans. Please pass our condolences on to the family. Thanks.

I sent a message back, telling flight control thanks for a good job. I printed out the message and gave it to the lead flight attendant to pass on to the father. The lead flight attendant was very thankful and told me, 'You have no idea how much this will mean to them.'

Things started getting busy for the descent, approach and landing. After landing, we cleared the runway and taxied to the ramp area. The ramp is huge with 15 gates on either side of the alleyway. It is always a busy area with aircraft maneuvering every which way to enter and exit. When we entered the ramp and checked in with the ramp controller, we were told that all traffic was being held for us.

'There is a team in place to meet the aircraft', we were told. It looked like it was all coming together, then I realized that once we turned the seat belt sign off, everyone would stand up at once and delay the family from getting off the airplane. As we approached our gate, I asked the copilot to tell the ramp controller, we were going to stop short of the gate to make an announcement to the passengers. He did that and the ramp controller said, 'Take your time.'

I stopped the aircraft and set the parking brake. I pushed the public address button and said: 'Ladies and gentleman, this is your Captain speaking: I have stopped short of our gate to make a special announcement. We have a passenger on board who deserves our honor and respect. His Name is Private XXXXXX, a soldier who recently lost his life. Private XXXXXX is under your feet in the cargo hold. Escorting him today is Army Sergeant XXXXXXX. Also, on board are his father, mother, wife, and daughter. Your entire flight crew is asking for all passengers to remain in their seats to allow the family to exit the aircraft first. Thank you.'

We continued the turn to the gate, came to a stop and started our shutdown procedures. A couple of minutes later I opened the cockpit door. I found the two forward flight attendants crying, something you just do not see. I was told that after we came to a stop, every passenger on the aircraft stayed in their seats, waiting for the family to exit the aircraft.

When the family got up and gathered their things, a passenger slowly started to clap his hands. Moments later, more passengers joined in and soon the entire aircraft was clapping. Words of 'God Bless You', I'm sorry, thank you, be proud, and other kind words were uttered to the family as they made their way down the aisle and out of the airplane. They were escorted down to the ramp to finally be with their loved one.

Many of the passengers disembarking thanked me for the announcement I had made. They were just words, I told them, I could say them over and over again, but nothing I say will bring back that brave soldier.

I know everyone who reads this will have tears in their eyes, including me. **RWP2: Me Too!!**

I respectfully ask that all of you reflect on this event and the sacrifices that millions of our men and women have made to ensure our freedom and safety in these United States of AMERICA.

Thank you all who have served, or are serving. ***We Will not forget!!!!***

WHAT BUBBA KNOWS: THE RIGHT SIDE OF THE ISSUES

There are those among us who would argue that we are in the midst of a second American revolution – a revolution to reject and discard conservative values and principles, our Constitution, and our freedoms. Those instigating the revolution, however, will not declare their full intentions until they are convinced that they have a virtual stranglehold on our country. To do otherwise, would be to awaken a sleeping giant.

And so, the time is now - for American conservatives and Tea Party patriots to awaken the giant. Yes, some successes are clearly visible, particularly in terms of recent election results and in the prospects for further election victories for conservatives in November. But mere voting will not suffice if we fail to address the complacency that allowed this cancerous revolution to grow in the first place. It exists not only in government, but more importantly, in our schools and our media. It is time to awaken America from its self-induced stupor of apathy. It is time for all freedom-loving Americans to pay attention to the world around them, to become better informed, and to take personal responsibility for maintaining our freedom.

We cannot afford to assume that good, honest people will guide our country as they have for the better part of 234 years. We cannot afford for people to turn off their listening to politics, whether it be for lack of understanding, lack of interest, or desire to avoid confrontation. We cannot afford to bypass voting in seemingly unimportant local and primary elections. We cannot afford a reliance upon 'the other guy' to serve in public roles or to be advocates for various issues. We cannot afford to blindly accept the biased drivel of liberal hacks in the media. And we cannot afford to allow the increasingly liberal influence in academia to destroy the learning and moral fiber of our children. We must understand what we believe in, take ownership for its manifestation and survival, and share information that furthers the success of that survival.

Obama's writing frequently about the liberal hijacking of our present society, I am often puzzled by so many pundits who have tiptoed around the use of definable terms such as socialist, Marxist, communist, collectivist, etc. Even in the 2008 presidential primaries and general elections, the closest most candidates or pundits would get to defining Obama was the 's-word'. Is it some McCarthy-like phobia that prevents the application of an all-to-accurate label describing a left-winger's ideology? We know that leftist political candidates shun the 'liberal' label – it's a known negative connotation to the majority of Americans. More recently, many lefties such as Obama and Hillary have donned the 'progressive' label. And thanks to our friend, Glenn Beck, that will soon likely become a new curse for politicians.

But why has there been such a hesitancy use to the 'communist' and 'Marxist' labels? To their credit, Beck, Levin, and Rush flirt with both of these labels, but this video by Victoria Jackson leaves little doubt and is much more than a hoot – it's a clarion call to all the sleepy-eyed, apathetic Americans who think the Obama/Pelosi/Reid triumvirate and all the socialist minions in Congress are a harmless, passing fad.

It's also a wakeup call for all Democrats who let their party loyalty create such a blind spot that they can't differentiate 'Hopey/Changey' slogans from Marxist ideology and who can't recognize a communist when they're spewing their propaganda right in front of them, lying through their teeth with every breath, and steadily, intentionally causing the collapse of our economy and freedoms.

Certainly, this video is not going to change minds on its own merit. One must also have been paying attention to the continual barrage of Obama's Marxist messages/actions and his cadre of radical associates and influences. Consider the following:

- The manifestation of Obama's collectivist doctrine of transformation in our schools. Glenn Beck's March 5th episode brought Obama's tactics into clear focus. A champion of freedom does not belittle the knowledge and influence of the parents nor subjugate their role in raising children to that of the state.

- His infamous SEIU address where he reaches into his oratorical bag of tricks for what Harry Reid would likely describe as his 'ghetto dialect' – and proceeds to offer a freedom-threatening, narcissistic message to his following of union goons on how he will overthrow this country.

- His pre-election proclamation that we are "five days away from fundamentally transforming America". It was not a promise of fighting for freedom and opportunity – it was a threat of chains and control.

- His insistence to undertake unfathomable debt – debt that no reasonable person would ever mimic in their personal finances and debt to which only a person who is hell-bent on collapsing our economy would aspire.

- His insistence to urgently pass a massive 'stimulus' bill that to this date remains largely unspent and exists as a convenient slush fund for his pet projects and 'negotiations'/bribes.

- His desire to reduce our nuclear defenses and to remove defensive shields in Eastern Europe.

- His gracious, unapologetic acceptance of a book from avowed Marxist Hugo Chavez – a true patriotic leader would have simply said "No thank you." and turned away.

- Apologizing for America's successes, our Exceptionalism, and our foundation of Christianity.

- Lying to shun the use of a 51-vote majority – except when it's convenient to pass healthcare legislation that the majority of the country opposes – to call it democracy in action, but conveniently forgetting that **we are not just a democracy, but a democratic republic.** He refuses to acknowledge the majority opposition in this country to his proposal to destroy healthcare and grow the government.

- His appointments of numerous communists and extreme leftists to his administration.

- His preference in school to associate with the Marxist professors.

- **His mentoring by communist Frank Marshall Davis** and his association with such societal deviates, radicals, and criminals such as William Ayers, Jeremiah Wright, Rashid Khalidi, and Tony Rezko.

True to his history, beliefs, and associations, Obama has left a trail of Marxist stains at every turn in his presidency. And to that minority of people who actually recognize and subscribe to the radical transformation that this president is attempting to impose upon us, be aware that those of us who cherish our country, our freedoms, and our Constitution are prepared to defend them with every ounce of energy and commitment that we can muster.

But we must act with determination now. This is not a mere contest of ideologies nor of compatible belief systems that can survive through bipartisanship – rather, this is a battle for the survival and control of our nation. And make no mistake about it, we will defeat whosoever gets in the way – one way or another.

WHEN WILL THE CHURCH TAKE A STAND FOR AMERICA?

March 27, 2010 from <u>Randy's Right</u> by Randy Dye

For months many of us have been perplexed by the refusal of the church to acknowledge the dire situation our nation is facing. Please understand, I hold the evangelical church in high regard. I believe it is passionate about introducing a lost world to the love of Christ and the salvation available through Him alone. So I just can't conceive of how it can remain silent at such a crucial time in our nation's history.

Our country is about to implode. Our currency is about to collapse. Corruption is rampant. Tyranny is at our doorstep. Violence is about to erupt. We are about to lose our freedoms. Potentially even our religious freedom. Quite simply, we will not make it without God. Yet, in this time of darkness, the church has remained inexplicably silent. Why?

Below is an article expressing the frustration many people have been feeling. It is a harsh article (admittedly too harsh), but the overall logic can't be refuted. Will the church ever take a stand on issues facing this nation? Will it ever denounce the ACLU's relentless attacks on men and women of faith? Will it ever stand up for Israel?

Will it ever scream "Heck, No!" to any attempt at taxpayer-funded abortion in the HC bill, Medicaid, or the Mexico City policy? **Will the church ever so much as simply PRAY for our nation?** I encourage you to read this article, and share it with your pastors: http://www.sodahead.com/united-states/prissy-pastors/blog-285703/

Please, pray for America, and encourage your pastor to issue an urgent call to prayer as well. We desperately need the church to acknowledge what is happening in America, to pray fervently, and to take a stand. The nightmare unfolding in our nation can no longer be ignored.

The **good news** is, regardless of the church's current inaction, Christians (as individuals) across this nation **are** praying:

- The now-famous verse, 2 Chronicles 7:14, has been sent through cyberspace repeatedly.

- Even self-proclaimed "not-very-religious" people are starting to pray.

- Faith-based political organizations are banding together to hold a prayer rally on May 1st at the Lincoln Memorial. They are appropriately calling this event "**May Day**" http://www.mayday2010.org/.

- Family Research Council (a faith-based public policy organization) recently held a "prayer-cast".

- Glenn Beck (a Fox News Commentator, for Pete's Sake!) has been urging his listeners to get on their knees and pray for God's forgiveness and mercy on our nation. (Shouldn't we be hearing this message from the pulpit??)

- There is prayer coming from many different sources in our nation, and I would love to see it also coming from the church as well.

As you pray for America, **I will caution you that prayer alone will not save us**. According to 2 Chronicles 7:14, there are four (4) conditions that must be met for God to hear our prayers and heal our land:

"...if my people, who are called by my name, will humble themselves and pray and seek my face and turn from their wicked ways, then will I hear from heaven and will forgive their sin and will heal their land."

~ 2 Chronicles 7:14 (NIV)

Here are a few more verses every American should be familiar with:

"If at any time I announce that a nation or kingdom is to be uprooted, torn down and destroyed, and if that nation I warned repents of its evil, then I will relent and not inflict on it the disaster I had planned."

~ *Jeremiah 18:7-8 (NIV)* "But any nation who refuses to obey me will be uprooted and destroyed. I, the Lord, have spoken!"

~ *Jeremiah 12:17 (NLTv2)* The wicked will go down to the grave. This is the fate of all the nations who ignore God.

~ *Psalm 9:17 (NLTv2)* Seek the Lord while you can find him. Call on him now while he is near. Let the people turn from their wicked deeds...Yes, turn to our God, for he will abundantly pardon.

~ *Isaiah 55:6-7 (NLTv1)* In righteousness you will be established: Tyranny will be far from you; you will have nothing to fear. Terror will be far removed; it will not come near you.

~ *Isaiah 54:14 (NIV)* Righteousness exalts a nation,

~ *Proverbs 14:34a (NIV)* Even the familiar words of "*God Bless America*" now hold new meaning to us:

God bless America

Land that I love.--Stand beside her, **And guide her, Through the night With the light From above**

Pray for God's light to guide us through this night. Pray for His forgiveness, His guidance, and His power. Pray that it's not too late.

WHISTLE BLOWER MAGAZINE

JANUARY 2013 – THE FIRST MUSLIM PRESIDENT

It started when Bill Clinton was famously called "the first black president" – not because of his skin color, of course, but because he supposedly exemplified so many "black" qualities and attitudes.

Since Barack Obama has been president, he's been showered with many such accolades – most recently when Newsweek crowned him "The First Gay President" for his election-year abandonment of his opposition to same-sex marriage. But the elite media, to commemorate other Obama affinities and policy positions, have also dubbed him "The First Hispanic President," "The First Asian-American President," "The First Jewish President" – and even "The First Female President."

But there's one "first" label conspicuously absent from all the media homage paid to the 44th president – perhaps, ironically, because there's more truth to it than the press is comfortable admitting – and that's the title Whistleblower confers on Barack Obama in its blockbuster January 2013 issue: "THE FIRST MUSLIM PRESIDENT." Highlights of "THE FIRST MUSLIM PRESIDENT" include:

- "The first Muslim president" by David Kupelian, on why an adoring press crowns Obama with every title – except this one

- "Muslim-American author embraces Obama as 'My Muslim President'" – and reveals most Muslims she knows regard Obama as a "Muslim brother"

- "U.S. policy defending Shariah – not American citizens" by Clare Lopez, in which the 25-year CIA veteran blows the whistle on Obama's brazenly pro-jihad policies

- "Rep. Allen West: Benghazi a result of 'appeasement' of the Islamic world" – the courageous Florida congressman speaks his mind on the president's pro-Islamist foreign policy

WHITE GUILT IS DEAD

By Tom Adkins

www.Commonconservative.com

Look at my fellow conservatives! There they go, glumly shuffling along, depressed by the election aftermath. Not me. I am virtually euphoric. Do not get me wrong. I am not thrilled with America's flirtation with neo socialism. But, there is a massive silver lining in those magical clouds that lofted Barak Obama to the Presidency. For today, without a shred of intellectually legitimate opposition, I can loudly proclaim to America: The Era of White Guilt is over.

This seemingly impossible event occurred because the vast majority of white Americans did not give a fluff about skin color, and enthusiastically pulled the voting lever for a black man. Not just *any* black man. A very liberal black man who spent his early career race-hustling banks, praying in a racist church for 20 years, and actively worked with America-hating domestic terrorists. Wow! Some resume! Yet they made Barak Obama their leader. Therefore, as of Nov 4th, 2008, white guilt is dead.

For over a century, the millstone of white guilt hung around our necks, retribution for slave-owning predecessors. In the 60's, American liberals began yanking that millstone while sticking a fork in the eye of black Americans, exacerbating the racial divide to extort a socialist solution. But if a black man can become President, exactly what significant barrier is left?

The election of Barak Obama absolutely destroys the entire validation of liberal white guilt. The dragon is hereby slain.

So today, I am feeling a little uppity, if you will. From this day forward, my tolerance level for having my skin color hustled is now exactly ZERO. And it is time to clean house. No more Reverend Wright's God Damn America , Al Sharpton's Church of Perpetual Victimization , or Jesse Jackson's rainbow racism. Cornell West? You are a fraud. Go home. All those black studies programs that taught kids to hate whitey? You must now *thank* Whitey. And I want that on the final.

Congressional Black Caucus? Irrelevant. Maxine Waters? Shut up. ACORN? Outlawed. Black Panthers? Go home and pet your kitty. Black separatists? Find another nation that offers better dreams. Go ahead. I am waiting.

Gangsta rappers? Start praising America. Begin with the Pledge of Allegiance. And please no more Ebonics. Speak English, and who knows where you might end up? Oh, yeah, pull up your pants. Your underwear is showing. You look stupid.

To those Eurosnots who forged entire careers hating America. I am still waiting for the first black French President.

And let me offer an equal opportunity whupping. I have always despised lazy white people. Now, I can talk smack about lazy black people. You are poor because you quit school, did drugs, had three kids with three different fathers and refuse to work. So when you plop your Colt 45-swilling, Oprah watching butt on the couch and complain *Da Man is keeping me down,* allow me to inform you: Da Man is now black. You have no excuses.

No more quotas. No more handouts. No more stealing my money because someone's great-great-great-great grandparents suffered _actual_ pain and misery at the hands of people I have no relation to, and personally revile.

It is time to toss that massive, obsolete race-hustle machine upon the heap of the other stupid 60s ideas. Drag it over there, by wife swapping, next to dope smoking. Plenty of room right between free love and cop killing. Careful don't trip on streaking. There ya go, don't be gentle. Just dump it. Wash your hands. It is filthy.

In fact, Obama's ascension created a gargantuan irony. How can you sell class envy and American unfairness when you and your black wife went to Ivy League schools, got high-paying jobs, became millionaires, bought a mansion and got elected President? How unfair is that??? Now, like a delicious O'Henry tale, Obama's spread-the-wealth campaign rendered itself moot by its own victory! America is officially a meritocracy. Obama's election has validated American conservatism!

So, listen carefully _Wham!!!_

That is the sound of my foot kicking the door shut on the era of white guilt. The rites have been muttered, the carcass lowered, dirt shoveled, and tombstone erected. White guilt is dead and buried.

However, despite my glee, there is apparently one small, rabid bastion of American racism remaining. Black Americans voted 96% for Barak Obama. Hmmm. In a color-blind world, shouldn't that be 50-50? Tonight, every black person should ask forgiveness for their apparent racism and prejudice towards white people. Maybe it is time to start spreading the guilt around.

Amen!

WILL ROGERS:

From lariat to laughter

November 01, 2009

Robert H. Schuller

"I will instruct you and teach you in the way you should go; I will counsel you with my loving eye on you." – Psalm 32:8

One of the great men of American history is the legendary Will Rogers. His big ambition in life was to be a circus cowboy. He was finally given an opportunity to perform in New York but his whole career hinged on one trick—a lariat trick. He was so excited to be in New York and performing for a large audience where he hoped his rope trick would make him famous. But he was so nervous that he lost control at a peak point and got tangled up in his own lariat. Everybody laughed.

Instead of panicking, Will quipped, "Gettin' tangled up in a rope ain't so bad—unless it's 'round your neck!'" Everybody laughed again and again.

In making this mistake, Will Rogers discovered a new talent in himself—the ability to make people laugh. And that discovery changed his destiny.

What talents have you discovered in yourself? How did you discover them?

This excerpt was taken from the
"Power for Life Daily Devotional

WINNING THE RACE: BEYOND THE CRISIS IN BLACK AMERICA
BY RICHARD IVORY

In his book, *Winning the Race: Beyond the Crisis in Black America*, the Manhattan Institute Fellow John Mcwhorter writes: "When I hear someone say something along the lines of 'why do we have to be talking about race? Why can't we just be people and let that stuff alone', I hear someone who hasn't had the occasion to think hard about how the past effects the present."

Today there is no better example of this avoidance of "race talk" than in the Republican Party where the very mention of race is viewed with suspicion. Republicans, who hold such a view, tend to be what I call color blind Republicans. They feel that anyone who even mentions race is guilty of race baiting.

This sort of accusation is leveled even if the issue of race is relevant to the topic at hand. The color blind Republicans often clash ideologically with what might be called the race conscious Republicans, a group that when the facts suggest race has no problem mentioning it. The race conscious Republicans are always reluctant to mention race amongst the color blind Republicans for fear of being accused of playing the race card.

I believe that the color blind Republicans, while well-meaning put our Party at a disadvantage when speaking in urban settings. I am speaking specifically of things like police brutality, health disparities and incarceration rates for example.

By not factoring in race we leave ourselves outside of the debate and to a mostly ethnic audience we appear insensitive on a whole array of issues. In other words, many Republicans have only one weapon in their arsenal when debating any subject surrounding race: simply state that it doesn't exist!

Unlike Republicans, Liberals see issues of race under every nook and cranny with the net result being a Democratic Party that is perceived of as being more of an advocate on behalf of minorities. In theory, it would be nice if everyone did not see one's race, but in practice we know that this is not the case. We all notice other people's race! It is, however, what we perceive in that person after meeting him/her which determines a great deal about how we continue to view that person. The same argument can be made about class as it relates to the way we view people less educated than ourselves.

While most Republicans see the avoidance of race and of class as a good thing, the perception interpreted by a largely minority and poor people is one of avoidance. Many perceive that Republicans by virtue of not bringing up race or class by default are both racist and hostile towards the working class. The prevalent "color blind theory", hurts Republicans in our efforts to micro - target diverse communities in order to bring them into the fold.

The Republican Party was formed to battle the hate crimes perpetrated on the Black Community by Democrats. The entire debates surrounding slavery and post-war reconciliation were issues of race. The current topic is a bit ironic given that the Republican Party's origins were directly related to the issue of race. John Charles Frémont, who was the first candidate of the Republican Party for the office of President, surely felt that race was appropriate to speak on when he become the first presidential candidate to ever include race in his platform. Abraham Lincoln was clearly cognizant of race when during Reconstruction he implemented The Freedmen's Bureau to help freed slaves in their transition to freedom. And let's not forget that The Constitution was very much aware of race when on February 3, 1870, Republicans passed the first Civil Rights bill called the Fifteenth Amendment (Amendment XV) which prohibited any State from denying a citizen the right to vote based on "race, color, or previous condition of servitude" (i.e., slavery).

There is no assurance that Republicans will come to the same conclusions as Democrats about the cause and effect of any given scenario that involves race. As with anything there will be times where race is a huge factor and others where it will have no factor. But, by ignoring history and its overall impact on the events of the day, we Republicans lose the intellectual battle in promoting a better vision of assimilation for all Americans regardless of race.

The Republican Party in the past led the way in ensuring that blacks, who had been demoralized by the intuitions of slavery, became empowered citizens. There is no reason why the same Party, in today's society, can't reclaim that mantle again and lead a solution based movement "with race in mind" which helps to lead minorities out of poverty and into individual empowerment.

Richard Ivory is the Publisher and Founder, of Hip-HopRepublican.com, a blog that delves into urban issues from centrist perspective. Mr. Ivory is a political consultant who has worked on dozens of political campaigns around the country. He has worked for both the Republican National Committee and was the College outreach director for **Republican Youth Majority**. He is presently the founder of **The John Langston Forum** and is the College outreach director for **Republicans for Black Empowerment**

WISDOM OF COACHES

#1. At Georgia Southern, we don't cheat. That costs money and we don't have any." Erik Russell / Georgia Southern.

#2. 'After you retire, there's only one big event left... And I ain't ready for that.' - Bobby Bowden / Florida State

#3. 'The man who complains about the way the ball bounces is likely to be the one who dropped it.' - Lou Holtz / Arkansas

#4. 'When you win, nothing hurts.' - Joe Namath / Alabama

#5. 'Motivation is simple. You eliminate those who are not motivated.' - Lou Holtz / Arkansas

#6. 'If you want to walk the heavenly streets of gold, you gotta know the password: 'Roll, Tide, Roll!'' - Bear Bryant / Alabama

#7. 'A school without football is in danger of deteriorating into a medieval study hall.' - Frank Leahy / Notre Dame

#8. 'There's nothing that cleanses your soul like getting the hell kicked out of you.' - Woody Hayes / Ohio State

#9. 'I don't expect to win enough games to be put on NCAA probation. I just want to win enough to warrant an investigation.' - Bob Devaney / Nebraska

#10. 'In Alabama , an atheist is someone who doesn't believe in Bear Bryant.' - Wally Butts / Georgia

#11. 'You can learn more character on the two-yard line than anywhere else in life.' - Paul Dietzel / LSU

#12. 'It's kind of hard to rally around a math class.' - Bear Bryant / Alabama

#13. When asked if Fayetteville was the end of the world. 'No, but you can see it from here.' - Lou Holtz / Arkansas ...

#14. 'I make my practices real hard because if a player is a quitter, I want him to quit in practice, not in a game.' - Bear Bryant / Alabama

#15. 'There's one sure way to stop us from scoring - give us the ball near the goal line.' - Matty Bell / SMU

#16. 'Lads, you're not to miss practice . . . .unless your parents died or you died.' - Frank Leahy / Notre Dame

#17. 'I never graduated from Iowa , but I was only there for two terms - Truman's and Eisenhower's.' - Alex Karras / Iowa

#18. 'My advice to defensive players: Take the shortest route to the ball and arrive in a bad humor.' - Bowden Wyatt / Tennessee

#19. 'I could have been a Rhodes Scholar, except for my grades.' - Duffy Daugherty / Michigan State

#20. 'Always remember . . . .Goliath was a 40 point favorite over David.' - Shug Jordan / Auburn

#21. 'They cut us up like boarding house pie. And that's real small pieces.' - Darrell Royal / Texas

#22. 'Show me a good and gracious loser, and I'll show you a failure.' - Knute Rockne / Notre Dame

#23. 'They whipped us like a tied up goat.' - Spike Dykes / TexasTech

#24. 'I asked Darrell Royal, the coach of the Texas Longhorns, why he didn't recruit me and he said: 'Well, Walt, we took a look at you and you weren't any good.' - Walt Garrison / Oklahoma State

#25. 'Son, you've got a good engine, but your hands aren't on the steering wheel.' - Bobby Bowden / Florida State

#26. 'Football is not a contact sport - it is a collision sport. Dancing is a contact sport.' - Duffy Daugherty / Michigan State

#27. After USC lost 51-0 to Notre Dame, his postgame message to his team: 'All those who need showers, take 'em.' - John McKay / USC

#28. 'If lessons are learned in defeat, our team is getting a great education.' - Murray Warmath / Minnesota

#29. 'The only qualifications for a lineman are to be big and dumb. To be a back, you only have to be dumb.' - Knute Rockne / Notre Dame

#30. 'Oh, we played about like three tons of buzzard puke this afternoon.' - Spike Dykes / Texas Tech

#31. 'It isn't necessary to see a good tackle. You can hear it.' -Knute Rockne / Notre Dame

#32. 'We live one day at a time and scratch where it itches.' -Darrell Royal / Texas

#33. 'Football is only a game. Spiritual things are eternal. Nevertheless, Beat Texas ' - Seen on a church sign in Arkansas prior to the 1969 game.

#34. 'We didn't tackle well today, but we made up for it by not blocking' - Wilson Matthews / Little Rock Central High School

#35. 'Three things can happen when you throw the ball, and two of them are bad.' - Darrell Royal / University of Texas

#36. 'I've found that prayers work best when you have big players.' - Knute Rockne / Notre Dame

#37. 'Gentlemen, it is better to have died as a small boy than to fumble this football.' - John Heisman

THINGS TO THINK ABOUT

1. You spend the first two years of their life teaching them to walk and talk. Then you spend the next sixteen telling them to sit down and shut up.
2. Grandchildren are God's reward for not killing your own children.
3. Mothers of teens now know why some animals eat their young.
4. Children seldom misquote you. In fact, they usually repeat word for word what you shouldn't have said.
5. The main purpose of holding children's parties is to remind yourself that there are children more awful than your own.
6. We childproofed our homes, but they are still getting in.

ADVICE FOR THE DAY:

Be nice to your kids.

They will choose your nursing home one day

AND FINALLY:

IF YOU HAVE A LOT OF TENSION
AND YOU GET A HEADACHE,
DO WHAT IT SAYS
ON THE ASPIRIN BOTTLE:
'TAKE TWO ASPIRIN' AND 'KEEP AWAY FROM CHILDREN'!!!!!

WORDS WITH TWO MEANINGS

1. THINGY (thing-ee) n..
2. Female...... Any part under a car's hood. Male..... The strap fastener on a woman's bra.
3. VULNERABLE (vul-ne-ra-bel) adj. Female.... Fully opening up one's self emotionally to another. Male..... Playing football without a cup.
4. COMMUNICATION (ko-myoo-ni-kay-shon) n . Female... The open sharing of thoughts and feelings with one's partner. Male... Leaving a note before taking off on a fishing trip with the boys.
5. COMMITMENT (ko- mit-ment) n. Female.... A desire to get married and raise a family.! Male...... Trying not to hit on other women while out with this one.
6. ENTERTAINMENT (en-ter-tayn-ment) n. Female.... A good movie, concert, play or book. Male...... Anything that can be done while drinking beer.
7. FLATULENCE (flach-u-lens) n. Female.... An embarrassing byproduct of indigestion. Male...... A source of entertainment, self-expression, male bonding.
8. MAKING LOVE (may-king luv) n. Female...... The greatest _expression of intimacy a couple can achieve. Male.. Call it whatever you want, just as long as we do it.
9. REMOTE CONTROL (ri-moht kon-trohl) n.
   Female.... A device for changing from one TV channel to another.
   Male... A device for scanning through all 375 channels every 5 minutes.
   AND;
10. He said . I don't know why you wear a bra; you've got nothing to put in it.
    She said . . You wear pants don't you?
11. He said . . .... Shall we try swapping positions tonight? She said That's a good idea - you stand by the ironing board while I sit on the sofa and fart!

12. He said ... What have you been doing with all the grocery money I gave you?
    She said .....Turn sideways and look in the mirror!
13. She said . . Why is it difficult to find men who are sensitive, caring and Good- looking?
    He said .... They already have boyfriends.
14. He said .. Why are <u>married</u> women heavier than <u>single</u> women?
    She said . . Single women come home, see what's in the fridge and go to bed. Married women come home, see what's in bed and go to the fridge.

WHY I LOVE MATHEMATICS

IT ALWAYS TELLS THE TRUTH AND IT ALWAYS TELLS IT THE SAME WAY!

The odds of winning the Florida lottery are 1 in 22,957,480.

The odds of winning the Powerball is 1 in 175,223,510.

The odds of winning Mega Millions is 1 in 258,890,850.

The odds of a disk drive failing in any given month are roughly one in

The odds of two different drives failing in the same month are roughly one in 36 squared, or 1 in about 1,300.

The odds of three drives failing in the same month is 36 cubed or 1 in 46,656.

The odds of seven different drives failing in the same month (like what happened at the IRS when they received a letter asking about emails targeting conservative and pro Israeli groups) is 37 to the 7th power .

The odds of the IRS disk failure is therefore 1 in 78,664,164,096. (that's over 78 Billion). In other words these odds are greater than those if you l win the Florida Lottery **342 times than having those seven IRS hard drives crashing in the same month.**

WHY MEN ARE NEVER DEPRESSED

1. Men Are Just Happier People-- What do you expect from such simple creatures? Your last name stays put. The garage is all yours. Wedding plans take care of themselves. Chocolate is just another snack.
2. You can never be pregnant. You can wear a white T-shirt to a water park. You can wear NO shirt to a water park. Car mechanics tell you the truth.
3. The world is your urinal. You never have to drive to another gas station restroom because this one is just too icky. You don't have to stop and think of which way to turn a nut on a bolt. Same work, more pay.
4. Wrinkles add character. Wedding dress $5000. Tux rental-$100.
5. People never stare at your chest when you're talking to them. New shoes don't cut, blister, or mangle your feet. One mood all the time.
6. Phone conversations are over in 30 seconds flat. You know stuff about tanks.
7. A five-day vacation requires only one suitcase. You can open all your own jars.
8. You get extra credit for the slightest act of thoughtfulness. If someone forgets to invite you, he or she can still be your friend.
9. Your underwear is $8.95 for a three-pack. Three pairs of shoes are more than enough.

10. You almost never have strap problems in public. You are unable to see wrinkles in your clothes. Everything on your face stays its original color.
11. The same hairstyle lasts for years, maybe decades. You only have to shave your face and neck.
12. You can play with toys all your life. One wallet and one color for all seasons.
13. You can wear shorts no matter how your legs look. You can 'do' your nails with a pocket knife. You have freedom of choice concerning growing a mustache.
14. You can do Christmas shopping for 25 relatives on December 24 in 25 minutes.

No wonder men are happier.

WONDERFUL SUMMARY OF ESSENTIAL TRUTHS

If God wanted us to vote, he would have given us candidates.
~ Jay Leno

The problem with political jokes is they get elected.
~ Henry Cate, VII

We hang the petty thieves and appoint the great ones to public office. ~ Aesop

If we got one-tenth of what was promised to us in these State of the Union speeches, there wouldn't be any inducement to go to heaven. ~ Will Rogers

Politicians are the same all over. They promise to build a bridge even where there is no river. ~ Nikita Khrushchev

When I was a boy I was told that anybody could become President; I'm beginning to believe it. ~ Clarence Darrow

Why pay money to have your family tree traced; go into politics and your opponents will do it for you. ~ Author unknown

Politicians are people who, when they see light at the end of the tunnel, go out and buy some more tunnel. ~ John Quinton

Politics is the gentle art of getting votes from the poor and campaign funds from the rich, by promising to protect each from the other. ~ Oscar Ameringer

I offer my opponents a bargain: if they will stop telling lies about us, I will stop telling the truth about them. ~ Adlai Stevenson, campaign speech, 1952

A politician is a fellow who will lay down your life for his country. ~ Tex Guinan

I have come to the conclusion that politics is too serious a matter to be left to the politicians. ~ Charles de Gaulle

Instead of giving a politician the keys to the city, it might be better to change the locks. ~ Doug Larson

There ought to be one day -- just one -- when there is open season on senators. ~ Will Rogers

WRONG MAN, WRONG JOB, WRONG COUNTRY, WRONG TIME IN HISTORY

by randy dye

The author was an ardent Obama supporter, is a Liberal, and is Editor-in-Chief of the U.S. News and World Report An article by Mort Zuckerman of U. S. News and World Report

In a January 20, 2010 editorial, the Editor in Chief of U.S. News & World Report, Mortimer Zuckerman, had this to say: "Obama's ability to connect with voters is what launched him. But what has surprised me is how he has failed to connect with the voters since he's been in office.

He's had so much overexposure. He was doing five Sunday shows. How many conferences? And now people stop listening to him... He's lost his audience.

He has not rallied public opinion. He has plunged in the polls more than any other public figure since we've been using polls.

He's done everything wrong. Well, not everything, but the major things... I don't consider it a triumph. I consider it a disaster." And that's what his friends are saying about him.

As the boy president occupied the White House on January 20, 2009 it was predictable that his presidency would last a year, at most, because the things he promised and the things he stood for were so uniquely un-American.

Looking back over his year in office, any reasonably precocious fourth grader could make a cogent argument in opposition to nearly everything he's done. In fact, his policies have been so extreme and so far outside the mainstream that he was destined to achieve the most spectacular fall from grace of any American president in history.

It was easy to see him serving out the final three years of his term as a virtual exile in the White House... afraid to venture out among any but the most rabid partisans.

Seeing his most ambitious initiative, healthcare reform, die in the flames of the Massachusetts Massacre, Obama made a hastily-planned "sortie" to Ohio for yet another Bush-bashing, self-aggrandizing stump speech on job creation. It was vintage Obama... full of left wing hyperbole and planted questions from the Kool-Ade drinkers in the hand-picked audience... but there were just two things wrong with it: 1) Almost everything he said was either wrong or an outright lie, and 2) He is so overexposed that no one in the television audience really wanted to see him.

Obama Kool-Ade drinkers in the media, and elsewhere, like to describe Obama as a "very bright man, a true intellectual (compared to George W. Bush and Sarah Palin, of course)." If that is the case, why has he demonstrated such a great inability to learn from his failures?

The strident words and the in-your-face attitude of his Ohio speech were proof that he has totally misread the meaning of the Scott Brown victory in Massachusetts.

Whatever hopes and dreams he had for his time in the White House, whatever grandiose plans he had for transforming the United States from a constitutional republic with a free market economy into a socialist dictatorship with a centrally planned economy, were all lost on Tuesday, January 19, 2010... one day short of a full year in office.

Yet, he appears to have learned nothing from the experience. Comedian George Gobel once asked, rhetorically, "Did you ever get the feeling that the world was a tuxedo and you were a pair of brown shoes?" In the context of 21st century American politics, and assuming that he has any capacity at all for honest self-examination, Obama must be feeling today very much like a pair of brown shoes at a black tie soiree.

When a politically naïve and totally inexperienced young black man, with a glib tongue and an exceptional ability to read words convincingly from a teleprompter, announced that he was ready to serve as President of the United States, liberals and Democrats saw it as a perfect opportunity to expiate whatever white guilt they may have felt... which was apparently considerable among those on the political left.

It didn't seem to bother them that, as one pundit has remarked, "every time he walks into a room he is the least experienced and the least qualified man in the room."

Nevertheless, his friends in the worldwide socialist movement and the international banking community figured out how to smuggle hundreds of millions of dollars in illegal campaign funds into the country, the black community rallied to his banner, and American liberals and the mainstream media jumped on board the bandwagon. Together, they made it happen for him.

But now, just one year later, Obama appears destined to become the unhappiest man in American politics... unhappier than even former Senator John Edwards, who runs a close second, and former president Bill Clinton.

Clinton will be the third unhappiest man because, after capturing the big prize, he frittered away whatever chance he had of ever being compared favorably with Franklin D. Roosevelt as one of the 20th century's greatest Democratic presidents. Not only was he a politician of unusual skill and insight, he was widely known as a policy "wonk" among policy wonks and he had the drive and the personal charm to be loved and respected around the world. Unfortunately, he was never able to put the public trust at the top of his priority list.

Instead, he surrounded himself with a large cadre of trusted enablers who allowed him to conduct himself as if he were, not the President of the United States, but the class stud on an extended spring break in Acapulco.

Now that he's been out of office for nearly a decade and he's married to the current Secretary of State, he spends his days trying to find something useful to do without calling an undue amount of attention to himself.

Having lied so shamelessly to the American people, having perjured himself in a court of law, having turned the Oval Office into a sexual playpen, and having suffered the humiliation of impeachment, he's smart enough to know that he has little reputation left to protect. So in order to protect whatever legacy remains, he walks a tightrope every day... and he has many more years to walk it without falling off.

Former Senator John Edwards is destined to be the second unhappiest man in American politics because he will be known forever as the most thoroughly despised scumbag in the political arena. A trial lawyer, Edwards amassed a $60 million fortune by winning large jury awards against doctors, hospitals, and corporations. His specialty was cases in which children were born with cerebral palsy, which he blamed on doctors who had waited too long to perform C-sections, a claim that doctors and medical researchers have described as "junk science."

Then, like Obama, he decided that his experience in the courtroom, his glib tongue, and his one term in the U.S. Senate qualified him to be President of the United States. He entered the 2004 Democratic presidential primaries, raising an incredible amount of money for a newcomer to elective office... most of it raised illegally by "bundlers" in plaintiffs' law firms across the country. He was unsuccessful in his quest for the Democratic nomination but was selected by his Senate colleague, John Kerry, as his running mate.

Two years later, in 2006, Edwards met a young blonde film producer, Rielle Hunter, and embarked on a love affair with her. On February 27, 2008, Hunter gave birth to a daughter, for whom Edwards has consistently denied paternity... until now Taking into account that all of this was happening while his wife was waging a long battle with breast cancer, Edwards now has the well-deserved reputation of being the sleaziest of the sleazy.

He is so universally despised that, if he is looking for a friend, he might as well resign himself to getting a dog... or moving in with O.J. Simpson. Terry Moran, host of ABC's *This Week*, put it all in perspective. He said, "What's interesting to note is that Edwards' latest admission (that he is the father of Hunter's child) came while he was in Haiti. As if the people of that sad place didn't have enough problems."

Clearly, the one thing Clinton and Edwards share that places them near the top of our list is their sexual peccadilloes, a shortcoming that Obama does not appear to share with them at least from what we know so far.

What we do know about Obama is that, since his teen years, he has been mentored by, gravitated toward, and surrounded by the most dangerous sort of America-hating socialists, communists, and Marxists... from Frank Marshall Davis and Saul Alinsky to Weather Underground terrorists Bill Ayers and Bernadine Dohrn, to Rev. Jeremiah Wright, George Soros, and countless radical left college professors.

What destines Obama for the top spot on the list of unhappiest American politicians... aside from the failure of his economic recovery program, the failure of his radical cap-and-trade proposal, his failed attempt to give labor bosses unprecedented power to intimidate blue collar workers, and his ill-fated attempt at healthcare reform... is the fact that he carries on his shoulders the hopes and aspirations of every black child in America.

It is unfortunate that, because he is so far outside the American mainstream, and because he carries so much hatred in his heart for the country he seeks to lead, his failures will be viewed by generations of black children, not as the failure of a black socialist attempting to bring down a constitutional republic, but simply as the failure of a black man.

A man can fail in the eyes of his countrymen and still be dearly loved by those closest to him. But in Obama's case, his wife and his two daughters will be there to suffer every agonizing step of his fall along with him. And for the rest of his life, each time he looks into their eyes, and into the eyes of black people everywhere, he will see the crushing disappointment that his ill-fated attempt at national transformation has caused them.

He will be the country's unhappiest man, living the rest of his life knowing that his daughters know that the whole world sees him as a failure.

He is simply the wrong man, in the wrong job, in the wrong country, at the wrong time in history.

X-NO X-RATED BUT SOME PG13 MATERIAL IN AMERICA

Y

YANKEES AND SOUTHERNERS ON A TRAIN TO ATHENS, GA

One morning three South Georgia 'good old boys' and three Yankees were in a ticket line at the Atlanta train station heading to Athens, GA for a big football game. The three Northerners each bought a ticket and watched as the three Southerners bought just one ticket among them.

"How are the three of you going to travel on one ticket?" asked one of the Yankees. "Watch and learn," answered one of the boys from the South.

When the six travelers boarded the train, the three Yankees sat down, but the three Southerners crammed into a bathroom together and closed the door.

Shortly after the train departed, the conductor came around to collect tickets. He knocked on the   bathroom door and said, "Ticket please." The door opened just a crack, and a   single arm emerged with a ticket in hand. The conductor took it and moved on.

The Yankees saw this happen and agreed it was quite a clever idea. Indeed, so clever that they decided to do the same thing on the return trip and save some money.

That evening after the game, when they got to the train station, they bought a single ticket for the return trip, while to their astonishment the three Southerners didn't buy even one ticket.

"How are you going to travel without a ticket?" asked one of the perplexed Yankees.

"Watch and learn", answered one of the Southern boys.

When they boarded the train, the three Northerners crammed themselves into a bathroom, and the three Southerners crammed themselves into the other bathroom across from it.

Shortly after the train began to move, one of the Southerners left their bathroom and walked quietly over to the Yankees' bathroom. He knocked on the door and said, "Ticket please".

There's just no way on God's green earth to explain how the South lost the Civil War.

YOURSELF, BELIEVE IN

By Robert H. Schuller

"For you have been my hope, O Sovereign Lord, my confidence since my youth." – Psalm 71:5

The glass elevator in our Tower of Hope was inspired by the El Cortez Hotel in San Diego. The owners of the elegant hotel decided they needed additional elevators, so they hired a group of architects and engineers to figure out the best location, both in terms of appearance and cost. If they put the elevators inside the hotel, they would have to cut a hole in all the floors. What a mess! Plaster dust would be everywhere.

As the planners stood deliberating over where to place the elevators, a janitor overhead the conversation. He thought about the horrible mess the hotel was going to be in while all the reconstruction was going on. And the more he thought about it, the braver he became. Finally he approached the group of men and said, "Why don't you put the elevators outside the building?" Nobody had thought of that! The professionals listened and the idea clicked in their imagination. "Why not?" they said. "It's never been done before, but let's try and see how we could do it." So the elevators were built outside the El Cortez Hotel. Since then, many well-known buildings have done the same thing!

Common people can be brilliant if they only believe in their own ideas! I don't care who you are. I don't care how poor you are. I don't care how educated you are. I don't care what your race it. I don't care where you are on the economic ladder. You have the same basic brain as any other human being! Believe in yourself.

Have you ever abandoned a "brilliant" idea because you lacked self-confidence? Maybe it's time to go back and take a second look!

Z

ZIG ZIGLAR

Born Hilary Hinton "Zig" Ziglar (November 6, 1926 – November 28, 2012) he was an American author, salesman, and motivational speaker.

Zig Ziglar was born in Coffee County in southeastern Alabama to parents John Silas Ziglar and Lila Wescott Ziglar. He was the tenth of twelve children. In 1931, when Ziglar was five years old, his father took a management position at a Mississippi farm, and his family moved to Yazoo City, Mississippi, where he spent most of his early childhood. The next year, his father died of a stroke, and his younger sister died two days later.

Ziglar served in the United States Navy during World War II, from 1943 to 1945. He was in the Navy V-12 Navy College Training Program and attended the University of South Carolina in Columbia, South Carolina.

In 1944, he met his wife, Jean, in the capital city of <u>Mississippi</u>, <u>Jackson</u>; he was seventeen and she was sixteen. They married in late 1946. Ziglar later worked as a salesman in a succession of companies. In 1968, he became a vice president and training director for the Automotive Performance company, moving to <u>Dallas</u>, <u>Texas</u>.

As of 2010, Ziglar still traveled around taking part in motivational seminars, despite a fall down a flight of stairs in 2007 that left him with <u>short-term memory</u> problems. <u>State Representative Chris Greeley</u> of <u>Maine</u> mentions Ziglar in the credits of his CD on public speaking.

Ziglar wove his <u>Christianity</u> into his motivational work. He was also an open <u>Republican</u> who endorsed former <u>Governor Mike Huckabee</u> for his party's presidential nomination in 2008. Ziglar, who had been suffering from <u>pneumonia</u>, died at the age of eighty-six at a hospital in <u>Plano</u>, Texas, on November 28, 2012.

Zig Ziglar's (partial) Library of Official Quotes

Go to <u>http://www.ziglar.com/quotes?page=7&splash=</u>

"You were designed for accomplishment, engineered for success, and endowed with the seeds of greatness. "

"Look back in forgiveness, forward in hope, down in compassion, and up with gratitude." - Zig Ziglar

"You don't have to be great to start, but you have to start to be great. " -Zig Ziglar

"There are no traffic jams on the extra mile." - Zig Ziglar

"There is no elevator to success...you have to take the stairs."
-Zig Ziglar

"Where you start is not as important as where you finish. "
-Zig Ziglar

"The choice to have a great attitude is something nobody or no circumstance can take from you." -Zig Ziglar

"If you don't see yourself as a winner, then you cannot perform as a winner." -Zig Ziglar

"You are the only person on earth who can use your ability. It's an awesome responsibility. " -Zig Ziglar

"Duty makes us do things well, but love makes us do them beautifully." -Zig Ziglar

"Each close you use should be an educational process by which you are able to raise the value in the prospect's mind." -Zig Ziglar

"You don't build a business --you build people-- and then people build the business." -Zig Ziglar

"Desire is what takes the hot water of mediocrity and turns it into the steam of outstanding success." -Zig Ziglar

"Anything worth doing is worth doing poorly until you learn to do it well." -Zig Ziglar

"Go as far as you can see. When you get there, you'll be able to see farther." -ig Ziglar

"The choice to have a great attitude is something that nobody or no circumstance can take from you. " -Zig Ziglar

"Yesterday ended last night. Today is a brand new day and it's yours." -Zig Ziglar

"Success is not measured by what you do compared to what others do, it is measured by what you do with the ability God gave you. " -Zig Ziglar

"When obstacles arise, you change your direction to reach your goal, you do not change your decision to get there. " -Zig Ziglar

"Success (a win) doesn't make you, and failure (a loss) doesn't make you." -Zig Ziglar

"If you do not see yourself as a winner, you cannot perform as a winner." -Zig Ziglar

"When you do more than you're paid for, eventually you'll be paid for more than you do." -Zig Ziglar

"A goal properly set is halfway reached." -Zig Ziglar

"If you can dream it, you can achieve it." -Zig Ziglar

"Some of us learn from other people's mistakes and the rest of us have to be other people." -Zig Ziglar

"How you see your future is much more important than what happened in your past." -Zig Ziglar

"You can build a successful career, regardless of your field of endeavor, by the dozens of little things you do on and off the job." -Zig Ziglar

"Honesty and integrity are absolutely essential for success in life -- all areas of life. The really good news is that anyone can develop honesty and integrity." -Zig Ziglar

"Success doesn't make you and failure doesn't break you. "
-Zig Ziglar

"If you learn from defeat, you haven't really lost. " -Zig Ziglar

"Success is the maximum utilization of the ability you have."
-Zig Ziglar

"You can't climb the ladder of success dressed in the costume of failure." -Zig Ziglar

"It was character that got us out of bed, commitment that moved us into action, and discipline that enabled us to follow through."
-Zig Ziglar

"For every sale you miss because you were too enthusiastic, you'll miss a hundred because you weren't enthusiastic enough."
-Zig Ziglar

"The more you complain about your problems, the more problems you will have to complain about." -Zig Ziglar

"Building a better you is the first step in building a better America." -Zig Ziglar

"You cannot tailor make your situation in life, but you can tailor make your attitudes to those situations." -Zig Ziglar

"If you don't know where you're going, you'll probably end up somewhere else." -Zig Ziglar

"Hope is the power that gives a person the confidence to step out and try." -Zig Ziglar

"You don't have to be great to start, but you have to start to be great." -Zig Ziglar

"There are no traffic jams on the extra mile." -Zig Ziglar

"When you throw dirt at people, you're not doing a thing but losing ground." -Zig Ziglar

"You are the only person on earth who can use your ability, it's an awesome responsibility." -Zig Ziglar

"If you don't see yourself as a winner, then you cannot perform as a winner." -Zig Ziglar

"Money isn't everything... but it ranks right up there with oxygen." -Zig Ziglar

"Money isn't the most important thing in life, but it's reasonably close to oxygen on the gotta have it scale."

"What you get by achieving your goals is not nearly as important as what you become by achieving your goals."

"When you do things the right way, you have nothing to lose because you have nothing to fear." -Zig Ziglar

"The foundation stones for a balanced success are honesty, character, integrity, faith, love and loyalty." -r

"Where you start is not as important as where you finish." -Zig Ziglar

"Among the things you can give and still keep are your word, a smile, and a grateful heart." -Zig Ziglar

"If you go out looking for friends, you're going to find they are very scarce. If you go out to be a friend, you'll find them everywhere." -Zig Ziglar

"Make today worth remembering." -Zig Ziglar

"You never know when a moment and a few sincere words can have an impact on a life." -Zig Ziglar

"Outstanding people have one thing in common: An absolute sense of mission" -Zig Ziglar

"If you learn from defeat, you haven't really lost." -Zig Ziglar

"It's not how far you fall. But how high you bounce that counts." -Zig Ziglar

"What you get by achieving your goals is not nearly as important as what you become by achieving your goals."

"Do it and then you will feel motivated to do it." -Zig Ziglar

"If you can dream it, then you can achieve it. You will get all you want in life if you help enough other people get what they want." -Zig Ziglar

"If you want to reach a goal, you must 'see the reaching' in your own mind before you actually arrive at your goal." -Zig Ziglar

"You may have made some mistakes, and you may not be where you want to be, but that has NOTHING to do with your future." -Zig Ziglar

"Positive thinking won't let you do anything, but it will let you do everything better than negative thinking will." -Zig Ziglar

"Every obnoxious act is a cry for help." -Zig Ziglar

"You cannot perform in a manner inconsistent with the way you see yourself." -Zig Ziglar

"This I do know beyond any doubt, Regardless of what you are doing, if you PUMP LONG AND HARD ENOUGH and

ENTHUSIASTICALLY ENOUGH, sooner or later the EFFORT will bring forth the REWARD." -Zig Ziglar

"You were born to win. But to be the winner you were born to be, you gotta plan to win, and prepare to win. Then, and only then, can you legitimately expect to win." -Zig Ziglar

"I'm not gonna give up, shut up, or let up... as a matter of fact, I'm just getting warmed up." -Zig Ziglar

"I'm not gonna give up, shut up, or let up... as a matter of fact, I'm just getting warmed up." -Zig Ziglar

"Your attitude not your aptitude will determine your altitude." -Zig Ziglar

"Don't become a wandering generality. Be a meaningful specific." -Zig Ziglar

"By altering our attitudes we can alter our lives." -Zig Ziglar

"Lack of direction, not lack of time is the problem. We all have 24-hour days." -Zig Ziglar

"Worry is interest paid before it's due." -Zig Ziglar

"If you learn from defeat, you haven't really lost." -Zig Ziglar

"Selling is essentially a transfer of feelings." -Zig Ziglar

ZZ Stop-

RWP2: I had to have a ZZ to end this book and had two with the help of Zig Ziglar quotes. So the title is not really about the long bearded musical group, ZZ Top. This ZZ Stop is about getting older and being "Vintage People" not the "Village People" another vintage musical group now. Below is what someone else said very well and was in an e-mail sent to Lewis Burns and forwarded to his many friends and me.

As I've aged, I've become kinder to myself, and less critical of myself. I've become my own friend.

I have seen too many dear friends leave this world, too soon; before they understood the great freedom that comes with aging. Whose business is it, if I choose to read, or play, on the computer, until 4 AM, or sleep until noon? I will dance with myself to those wonderful tunes of the 50, 60 & 70's, and if I, at the same time, wish to weep over a lost love, I will.

I will walk the beach, in a swim suit that is stretched over a bulging body, and will dive into the waves, with abandon, if I choose to, despite the pitying glances from the jet set.

They, too, will get old. I know I am sometimes forgetful. But there again, some of life is just as well forgotten. And, I eventually remember the important things.

Sure, over the years, my heart has been broken. How can your heart not break, when you lose a loved one, or when a child suffers, or even when somebody's beloved pet gets hit by a car? But, broken hearts are what give us strength, and understanding, and compassion. A heart never broken, is pristine, and sterile, and will never know the joy of being imperfect. I am so blessed to have lived long enough to have my hair turning gray, and to have my youthful laughs be forever etched into deep grooves on my face. So many have never laughed, and so many have died before their hair could turn silver.

As you get older, it is easier to be positive. You care less about what other people think. I don't question myself anymore. I've even earned the right to be wrong.

So, to answer your question, I like being old. It has set me free. I like the person I have become. I am not going to live forever, but while I am still here, I will not waste time lamenting what could have been, or worrying about what will be. And I shall eat dessert every single day (if I feel like it).

RALPH W. "PETE" PETERS JR.

Founder-President: The Maintenance Excellence Institute International (TMEII)
-10302 Dapping Drive, Raleigh, NC 27614
-2625 East Beach Drive, Oak Island, NC 28465
US Office/Cell : 919-270-1173 **E-Mail:**
RalphPetePeters@gmail.com
www.PRIDE-in-Maintenance.com
Skype: PRIDEnWork

Summary: Ralph "Pete" Peters is a highly recognized author,-trainer and leader around the World after his 48 years in the areas of implementing maintenance and manufacturing best practices, developing effective productivity measurement systems and initiating long term sustainable operational improvement processes. He has also supported both the public and private sectors. He is the author of two major books; *Maintenance Benchmarking and Best Practices* from McGraw-Hill and *Reliable Maintenance Planning, Estimating and Scheduling* from Elsevier. He has written a number of E-Books and chapters for five major handbooks plus over 200 articles and publications. And as a frequent speaker, he has delivered speeches and TrueWorkShops™ on maintenance and manufacturing excellence related topics Worldwide in over 40 countries to over 5,000 people.

This is his first non-maintenance related book <u>with all profits</u> going to the nonprofit he cofounded with son Brian Peters; Adventurers for Special Needs at www. adventurers4specialneeds.com .

Worldwide Maintenance Consulting and Training Services: TMEII has helped such diverse operations such as Sanofi Pasteur, Campbell Soup, British Petroleum, EcoPetrol (Columbia), Nigeria Liquid Natural Gas, TOTAL, DP World, Dubai International Airport, Marathon Oil Corporation, SIDERAR Steel (Argentina) and Atomic Energy Canada Ltd,.------ and many more.

Education: He received both his BS Industrial Engineering and Masters of Industrial Engineering focused upon management information systems from North Carolina State University. He is also a graduate of the US Army Command and General Staff Course, the Engineer Officers Advanced and Basic Courses, the Military Police Officers Course and the Civil Affairs Officer Course. He is certified as a Total Quality Management facilitator for the National Guard Bureau and the North Carolina Army National Guard.

Personal: Married to Joyce Peters for 53 years with 2 sons: Jay and Courtney Peters with two grandchildren (Dylan and Olivia) and Brian and Jennifer Peters with one grandson (Cameron). Member of North Raleigh United Methodist for 42 years, serving a 3rd grade Sunday school teacher and as member of the first building committee and charter member of the early 7 am bible study.

Sports: Starter in all three sports in junior high/high school (baseball, football and basketball) with 95% winning season; Won 20 Lost 0 in junior high. Was 6' 4' proving "white men can really dunk" While at Brevard College 2 years basketball, Co-Captain Sophomore year, All Conference 2 years. 1964 we went to the NJUCO finals in Hutchinson, KA and finished 9th in the nation. The next year we were conference champs and was MVP but we lost in district play. Voted into the Brevard College sports Hall of Fame in October 2014 and to the Northern Highs school Hall of Fame in 2019.